Praise for

THE ECONOMIST'S CRAFT

"At long last, young scholars interested in economics have a much-needed resource that explains how to produce new knowledge, the core mission of researchers. *The Economist's Craft* is comprehensive in scope and filled with insights that have helped me to reflect on and improve my research process."

—**Yueran Ma**, Booth School of Business, University of Chicago

"This book provides excellent insights into navigating graduate school, constructing effective journal articles, and making good conference presentations. The adoption of even 50 percent of the recommendations woven through these chapters will transform both the economics literature and the careers of young economists. I would like to see a copy of this book in the hands of every one of our PhD students."

—**Steven G. Medema**, Duke University

"Weisbach goes beyond mere tactical advice to deliver a highly substantive and engaging work of professional guidance. If I had read this book in graduate school, I would have avoided many mistakes. I recommend *The Economist's Craft* to any and all PhD students in economics and allied fields."

—**Luigi Zingales**, University of Chicago and coauthor
of *Saving Capitalism from the Capitalists*

THE ECONOMIST'S CRAFT

SKILLS FOR SCHOLARS

The Economist's Craft: An Introduction to Research, Publishing, and Professional Development, Michael S. Weisbach

The Book Proposal Book: A Guide for Scholarly Authors, Laura Portwood-Stacer

The Princeton Guide to Historical Research, Zachary M. Schrag

You Are What You Read: A Practical Guide to Reading Well, Robert DiYanni

Super Courses: The Future of Teaching and Learning, Ken Bain

Syllabus: The Remarkable, Unremarkable Document That Changes Everything, William Germano and Kit Nicholls

Leaving Academia: A Practical Guide, Christopher L. Caterine

A Field Guide to Grad School: Uncovering the Hidden Curriculum, Jessica McCrory Calarco

How to Think like Shakespeare: Lessons from a Renaissance Education, Scott Newstok

The Craft of College Teaching: A Practical Guide, Robert DiYanni and Anton Borst

The Economist's Craft

AN INTRODUCTION TO RESEARCH, PUBLISHING, AND PROFESSIONAL DEVELOPMENT

MICHAEL S. WEISBACH

PRINCETON UNIVERSITY PRESS

PRINCETON & OXFORD

Published by Princeton University Press
41 William Street, Princeton, New Jersey 08540
6 Oxford Street, Woodstock, Oxfordshire OX20 1TR

press.princeton.edu

All Rights Reserved

Library of Congress Cataloging-in-Publication Data

Names: Weisbach, Michael S. (Michael Steven) author.
Title: The economist's craft : an introduction to research, publishing, and
    professional development / Michael S. Weisbach.
Description: Princeton : Princeton University Press, 2021. | Series: Skills for
    scholars | Includes bibliographical references and index.
Identifiers: LCCN 2021013447 (print) | LCCN 2021013448 (ebook) |
    ISBN 9780691216485 (paperback) | ISBN 9780691216492 (hardback) |
    ISBN 9780691216584 (ebook)
Subjects: LCSH: Economics—Research. | Social sciences—Research—
    Methodology. | BISAC: BUSINESS & ECONOMICS / Economics /
    General | STUDY AIDS / General
Classification: LCC HB74.5 .W435 2021 (print) | LCC HB74.5 (ebook) |
    DDC 330.023—dc23
LC record available at https://lccn.loc.gov/2021013447
LC ebook record available at https://lccn.loc.gov/2021013448

British Library Cataloging-in-Publication Data is available

Editorial: Peter Dougherty and Alena Chekanov
Production Editorial: Ali Parrington
Jacket/Cover Design: Matt Avery (Monograph LLC)
Production: Erin Suydam
Publicity: James Schneider
Copyeditor: Cynthia Buck

This book has been composed in Arno

Printed on acid-free paper. ∞

Printed in the United States of America

10 9 8 7 6 5 4 3 2 1

To my students and coauthors, who taught me most of
what is in this book

CONTENTS

Preface   ix

1 Introduction—How Academic Research Gets Done   1

PART I. SELECTING A TOPIC

2 Selecting Research Topics   21

3 Strategic Issues in Constructing Research Portfolios   37

PART II. WRITING A DRAFT

4 An Overview of Writing Academic Research Papers   53

5 The Title, Abstract, and Introduction   68

6 The Body of the Paper: The Literature Review, Theory,
   Data Description, and Conclusion Sections   87

7 Reporting Empirical Work   99

8 Writing Prose for Academic Articles   116

PART III. ONCE A DRAFT IS COMPLETE: PRESENTATIONS, DISTRIBUTION, AND PUBLICATION

9 Making Presentations   135

10 Distributing, Revising, and Publicizing Research   153

11 The Journal Review Process   169

PART IV. BEING A SUCCESSFUL ACADEMIC

12 How to Be a Productive Doctoral Student   199

13 How to Be a Diligent Thesis Adviser   231

14 Managing an Academic Career   247

    Epilogue—Academic Success beyond the PhD   279

            Bibliography   285
               Index   291

PREFACE

WHEN I MOVED to Tucson, Arizona, in 1994 to teach at the University of Arizona, I started teaching a doctoral course on corporate finance, which covered research about how firms raise capital, corporate governance, and related issues. In the twenty-six years since that time, I have taught some variant of that course almost every year during my time on the faculties of three different universities. The students in these classes were almost always smart and hardworking, and the vast majority wanted a career as academics themselves. Yet many did not succeed in that goal. Some were unable to complete their programs, some could not get an academic job following graduation, and some were unable to publish their work once they became junior faculty.

There are a limited number of tenure-track positions in academia, so it is not possible for every entering doctoral student who wants an academic career to have one. To become a productive academic scholar, talent and a drive to succeed are necessary, but not sufficient. For the majority of young scholars who do not succeed in becoming successful academics, the problem is not a lack of ability or effort. Instead, the problem is that they do not go about their task as graduate students, and then as junior faculty, in the best way. Being a professional scholar is completely different from almost any other profession, and many people who want to become academics never figure out important aspects of the job.

In light of this observation, I started including short segments in my doctoral course about how best to approach the task of becoming a successful academic. I covered topics such as what to spend time on as a doctoral student: starting research programs, convincing readers that they should care about your papers, writing English prose, presenting research, and acquiring the human capital necessary for a successful career after finishing the dissertation. After a few years, I began to notice that the students were paying more attention during these short segments than they were during the rest of my lectures. Students appeared to be more interested in the advice I had for them about the way they should approach their time in the program and their future careers than in what I had to tell them about corporate finance.

Doctoral students are always justifiably nervous that they aren't making optimal use of their time in the program, so they are almost always very appreciative of whatever guidance they can get from faculty. Over the years I have found a demand for advice coming not just from the students I have taught but also from students and younger faculty I have met while visiting other universities around the world. In fact, the demand for advice is so great that many young scholars even turn to internet message boards, where they ask for the opinions of anonymous strangers who usually know as little as they do.

A second observation I have made over the years is that, perhaps because of a lack of good advice, many scholars, both doctoral students and faculty members, constantly make the same mistakes. Far too many publicly circulated papers contain incredibly long, mind-numbingly dull literature surveys; introductions that go on and on before they tell the reader what the point of the paper is and why the reader should bother to waste her time on it; data descriptions containing insufficient detail for a third party to replicate the results; tables that are unnecessary, badly labeled, or hard to understand; or overly dry prose written in the passive voice and apparently designed to put the reader to sleep. In addition, many scholars manage their time so badly when giving presentations that they do not get to the main results of their paper until the last five minutes of the talk. Their presentations are often poorly designed, with slides that are incomprehensible or even unreadable owing to their use of fonts so small that participants sitting more than a few rows back cannot read them. Young faculty routinely mismanage their career by not having a coherent research agenda, not getting their papers to journals, or not making connections with people in their field who teach at other universities. Sometimes they do not even bother to show up for seminars in their field at their own university.

Writing papers, making presentations, and communicating with other scholars are basic parts of a professor's job. Yet, while there are books and courses on how to do almost anything in the world, very little has been written on how to be a successful academic. The irony is that, as academics, we spend our lives teaching other people skills for all sorts of non-academic jobs. But rarely does anyone teach us how to do ours. Usually what a scholar has learned about how to do her job is what she's been lucky enough to absorb from faculty advisers, friends, and colleagues; the rest she figures out on her own.

Doctoral programs in economics and related fields usually do a reasonably good job teaching the *science* involved in research—that is, programs teach theory, econometrics, and the literatures in applied fields fairly well. Where they are lacking is in how they teach the *craft* of research. Like other kinds of craftsmanship, writing a good research paper can be thought of as a craft, one that involves a combination of time-tested techniques, strategic thinking, imagination, ethics, and attention to details that are often overlooked.

The observation that doctoral students and young faculty members often do not learn the craftsmanship necessary to do their jobs well made me think: *Someone should write a book explaining to academics how to do research and manage their careers.* After teaching in five research-oriented departments and seeing the successes and failures of my students and colleagues, I decided that I would try to be that someone. What you are about to read is my attempt.

The purpose of this book is to provide a guide for a scholar who wishes to pursue a career in academia. The primary focus is on research—how a scholar selects research topics, does the analysis, writes her papers, and publishes them—though the book marries research and publishing with professional development. Throughout the book, I encourage scholars to think of each of their papers as part of a larger research program. A scholar's goal should be to structure her research so that the profession learns more from her body of collected research than from the sum of the contributions of each individual paper.

When writing this book, I tried to make each chapter more or less self-contained, with each covering a different aspect of a scholar's job.

The idea is that whenever a scholar stumbles across an aspect of her job about which she is uncertain, she can turn to a chapter in this book that can help her address the issues she is confronting. So, for example, if a scholar is trying to write the introduction to a paper, she can turn to chapter 5 and read my discussion about writing an effective introduction. Or if she is contemplating how to present her empirical results, she might look to chapter 7, where I describe ways to present empirical results in a clear and compelling manner.

Since my background is in economics and finance, the book is most relevant to scholars working in those fields. For scholars in other fields who might be considered part of the broader economics ecosystem, such as accounting, some aspects of public policy, and related social sciences, the book should be equally relevant. My hope is that much of what I say will be valuable to academics working in other fields and also to non-academics who do research and try to publish it.

How the Book Came to Be

Much of the book explains the process of writing a paper from the idea stage through publication. It describes the transformation of an idea into a research project, then into a draft of a paper, then through the many revisions prior to submitting the paper to a journal, then through the further revisions that follow submission, and eventually to acceptance by the journal and publication. It also explains why a scholar should think of each paper as a part of a coherent research program that defines her career, and how she should manage that career to maximize her own welfare. At each step, I present techniques that a scholar can use to accomplish this step of the research project.

When writing this book, I tried to approach it as I would a research project and to utilize the very techniques I was writing about. So, when I was starting out and wondering whether I should write it at all, I decided to follow the advice I would eventually include in chapter 3. I gave myself some time to write an introduction and see if I could make it something that others might find interesting.

I began my attempt during a vacation, so that I could write without any work-related distractions. On a cruise down the Dalmatian Coast in the summer of 2017, I sat for days in the boat's lounge with a computer on my lap, trying to write something I liked. The other passengers often came up to me and asked what I was doing. At first, I told them I was working, but they would glare at me for committing the faux pas of working on a cruise, especially in a public place where it would make the other passengers feel guilty. After a few days, I started saying that I was writing; the other passengers were fine with that. Writing can be fun, so it's an acceptable thing to do on vacation. In fact, the sooner a scholar believes that writing really is fun, the better her papers will be!

Two years later, I finally had something I liked, which was an early draft of chapter 1. I showed it to a few people. As I mention in chapter 13, one of the first people I showed it to was my former thesis adviser, Jim Poterba of MIT. In addition, my close friend and coauthor Ben Hermalin of Berkeley gave the draft a careful read, as did a few other coauthors, students, and colleagues I asked to have a look at it. All of these people agreed that what I was doing was worthwhile, and they encouraged me to proceed. So I nervously wrote a tentative outline and gave it a try.

I decided to write each chapter as a more or less self-contained essay on one aspect of being an academic. After writing an initial draft of a chapter, I used the approach discussed in chapter 10: I distributed it sequentially to students and colleagues rather than giving it to all of them at the same time, hoping to minimize duplication of the suggestions I would receive. I was fortunate to have Hyeik Kim, one of our excellent doctoral students, assigned as my research assistant for the academic year. Hyeik was always the first person who saw the initial draft of a chapter. She fixed many mistakes and gave me her opinion on the strengths and weaknesses of the chapter. She seemed to take great joy in catching me violating one of my rules for English prose discussed in chapter 8, such as overusing the passive voice or, God forbid, using "this" as a noun rather than as a modifier. I dropped or completely rewrote several chapters before anyone else saw them because of Hyeik's reaction to them. I could never have completed the book without her.[1]

---

1. Toward the end of the writing process, two other doctoral students, Dongxu Li and Rui Gong, also provided invaluable help improving the manuscript.

After Hyeik was finished with a chapter, I forwarded it to two former doctoral students, Murillo Campello and Shan Ge. Murillo and Shan each read every chapter carefully and offered invaluable detailed suggestions that substantially improved the text. After a while, my colleague Lu Zhang and my coauthor Tracy Wang joined in; both read the entire draft while giving me detailed comments. Throughout this process, I also received feedback from a number of friends and colleagues on various chapters. Ben Hermalin, Steve Kaplan, Mervyn King, Josh Lerner, Ron Masulis, and Jim Poterba were especially helpful.

Around the beginning of 2020, after I had written about half of the book, I realized I had to find a publisher. I realized fairly quickly that the appropriate publisher for this book was likely to be a university press, since the target audience is academics. Similar to the journal review process described in chapter 11, these presses all require that manuscripts be reviewed by several scholars. However, unlike journal articles, book manuscripts are normally sent to multiple publishers at the same time. So I sent the paper to some well-known university presses and received favorable feedback from a number of them. Eventually, four prestigious university presses agreed to send the manuscript to reviewers.

While all the editors I dealt with were very professional and helpful, one who stood out throughout this process was Peter Dougherty of Princeton University Press. I often teach students in my private equity class that the best venture capitalists begin to add value even before they sign a contract; it turns out that the same is true for the best editors. One Sunday morning at 8:00 a.m., I received my first email from Peter, which contained substantive suggestions for ways I could improve my manuscript. Before even sending it to reviewers, he convinced me to change the title and to focus on economics-related disciplines. (I had been trying to write a book focusing equally on all fields.) When Peter called with an offer to publish the book at Princeton University Press, I accepted it immediately, without hearing whether the other publishers would be willing to offer contracts.[2]

2. It was my wife Amy's suggestion to accept immediately. My natural inclination would have been to foolishly drag the process out longer than necessary. Amy was incredibly supportive throughout the project, and I could not have finished it without her help.

The reviews from Princeton University Press were incredibly valuable. They led me to rethink several sections of the book and to address a number of new topics. Yueran Ma, Steve Medema, Jonathan Wight, and John Cochrane were all particularly helpful. John Cochrane even wrote an amusing entry on his blog about the book, which can be seen at: https://johnhcochrane.blogspot.com/2020/04/weisbach-advice .html. The book would not have been the same without the reviewers' help, for which I am eternally grateful.

I would be remiss if I did not mention that there are other sources that also provide useful advice for young scholars. A book with a title very similar to mine is William Thomson's *A Guide for the Young Economist*.[3] However, the overlap between the two books is surprisingly small. I would recommend that scholars look at Thomson's book if they have a question about an issue that I do not address here satisfactorily.

There are of course many wonderful books about how to write. William Zinsser's *On Writing Well* is excellent. The classic guide to writing about economics is Deirdre McCloskey's *The Rhetoric of Economics*. John Cochrane's *Writing Tips for PhD Students* is a very good guide, and not just about writing: it also discusses many of the other topics covered in this book.[4]

One last thing I would like to emphasize is that my recommendations in this book are a matter of opinion, not fact. My guess is that most readers will agree with much of what I say and disagree with me on a few points. There is more than one way to do research and more than one way to approach a career. Many academics have had excellent careers doing the opposite of what I recommend.

Nonetheless, many scholars do drift through their career without thinking much about the issues I discuss. They go from project to project giving little thought to how the work fits into a research portfolio and whether any of it might be influential. These scholars usually think

---

3. W. Thomson, *A Guide for the Young Economist* (MIT Press, 2001).

4. W. Zinsser, *On Writing Well: The Classic Guide to Writing Nonfiction* (Harper Perennial, 2016); D. N. McCloskey, *The Rhetoric of Economics* (University of Wisconsin Press, 1998); J. H. Cochrane, "Writing Tips for PhD Students," June 8, https://static1.squarespace.com/static /5e6033a4ea02d801f37e15bb/t/5eda74919c44fa5f87452697/1591374993570/phd_paper_writing .pdf.

that when they have finally gotten a likelihood function to converge or proved a theorem that they have worked on for a long time, their work is done.

At this point, however, the work is only beginning. How a paper is written up, presented to an audience, marketed to a journal, and packaged with other related work as part of a research portfolio will determine the work's impact and the value it will add to the scholar's career. If scholars consider what I have to say in the following pages but decide that I am wrong about every point I make, that is fine with me. These scholars will still be much better off having spent time thinking about these issues and the best ways to address them, so the book will have accomplished its purpose.

THE ECONOMIST'S CRAFT

1

Introduction—How Academic Research Gets Done

WHEN WE THINK about the way in which we do academic research, we might think of the mathematician Andrew Wiles, who won the Abel Prize in 2016 for proving Fermat's Last Theorem. This "theorem" was originally stated by Pierre de Fermat in the seventeenth century, although Fermat did not provide a proof.[1] For over three hundred years, no one could prove that Fermat's Last Theorem was true, nor provide a counterexample to show it was false. Fermat's Last Theorem would baffle many of the world's greatest mathematicians—including Leonhard Euler and David Hilbert, each of whom spent several years attempting to solve it—and it became one of the greatest unsolved problems in mathematics, or really in any field. A German industrialist and amateur mathematician who himself had tried and failed to solve the problem established the Wolfskehl Prize at the end of the nineteenth century—a substantial financial reward to be given to the scholar who solved the problem. A century later, Wiles, who was a professor at Princeton at the time, worked on proving Fermat's Last Theorem in total secrecy for a number of years, letting only his wife know that he

---

1. Fermat famously wrote in the margin of a book: "I have a truly marvelous demonstration of this proposition which this margin is too narrow to contain." For Wiles's formal statement of the problem and presentation of his proof, see A. Wiles, "Modular Elliptic Curves and Fermat's Last Theorem," *Annals of Mathematics* 141(3, 1995): 443–551.

was working on the problem. One can only imagine what the conversations were like at lunch when his colleagues or students asked Wiles about his research. When Wiles finally announced the solution in 1993, it was generally considered one of the greatest mathematical discoveries of all time.

Those of us who become academic researchers in any field look to Wiles's discovery as the "Holy Grail" of what we would like to achieve with our scholarship. We all would love to solve a famous problem that was formulated by someone else, especially one that many others have unsuccessfully attempted to solve. Such an accomplishment would represent a substantial contribution to knowledge, and the scholar who solved the problem would become an "academic celebrity." Many of us get our PhD with the dream of making a discovery like Wiles's and gaining a similar kind of acclaim.

However, the actual experience of the vast majority of researchers, even the most successful ones, is nothing like Wiles's. Not only are most researchers far less successful than Wiles, but the approach they take to research is very different. Indeed, what is relevant to most researchers about Wiles's remarkable discovery is that it illustrates what most research is not. There are important differences between his experience and the approach most of us have to take to become successful researchers. At least three such differences are worth highlighting.

First, most problems we solve were not stated by someone else, and certainly not three hundred years ago by someone as famous as Fermat. Most of the time, at least half of the battle is coming up with the right questions to ask and the right way to ask them. In fact, once a question is asked, answering it is often quite straightforward. In 1937, Ronald Coase asked a question no one had asked before: "What determines the boundaries of the firm?" His paper asking this question led to the development of the field of organizational economics. Coase earned the 1991 Nobel Prize in Economics in large part because he had the foresight to be the first person to ask such an important question. Coase also proposed reasons for the boundaries of firms, but his explanation was fairly straightforward. Once the question was asked, many people would have come to the same conclusion he did. The brilliant part of Coase's paper was the asking, not the answering.[2]

Second, unlike Wiles's experience, research in most fields is intensely collaborative. In the sciences, research is usually centered on a laboratory or a research group working together on related problems. In the social sciences, the collaboration tends to be less structured but is no less important. Most papers are coauthored, and even sole-authored papers go through many rounds of revision based on discussions with colleagues before they are published. In most fields, it is very rare for someone working alone in secret to come up with an important discovery.

Third, the discussion following Wiles's discovery was about whether his proof was in fact correct, since there was no question about the importance of the problem he was trying to solve. However, the discussion about most academic papers usually centers on the nature of the contribution, the questions the paper asks, and the limitations of the analysis. Frequently the most important question in an academic seminar, and the one for which the author most often does not have a good answer, is "Why do we care about this paper?"

The burden of any researcher is to explain why the question she is asking is important and why she did what she did to answer it.[3] Most importantly, she should explain why the results tell us something we want to know, or should want to know, about the world around us. The ability of a researcher to provide such explanations can, and often does, determine the success of a particular research project. A paper that fails to explain why its contribution is important will have trouble getting

2. See Ronald Coase's "The Nature of the Firm," *Economica* 4(16, 1937): 386–405. Coase's Nobel Prize also was awarded for his other seminal contributions, especially "The Problem of Social Cost," *Journal of Law and Economics* 3(1960): 1–44.

3. For ease of exposition, I have tried to be consistent with my use of pronouns throughout the book. I use feminine pronouns when referencing researchers and authors, and male pronouns for readers. When I discuss doctoral programs and journal submissions, I have made advisers male and editors female. I have made these choices for consistency and not to make any statements about the empirical distribution of genders in the profession.

published, and even if it does get published, it will have little impact. Sometimes a researcher lacks an adequate explanation because the paper does not tell us anything particularly important. But often a researcher lacks a good explanation because she failed to "put her best foot forward" in explaining to a reader why he should care about the paper's results.

When I was a doctoral student, I was the beneficiary of the spectacularly good training provided by the MIT Economics Department. In my classes, I learned how to solve models, derive properties of estimators, and critique other people's work, as well as many other useful skills. What I did not learn in class was how actually to do research. That I learned by going to the National Bureau of Economic Research (NBER) office in Cambridge, Massachusetts, every evening, where I hung out with some of the best faculty and doctoral students from both Harvard and MIT. We spent hours and hours talking about what was good research and what was not, what we thought were the important questions yet to be solved, and whether the seminar presentation we heard that day made any sense. We also read each other's papers carefully and helped one another become successful scholars.

One thing I have observed over the years is that most graduate programs tend to prepare students for problems like the one Andrew Wiles solved, not the ones they are much more likely to deal with in their future careers. Traditional classes in graduate programs teach students to solve problems that have been posed for them, which is what they have to do to pass their qualifying exams. Solving a well-known question is what Wiles did when he solved Fermat's Last Theorem, although the challenge, of course, was on a totally different scale than passing a qualifying exam.

Where many graduate programs struggle is by not providing young researchers with the experiences and insights that are necessary to be successful researchers. They do not, for the most part, teach students the *craft* of being a scholar. In particular, they do not teach students how to pick research projects that will have lasting impact, how to communicate why a project will be important, how to handle data properly, how to write up results in an appropriately scientific yet readable manner, and how to interpret results in a way that others will find reasonable. Most scholars learn these skills as doctoral students in an apprenticeship-type relationship with their thesis adviser, from other faculty, and from fellow students.

Young scholars often ask my advice on various aspects of the research process. Their questions tend to arise from the craft rather than the science of economics. Young scholars want to know how they should pick research topics, find coauthors, write readable and interesting prose (in English), structure academic papers, present and interpret results, and cite other scholars. Most frequently, they have questions about all aspects of the publication process. In addition, academics of all ages do not think enough about their own professional development and do not invest in the human capital that would allow them to enjoy their jobs throughout their career.

Learning the economist's craft—how to do research and how to proceed in career development—has historically been a random, word-of-mouth process. Some scholars are fortunate enough to have someone to teach them the craft of the profession, while others go their entire career without figuring it out. There is no reason why something this important must be communicated in a haphazard manner by word of mouth. It can and should be written down.

The State of Academic Research

Before getting into the particulars of how to do research, it is important to understand the market in which we work and how it has affected research. While basic research in some fields is done by the corporate and government sectors, in most fields it tends to be dominated by universities. Universities reward faculty in large part based on their research, so faculty have substantial incentives to do research and publish their findings in the most prestigious outlets possible.

The academic marketplace can be summarized by three main trends: First, there has been substantial growth in academic research globally. Many universities, both in the United States and, especially, in other countries, have decided that they should improve their research reputation and are strongly encouraging their faculty to become more active scholars. Second, this growth has led to more competition among faculty for research ideas. This competition, in combination with the maturing of most fields of study, has led faculty to become increasingly specialized. Third, the growth in the number of top-level journals has not matched that of research-active faculty, so it has become increasingly difficult to publish a paper in a "top-tier" journal.

THE GROWTH IN ACADEMIC RESEARCH

Many universities have cut back on the number of their tenure-track faculty as a way of saving money, but others are trying to gain prestige by increasing their research presence. In the thirty-plus years since I left graduate school in 1987, the number of universities expecting their faculty to publish in top outlets has increased dramatically. While my PhD is from an economics department, I have focused my research on financial economics, a subfield of economics that is mostly taught in business schools. I have observed a number of changes in the structure of finance academia since I left graduate school. Similar changes have occurred in economics departments and also in related fields such as accounting.

In 1987, little research was published in the top journals that came from outside the top twenty or twenty-five US departments. Now there are probably at least one hundred US departments that require publication in top journals as a condition of earning tenure. Internationally, the growth in this expectation has been even larger. In 1987, only two European finance departments consistently produced top finance research, London Business School and INSEAD. Today there are probably at least ten or fifteen departments with as many active researchers as London Business School and INSEAD had in 1987. In Asia, little serious finance research was going on in 1987. Now there are at least three very good departments in Singapore and four or five in both Hong Kong and Seoul. In mainland China, academic research activity has grown so much that it is virtually impossible to keep track of all the good departments unless you live there.

Growth in doctoral programs has mirrored the increase in high-quality departments. In the 1980s and 1990s, with rare exceptions, most of the best finance PhD students graduated from the top ten US departments. Now the best students on the academic job market come from all over the world. European departments regularly place students at the top five US departments, and US departments ranked outside the top fifteen or twenty regularly produce extremely good students who land jobs at top departments. Students from Asian programs are getting better every year, and it is only a matter of time before, like their European counterparts, they are regularly placing at the top of the market. As a result of this growth in doctoral programs, there are many more active researchers in the world today than when I began my career, and that number is growing at an accelerating rate.

SPECIALIZATION IN RESEARCH

What about the problems that are being studied? In most fields, contributions tend to become narrower and narrower over time as researchers become increasingly specialized. The basic questions in any field remain the same, so researchers discover the most fundamental contributions first, then refine them over time.

Occasionally, there is a seminal event, research breakthrough, or technological innovation that spurs new research. In my field, one such event was the Financial Crisis of 2008. While catastrophic for the world economy, the crisis led to an important burst of research seeking to understand its causes, the effect of new financial products on the economy and how they should be regulated, potential government interventions during a financial crisis, whether banks should be allowed to be "too big to fail," and similar issues.

Recently, the availability of immense amounts of data and the computing tools to work with such data have revolutionized many fields. Much recent research in many fields of economics has been based on newly available large databases, dramatically increased computing speed, and new approaches to data analysis, such as machine learning. These developments have pushed economics and related fields toward applied empirical work. Roger Backhouse and Béatrice Cherrier point out that ten of the previous twelve winners of the John Bates Clark Award, which is given to the top American economist under age forty, focus on empirical or applied work.[4] This pattern is in marked contrast to the early years of the award, when it most often recognized work in theoretical economics or theoretical econometrics.[5]

These examples of "quantum jumps," however, are more the exception than the rule. The general rule is that academic fields tend to become more narrow and more specialized over time. In some fields, such as math, biology, psychology, and economics, the subfields have essentially become fields of their own, with the faculty becoming so specialized that there is sometimes little interaction across subfields.

For example, in finance most of the leading lights of the generation previous to mine, such as Fischer Black, Gene Fama, Mike Jensen, Bob Merton, Merton Miller, Steve Ross, and Myron Scholes, worked in a number of different areas of finance.[6] Academic finance was in its infancy when they were beginning their careers, and all of these individuals made important contributions across the main subfields of finance. In my generation, a few of the very best finance researchers, such as Andrei Shleifer, Jeremy Stein, and Robert Vishny, have also made important contributions across the major subfields. Most of us, however, specialize in one subfield or another. In the generation after mine, scholars have become even more specialized: a typical new PhD comes out of graduate school as a "macro-finance person," a "dynamic-contracting scholar," or a "time series econometrician specializing in asset prices."

4. R. E. Backhouse and B. Cherrier, "The Age of the Applied Economist: The Transformation of Economics since the 1970s," *History of Political Economy* 49(2017): 1–33.

5. For the American Economic Assocation's list of recipients of the John Bates Clark Medal, see https://www.aeaweb.org/about-aea/honors-awards/bates-clark.

6. Economists will immediately recognize these names. Non-economist readers should be aware that of the individuals on this list, Fama, Merton, Miller, and Scholes are recipients of the Nobel Prize in Economics. Black and Ross tragically passed away before they received the prize but undoubtedly would have received it at some point had they lived longer. Jensen's prize will hopefully be awarded at some point in the near future.

Owing to this specialization, however, scholars who do excellent work in one subfield of finance sometimes lack a basic level of competence in other related subfields. For example, people who are strong in macro-finance often fail to keep up with new empirical results related to investments, nor are they fluent in behavioral research, even though each of these subfields has important things to say about the determinants of asset prices. I fear that finance is heading in the direction of many other fields that find themselves populated by scholars in the same department who cannot understand each other's work.

THE PUBLICATION PROCESS

In contrast to some other fields in which the most important publications can be books or conference proceedings, by far the most important method of disseminating research in the economics-based fields is through refereed journals. These journals differ substantially in both their quality and the style of research that they tend to publish. Higher-ranked journals are much more prestigious, and many departments promote only faculty who publish in the few journals that they consider top-tier. Consequently, the ability to publish in top journals is an important element of an economics scholar's success.

Since I entered the profession in 1987, the number of journals has grown with the size of the profession, but the ones considered top-tier have not changed. In economics, the top general-interest journals in 1987—*Journal of Political Economy, American Economic Review, Quarterly Journal of Economics, Review of Economic Studies,* and *Econometrica*— retain that status today. While more specialized "field" journals have grown in both quantity and quality since 1987, most research-oriented economics departments expect junior faculty to publish at least some of their work in the top general-interest journals if they are to earn tenure.[7]

In finance, we have the same three top-tier journals as we had in 1987: *Journal of Finance, Journal of Financial Economics,* and *Review of Financial*

---

7. See D. Card and S. DellaVigna, "Nine Facts about Top Journals in Economics," *Journal of Economic Literature* 51(1, 2013): 144–61.

Studies. Similarly, in accounting the same three journals dominate the field today as in 1987: *Journal of Accounting and Economics, Journal of Accounting Research,* and *Accounting Review.* These journals usually publish more papers per year than they used to, but not nearly enough to compensate for the increasing number of scholars in the field. Most of the top departments expect the majority of their faculty's research to be published in these journals or in comparable ones from related fields.

Whatever the reason, journal reputation is extraordinarily sticky (a topic, not surprisingly, about which academics love to speculate). Top journals not infrequently make questionable editorial decisions and sometimes provide terrible service to authors. Nonetheless, it is virtually impossible for a new journal or a lower-ranked journal, even if such a journal provides excellent editorial service and publishes first-rate papers, to break into the top tier in the eyes of tenure committees and university administrators.

As an economist, I am depressed by the failure of market forces to ensure quality in our own industry, in contrast to both the principles of economics and the experiences of real-world industries. For example, when American automobile manufacturers produced mediocre cars that had terrible gas mileage in the 1970s, a subsequent influx of better cars produced by Japanese competitors prompted American manufacturers to increase quality. This pattern regularly occurs in many different industries and is one of the hallmarks of a successful free-market economy. But in academia, a journal can regularly take more than a year to get back to authors and still be considered top-tier by universities. Faculty will continue to submit their top papers to such journals regardless of the poor service they receive, and the journal will feel little market pressure to improve its service to authors.

Changes in Academia and the Research Process

How has the research process been affected by the changes in the publication environment? One effect of contributions becoming narrower and more specialized is a shrinking pool of potential reviewers for papers. Smaller pools of reviewers increase the potential for politics and the creation of cliques. In some subfields, reviewers seeking to promote their subfield (to the benefit of those in the clique) tend to be more positive; in fields where various turf wars are raging, reviewers tend to be overly negative. Overall, the academic research world has become increasingly competitive, since there are more and more scholars pursuing narrower and narrower research topics, and all are competing for space in the same journals. There is every reason to think that it will become even more competitive in the future.

If you are reading this book, you probably are an academic or are considering becoming one. Therefore, you probably find this discussion disquieting, if not outright depressing. In some ways, it is certainly depressing: an academic research career is becoming a more and more difficult way to earn a living. However, academia remains a wonderful profession in which you can have a fantastic life. Scholars can contribute to society in any number of ways—educating good students, increasing humanity's body of knowledge, providing insights that can improve public policy. Tenure enables us to present unpopular ideas without worrying about retribution from bosses. Our friends in the private sector are often jealous of our academic freedom to express such unpopular opinions publicly.

Responding to the Competitive Environment

How should the increasingly competitive nature of the academic labor market affect our behavior? In other words, how does a newly minted PhD or faculty member survive and even thrive in this environment?

There are always factors that are out of your control that affect your success. But there is much that can be done to advance your career, often in ways that might seem obvious but are ignored by young academics. It is somewhat ironic that in business schools we spend considerable time teaching our MBA students how to improve their career prospects but little time thinking about our own.

Faculty often pursue haphazard research strategies. Some start too many papers, others start too few. Some essentially rewrite the same paper over and over, while others constantly start papers in many different subfields and never publish any of them. Academics make many other correctable mistakes when managing their research career. While my experience is mostly with business school faculty and economists, I am confident that the same issues affect faculty in all fields.

Helping young academics survive the pressure they face and put their best foot forward when doing research is the overarching theme of this book. Here are a few principles that I will touch on throughout the book that are likely to help young scholars develop a successful research portfolio.

1. UNDERSTAND YOUR PRODUCTION FUNCTION

Economists characterize the way a producer can convert inputs (materials, labor, capital, and so on) into outputs as a "production function." Formalizing this production process helps economists study firms, as well as the markets in which firms operate.

But the notion of a production function is also much more general, and a useful way for academics to understand how they go about doing research themselves. We each have a certain set of skills that allow us to contribute usefully to research projects. Some of us work well by ourselves, while others prefer being part of a team. Some people are very creative and come up with novel ideas, while others are better at performing analyses suggested by others.

Perhaps the most important aspect of an academic production function that academics misunderstand is the notion of capacity. There are only twenty-four hours in a day, and most of us like to spend some of them enjoying life outside of work. Moreover, research is an intense activity; it is hard to focus on more than one or two things with sufficient intensity at any time. There are tricks to managing your workload. Personally, I try to work hard on one paper at a time; I then return it to my coauthors and focus next on another paper while the coauthors take their turn editing the paper. That way I can work diligently on a number of papers simultaneously.

Nonetheless, there is a limit to the number of papers that any of us can work on at any point in time. This number varies across individuals, but each of us has a "capacity." I believe that it is important for people to know their own capacity, because committing to research projects that exceed your capacity can be a serious mistake. Some scholars constantly start new projects and work on many papers at once, but too often they frustrate their coauthors, produce sloppy work, and never finish many of their research projects. Of course, the opposite is true as well: some scholars are such perfectionists that they never start anything that they don't think will win them a Nobel Prize. Usually, such projects never arrive, but these perfectionists nonetheless like to boast of having higher standards than other people despite their lack of production.

2. PROCEED WITH A PLAN

In business schools, we teach young entrepreneurs to start with a well thought out business plan for their new enterprises. Such a plan involves setting very specific goals, such as customer acquisition, development of beta versions of software, and a date by which the firm will be profitable. Such plans can be thought of as a route to becoming a successful firm in a specified (but narrow) sector of the economy. Entrepreneurs, even successful ones, do not always end up following the plan. Sometimes the plan is found to be overly ambitious; even if the firm makes good progress, it is often not as rapid as the entrepreneur had hoped for. And sometimes the plan turns out to be somewhat misguided and the firm has to shift its focus to be profitable. Nonetheless, having a business plan is important, principally because it forces the entrepreneur to keep his focus on the end goal and requires him to have a very good reason to depart from the original plan.

I see no reason why young academics shouldn't take a similar approach. Suppose you are a doctoral student who finished your exams and now needs to write a dissertation, or a young assistant professor looking to establish a research reputation, or even a full professor looking to remain active in research. Why not follow the same process as a new entrepreneur? Decide where your interests lie and what big-picture question you want to address. Then make a "market map" that shows what has been learned about the question, what remains unknown, and, perhaps, why some questions have not been addressed yet. Through this process, you will hopefully hit on a research idea or two. Decide what you are likely to learn from the idea and make sure it is sufficiently important to be worth your time. Then set a timetable for when you think you will be able to complete drafts of each research project, and try your best to keep to this timetable. Your ultimate output might not look like the plan you made, but having such a plan is likely to make you happier with the output you do produce.

I realize that approaching research in such a systematic fashion probably sounds simpler than it will prove to be in practice. My point is not to make the research process seem easy or formulaic. Rather, my intent is to get scholars to think systematically about where their research is going and how they are going to get it there. Many young scholars proceed in a rather random and haphazard fashion, looking only at whatever topics happen to occur to them. I know this problem well, because I did the same during my first few years as a faculty member. Once I defined my areas of research more tightly and focused on becoming one of the main participants in these areas, I became a much more productive scholar.

3. FINISH PROJECTS

The vast majority of academics enter the profession because they love to learn. We all did well in school and were fascinated by problems for which we did not know the answers. Solving them was a lot of fun. Research came naturally to us because we loved solving new problems and developing new ideas.

Starting research projects epitomizes what we love about academia. A scholar starts a research project because she is thinking about a problem she does not know the answer to and she hopes to come up with a way to answer it. Sometimes she will get interesting results and learn something; other times the analysis just makes the question murkier. But at some point in the analysis, she learns whatever she is going to learn from the question.

At this point, research stops being fun and starts being work. The scholar will go down blind alleys, then have to retrace her steps when that approach does not work. She will have to get around to writing the paper, hopefully, in a way that helps others understand what she did, why she did it, and what she found. She will have to present the paper in seminars and deal with people—some of them lacking the usual social graces—who question her analysis. She may have to wait as long as a year to hear about her submission to a journal, only to get two short referee reports of limited value and a terse note from the editor saying the paper might be reconsidered for publication if she is responsive to the referees.

Usually an author pretends to enjoy being questioned about her paper's basic premises as well as every step of its logic. Sometimes she really does enjoy the criticism, and sometimes it actually is helpful. The author is more likely, however, to publicly thank the critics politely but secretly want to strangle them. How can they not understand the point of what is in the paper, and why won't they just shut up and realize how brilliant it is? And worse, because referees are anonymous in many fields, they often feel no constraints about being harsh toward the paper they are reviewing (whose author becomes the dog they get to kick as they steam about the referee reports they just got on their own papers).

Young scholars can feel tempted to throw up their hands and start another paper. After all, starting papers is fun, but finishing them can be painful. *Do not give in to this temptation.* An author has to understand why people have responded negatively to her work, even if she thinks they are horribly misguided in doing so. Unless the author has proved Fermat's Last Theorem, she will have to expend a fair amount of effort explaining why her result is important and why a reader should care about it. The key to success in the face of negative criticism is persistence. The author has to learn how to understand and elucidate her paper's contribution so clearly that others will find it difficult to object.

Ultimately, an academic has to publish her papers. In academia, little weight is given to unpublished work. Even in fields like economics and finance, where unpublished but circulating working papers can have influence, promotion and tenure committees want to see the "certification of quality" that comes with publication. And after a paper has remained unpublished for a few years, the author's peers will stop feeling an obligation to cite it. In other words, both the paper (which takes on a life of its own) and the author benefit substantially from publication.

Sometimes authors refuse to publish a paper if they cannot get it accepted in one of the journals considered top-tier. I believe this attitude is a mistake. There are many journals, and a paper will have a much larger impact if it is published in a good journal, even one that is not considered top-tier, than if it is not published at all.[8] Many good papers are never published because the authors lack the persistence to see it through, or because they do not understand the paper's contribution and limitations and try to market the paper in an inappropriate manner.

4. BE PROFESSIONAL IN YOUR INTERPERSONAL RELATIONSHIPS

For reasons that I do not understand, a very close friend of mine has gone into administration and now is a vice provost at one of the top universities in the country. He always tells me that the biggest surprise he finds in his job is the immature behavior of brilliant scholars, who regularly act like five-year-olds. With the advent of social media and the internet, every mistake you make risks becoming not only widely known but unforgettable. (Like most great innovations, Google is both a blessing and a curse.) Every few months there seems to be a new scandal that people discuss over the internet. For example, one big name might accuse another of stealing his idea while they are socializing, and before long there is a nasty email trail that everyone in the profession

---

8. Not everyone agrees with me on this point. One of my favorite coauthors commented: "Pushing a paper through in a below top-tier journal often takes a great amount of time as well. Yet papers in non-top-tier journals do not count towards tenure, and do not attract quality citations. In many places, publishing on lower-tier jounrals is even considered a bad signal about the author. So we often wonder whether it is worth the time or [whether] we can put the time into a more promising project."

has seen. Or a prominent faculty member writes a paper that cannot be replicated, the entire profession soon knows the story, and the faculty member's reputation is damaged.

A faculty member or even a doctoral student must always remember to be a professional scholar. As in all professions, the standards about anything related to one's job are much higher for professionals than for amateurs. It is fine for economics professors to go to a bar and karaoke out of tune, but a tape of a professional singer engaged in such activity could be harmful to her career.

As academics, we are on display all the time, especially when we discuss anything related to our specialty. If we produce a result and post it publicly, we have to make sure it is correct, double- and triple-checking the code before posting. Once it is online, it is there forever and people can (and will) find it. Everyone makes honest mistakes, but if we make too many mistakes, even honest ones, people will stop believing anything we do. If we blog or tweet, we try to do so intelligently. If we say things through social media that do not stand up to the standards of logic that we expect in an academic dialogue, we shouldn't expect people to take us seriously when we try to contribute to more serious discussions in other settings.

Why Do Academic Research?

So why do you do academic research?[9] Why embark on this path in life? There is only one really good answer to this question: *because you love it*. You love playing with new ideas, understanding things you didn't understand before, learning something new about the world, but also communicating that to other people, teaching them the new idea, shepherding new ideas to their place in the world. Yes, it will take some ambition, some working the system. And there will be drudgery— cleaning data, answering referee reports, doing your social personal and professional duties.

9. This subsection is copied (with minor edits) from the review of this book that John Cochrane wrote for Princeton University Press.

As an ambitious academic, you should also enjoy the accolades of people reading and following your work. You should not write just to publish papers; you should write to have people read them, cite them, think about them, and change the way they think. You want to make an impact beyond having someone remark at your funeral on how long your vita was.

If you love it, academic research is liberating. You have time to pursue ideas of your own choosing. But if you are like 99 percent of people on this planet, being told to "go to your office and think up something great" is a paralyzing and terrifying mandate. Most people need to be told what to do, told when to work, told when it's okay not to work, and told what to think about. Most people need daily pats on the back and the incentives that business is good at providing.

Only people who love academic scholarship—who love playing with ideas and who love the hard process of refining them, writing them, presenting them, and interacting with others about them—actually produce good work. Do you love academic scholarship? Then you should do it.

PART I

Selecting a Topic

2

Selecting Research Topics

BEFORE YOU CAN begin a research project, you must first find a topic to study, and a specific question within the topic to address. Coming up with good research questions is often the hardest and most important part of a researcher's job. A good research project should address an issue that is not completely understood by the existing literature, and one to which the researcher has a chance of making a meaningful contribution. It also should be something that the researcher finds interesting and fun, and that fits well into her personal research portfolio.

Scholars often ask me for advice about picking research topics. I usually answer that you should pick research projects in the context of your broader research goals. While there is no magic formula for coming up with a research topic, there are general principles that can aid you in choosing a project that is likely to be successful. You can and should think systematically about the research projects you undertake.

The choice of any research project should be predicated on your background, knowledge, and prior research history. The quality of a research project is individual-specific: what is a good project for one scholar might be a bad one for another scholar, even if they are in the same field. For a number of reasons, research projects are more valuable when they are part of a stream of related research. The overall importance of a series of projects tends to be greater when they complement each other.

It is important for every researcher to define her own identity in terms of the set of issues and methodological approaches that she wishes to explore over a relatively long period of time. These issues are known as a "research agenda," or "research program." Once a scholar has a moderately well defined research agenda, she can pick individual projects that fit into this agenda. Occasionally, it will make sense for her to depart from her research agenda if she comes across a sufficiently high-quality research opportunity. But as I discuss in detail later, such departures should be the exception: the majority of your work should be determined by a coherent research agenda.

I think of the issue of picking research projects as a two-part process: a researcher first needs to define her research agenda—the long-term set of goals she wishes to accomplish with her research—and then, conditional on a research agenda, she is ready to select individual research projects. Each of these choices can be difficult, but they ultimately will have a huge impact on a researcher's career, so she should take them extremely seriously.

Why Specialize?

Graduate programs, regardless of field, are usually designed to expose students to most of the important work in the field, including the major subfields. A good student will find many of the topics she learns about to be interesting and is likely to have ideas as to how knowledge could be extended in a number of them. Many other students begin research projects in a number of different areas because they do not know exactly what they want to specialize in. Either way, this is how most students are introduced to research.

Nonetheless, for a number of reasons, it is usually advisable for researchers to specialize and focus on a relatively narrow set of issues in their research. First of all, in any literature, there are usually many papers that have already been written. To make progress and advance the literature, a scholar needs to know these papers extremely well. Moreover, every literature has issues that participants know about and that are not easily learned by reading papers. Some papers published in top journals are not taken seriously because participants in the literature know that there is something wrong with them. Sometimes what seems like an obvious approach is found to have flaws once it is examined more closely; a new researcher in the literature might find this out the hard way by spending time on the approach before realizing that it does not work. The learning curve for doing first-rate research in any literature is steep, and it is doubly hard to keep up for those who work in multiple literatures.

Once a scholar's research has been recognized as a contribution to a literature, it can be easier for her to make subsequent, related contributions. Often she can write a paper that is a natural "follow-on" to the first one. Sometimes it turns out that the project that she was originally working on was interesting, but not as interesting as a second idea she has had while working on it. Once a scholar has made an investment in the first paper, she has a comparative advantage in writing subsequent related papers.

In addition to the advantages in the production of new research by specialization, there are other advantages to research specialization in the marketing, distribution and eventual impact of the research. After writing a paper, a researcher must turn to the important task of marketing the paper to others in the field. It is not enough for a scholar to do the research: she must also communicate to others what she has done and convince them that the work is important. She should present the paper at other universities and at conferences and figure out how to get others doing related work to pay attention to it. The sad fact is that people pay more attention to the work of people who are well known in a particular area than the work of others, even if the others are high-quality researchers who produce good papers. All other things equal, work that a scholar pursues inside her area of specialty is likely to receive more attention and citations than work she pursues outside her main area.

Finally, the politics of academia favors those who specialize. At Ohio State, I think we are fairly typical in that we hire new faculty who fill a particular area of need. We judge them by whether they have the potential to be a well-known scholar in that area. Of course, it is nice if the candidate has done additional work outside that area. But the most important thing is having a body of related work to demonstrate to us that she is likely to become an important scholar in that area. For this reason, having a second paper related to her main paper would usually benefit a candidate more than having a second paper in a completely different area.

When it is time to consider faculty for promotion and tenure, it again is to the candidate's advantage to be at least somewhat specialized. An important part of the process is receiving letters of evaluation from scholars outside the university. It is much easier to get strong letters from outside scholars if the work is relatively concentrated. When asked to write a letter of evaluation, outside scholars almost always prefer to be already familiar with the bulk of the candidate's work before sitting down to write the letter, which is usually a time-consuming and uncompensated chore. It can be awkward if the letter-writer says that he knows one of the candidate's papers but cannot comment on the remainder because they are far from his area of specialty. Since letter-writers are often besieged with requests for promotion and tenure letters, sometimes getting more than ten such requests in a given academic year, they are often unable or unwilling to spend much time learning work that is new to them for the purpose of writing these letters.

For all these reasons, I usually encourage young scholars to organize their research around a coherent research program, especially when they are starting out. It is much better to focus your research on a big issue such as "the effect of machine learning on advertising," or "the causes and consequences of countries adopting the euro," than to write a series of unrelated papers. A research program does not have to last forever; scholars' interests change over time, and particular fields go in and out of fashion. Most of us will pursue a number of different research programs over our careers, and sometimes we simply find it enjoyable to work on projects outside our major research programs. But at any point in time, it is probably advisable to have most of your work concentrated on a group of somewhat related projects.

Be an Academic Hunter, Not an Academic Farmer

A very popular guest speaker who regularly guest-lectures in my class used to be a partner in one of the most famous venture capital firms in Silicon Valley. This venture capitalist provided financing for some of the tech companies that most readers probably deal with on a daily basis. One thing he always tells the class is that at his Silicon Valley firm (and at the new firm he started as well), "we are hunters, not farmers." What he means is that these firms make decisions about which markets are likely to take off, then actively search for firms they think will dominate these markets. He and his partners map out all the subsectors of that market, decide the characteristics of the firm they would in principle like in each subsector, and then search for such a firm. Sometimes it does not exist, so they create the firm themselves. Once his firm found two MIT PhD students who were working on a technology that fit what they thought would be valued by the market, so they approached the students and convinced them to start a company that their firm (very profitably) funded. Another time, when his current fund was unsuccessful in convincing established firms to use a technology that he and his partners thought would revolutionize an industry, they created their own company to use this approach.[1]

The alternative, more traditional way to do venture investing is what my guest speaker calls "farming." In this more passive approach, venture capitalists sort through the thousands of business plans that cross their desks and choose the best ones in which to invest. Many venture capitalists follow this approach and are successful. These venture capitalists do limit their investments to companies in certain industries and companies of a certain age, whether early-stage or more mature companies. But they are less aggressive at seeking out companies that do not contact them, and they are more likely to invest in firms they happen to know about through personal contacts.

How does this discussion of venture capital relate to academic research? I think that since venture capital firms and academics both make risky investments in innovative projects, many of the same principles apply. An important difference between professional investors and academics, however, is that professional investors spend a lot of time thinking about the investment process and academics tend to take a more haphazard approach.

Almost all academics are very smart and have learned the material taught in the courses they took as students. But they often have different strategies for coming up with research ideas. Some people get ideas

1. This company went public around the time of this writing with a valuation well into the billions of dollars.

from papers they have read or heard at seminars. Perhaps they detect mistakes in these papers that need fixing, or see a way to extend them. Sometimes they rely on lunch conversations with their colleagues or wait for friends to suggest projects they can coauthor. This approach might be called what my guest speaker would refer to as "farming." Many successful research careers have evolved, however, through strategies like these.

The key distinction between hunters and farmers is that a hunter knows what she wants to accomplish, what questions she wants to address, and what methods she wants to use. Hunters are proactive. In contrast, farmers are reactive. They are motivated by others' work, perhaps fixing mistakes or providing extensions. Or they will join several unrelated projects with their friends and get publications that way. Sometimes this distinction is not clear-cut; for example, a conversation with a colleague or a reaction to an important paper can lead to a lifetime of work. Nevertheless, I think these are important distinctions in how academics think about their research.

I believe that most successful scholars have a well-defined research program centered on a specific question or research approach. It is not usually a response to others' research but instead a scholar's own drive and search for answers that motivate the best research. The scholar will "hunt" for the truth wherever clues can be found and will usually pursue this research program with single-minded energy. The research itself becomes a goal, rather than a means to an end. In other words, the most successful researchers do not do research because they want to get promoted or become famous or increase their salary; they do research because they want to know the answer to the questions they ask.

Two Successful Research Programs

Many successful academic researchers have adopted such a "hunting" strategy. Two particularly successful ones highlight the importance of a targeted and specialized research strategy. Both could be described as "hunters," as each spent his career seeking out novel approaches to problems rather than focusing on the problems that happened to be available to him.

Daniel Kahneman's book describing his work, *Thinking, Fast and Slow*, is one that every scholar should read, regardless of their field.[2] Kahneman is a psychologist who, together with his longtime collaborator Amos Tversky, spent his career studying how humans make decisions.[3] In an influential series of experiments, Kahneman and Tversky presented compelling evidence that human decision-making can be characterized by what they refer to as "prospect theory," which departs from rationality in predictable ways. This work has revolutionized both psychology and economics; prior to their work, economic analysis always started from the presumption that individuals are rational.

The thing that struck me when I read Kahneman's book, aside from the brilliance and importance of the work itself, was how Kahneman and Tversky went about doing their work. They started working together after Tversky gave a guest lecture in Kahneman's class. What is surprising to many is that Kahneman absolutely hated Tversky's talk. The two of them ended up arguing about the issues in the lecture endlessly and eventually came up with experiments that enabled them to distinguish between their alternative views. The issues raised in these discussions, about the way individuals make decisions, became the life's work of each scholar. Within this broad research agenda, Kahneman and Tversky pursued many individual projects, a number of which involved other coauthors as well.

Kahneman and Tversky's research agenda came about because of disagreements, both with each other and with the prevailing "rational" view of behavior. They wanted to know how and why people behave the way they do. What they did not do was to ask: What are the journals publishing nowadays? What issues are hot? What issues can we get research funding for? The impetus for the work was their desire to understand the question of how people make decisions, not the rewards that would ultimately accrue to its authors. Kahneman and Tversky started with a question, hunted for the answer to that question using approaches that were unconventional at the time, and were ultimately rewarded for it.

---

2. D. Kahneman, *Thinking, Fast and Slow* (Farrar, Straus and Giroux, 2011).

3. For an entertaining treatment of Kahneman's and Tversky's lives and the relationship between the two, see Michael Lewis's *The Undoing Project* (W. W. Norton, 2016).

While Kahneman's research centered on one particular question, other very successful researchers have centered their research on a particular method, or on a style of answering questions. One such scholar whose work follows this pattern is Alan Krueger, a labor economist whose unique style of research led him to a number of important insights.

Traditionally, labor economists have relied on large, publicly available databases to draw inferences about labor markets. Krueger sometimes used this approach, but more often he collected his own data so that he could address a question he was interested in. Krueger and a group of like-minded labor economists who often coauthor together have popularized a number of methods that allow for drawing causal inferences. The issue of how one makes causal inferences from real-world data is a key issue in economics (and really in all the social sciences). His research program has used unique and often hand-collected data to draw causal inferences about some of the most important issues about labor markets.

What is perhaps Krueger's most celebrated (and controversial) paper was coauthored with David Card and concerns the effect of the minimum wage.[4] Every economics textbook has historically taught that the minimum wage leads to lower employment because it increases the incremental cost of each additional worker. Card and Krueger challenged this view by analyzing what happened when, in 1992, New Jersey raised its minimum wage and neighboring Pennsylvania did not. They found, counter to the standard textbook prediction, that employment at fast-food restaurants that paid minimum wage increased more in New Jersey than in Pennsylvania. This finding generated an incredible amount of interest, primarily because of Card and Krueger's strategy of actively seeking data that would provide insights about an important question.[5]

4. See D. Card and A. Krueger, "Minimum Wages and Employment: A Case Study of the Fast Food Industry in New Jersey and Pennsylvania," *American Economic Review* (84, 1994): 772–93.

5. Card and Krueger's findings on the minimum wage are not universally accepted. For an alternative view, see D. Newmark and W. Wascher, "Minimum Wages and Employment: A Review of Evidence from the New Minimum Wage Research," Working Paper 12663 (National

An important methodological concern in economics is called "unobservables," which are variables that affect economic outcomes that outsiders cannot see. For example, if we are interested in estimating the returns to schooling, it is difficult to distinguish between the view that schooling *causes* better outcomes or the possibility that the better outcomes are associated with more schooling because more talented people stay in school longer. To address this issue, Krueger, together with Orley Ashenfelter, gathered a sample of identical twins, whose DNA is exactly the same.[6] They actually went to a convention of twins, in a place called Twinsburg, Ohio, and interviewed the twins themselves about their education, life history, and earnings. With these data, they were able to provide estimates of the returns to schooling that they knew were not caused by unobservables. As in the previous example, Krueger's strategy of actively seeking new data from creative sources to identify causal answers to fundamental questions yielded an important contribution.

How to Develop a Research Agenda

Perhaps it is a bit unfair of me, when discussing the importance of a research agenda, to give examples of academics who are among the most successful in their fields. A reader might think that these scholars were obviously brilliant and would have been successful no matter what strategy they pursued. But in academia, there are many brilliant people, and very few are as successful as Kahneman and Krueger. What distinguishes them is that they knew what they wanted to learn from their research, developed a style of their own, and were able to make a substantial contribution to our knowledge.

Most young scholars enter graduate school with a vague idea of what they want to study but no particular research agenda in mind. Coming up with a coherent research agenda is possibly the most difficult task

Bureau of Economic Research, 2006); and D. Newmark and W. Wascher, *Minimum Wages* (MIT Press, 2008).

6. See O. Ashenfelter and A. Krueger, "Estimates of the Economic Return to Schooling from a New Sample of Twins," *American Economic Review* 84(5, 1994): 1157–83.

facing a young researcher, but might also be the most important. The scholar's research agenda defines who she is as an academic. It is what she spends the majority of her time working on, and what others think of when her name comes up. When starting an academic career, a scholar should put substantial effort into thinking about what she wants her research agenda to be going forward, and how she will go about achieving it. In addition, as she gets older she should always be asking herself these sorts of questions about her research agenda: Is her agenda still exciting to her? What about it is getting boring from being done over and over again, both by her and by others? Are there new areas she would like to explore? If so, is it worth the up-front cost of acquiring the background and skills to study these areas?

I entered an economics PhD program with little knowledge of finance. I was an undergraduate mathematics major who had taken a lot of economics courses and worked as a research assistant to a number of faculty in the mathematics, economics, and finance departments. What I did know about finance was through my work as a research assistant on work about option pricing, which is an area of finance on which I ultimately chose *not* to focus my research.

When I entered graduate school, I was interested in economics and had the skills to succeed at it, but did not really know what I wanted to study. Motivated by the 1980s takeover wave that was occurring while I was a graduate student, I wrote my dissertation about corporate governance. This work led to research in more mainstream corporate finance and, after I moved to the University of Illinois in the early 2000s, to an interest in private capital markets and the ways in which they are used to finance new companies and acquire existing ones. As is fairly typical of many academics over the course of their career, my research agenda evolved based on what I happened to be interested in at the time.

How do you get started on a research agenda? The answer varies a lot by field. In some fields you are limited by your university's lab facilities or by the knowledge and interests of the faculty in the department. In those fields, a student might enter graduate school receiving funding from a particular professor so that she can work in his lab doing research he directs. Or she could have such specialized interests that she knows with fairly high certainty which faculty member will be her adviser. But in most departments in the economics-oriented fields, the burden of finding a research program is on the student or the young faculty member. Sometimes a scholar's research program mirrors that of her thesis adviser or mentor. The mark of a successful scholar, however, is independence: a scholar should try to have her own unique approach that is somewhat different from that of her adviser. Her goal is to make contributions for which she will be known individually.

I have always encouraged my doctoral students to take advantage of their unique knowledge and talents and to pursue a research program that takes advantage of their natural comparative advantage. To use a bad sports analogy, if you are seven feet tall, it is usually not such a good idea to play shortstop, since focusing on basketball would probably lead to a better outcome. Thinking about the topics of recent doctoral dissertations I have helped to advise, most of my students, with my encouragement, have taken advantage of their own individual strengths. One student worked on Wall Street prior to graduate school and had a deep understanding of how loans are securitized; he wrote a fine dissertation on this topic and pursued a successful research program focusing on securitization. Another student had the ability to pick up Bayesian statistics and related programming as easily as most of us learn basic algebra; he eventually wrote a fine dissertation taking advantage of these skills. Most recently, a student came into the program with connections and knowledge of real estate private equity funds and started a research program in that area. These students and many others started their academic careers in good shape because they were able to find a research agenda that matched their skills and interests.

However, students should not feel limited by what they know when they enter graduate school. The real purpose of graduate school is to enable students to pick up new interests and skills that they did not have when they arrived on campus. Students should take advantage of opportunities to learn new areas and develop new skills. A good strategy for deciding what to learn is to observe what the best young faculty are working on and the skills they are using.

If you are one of those students (or faculty) who cannot seem to focus their research ideas around a central theme, I would encourage you to think about the following questions: Why did you enter the program in the first place? What was it about that field that excited you and inspired you to go into it? Is the field still exciting to you? Are there a number of unsolved issues that you can address? Ultimately, you want to find a niche where you can contribute something beyond what the profession already knows, preferably about something sufficiently important that the profession will care about what you do.

One approach to starting a research program is to think of a classic puzzle that the literature has been considering for a long time. Although sometimes celebrated research comes from this approach (such as solving Fermat's Last Theorem), it often can be difficult to make progress on such topics. As John Cochrane puts it: "There are thousands of papers, they probably thought of any idea you might have, and you'll have to master them before you publish."[7] Cochrane also cautions against extensions of well-known papers for the mere purpose of generalizing them rather than drawing any new implications from them—for instance: "I'm going to add recursive preferences and estimate the Campbell-Cochrane model on Korean data."

Another approach is to focus your research on large events that are going on in the world and their implications for economics (or whatever field you are studying). As I write, the world is in shutdown from the Covid-19 virus, and academics have been besieged by many papers inspired by the virus. These papers were put together remarkably quickly—some papers were *published* in 2020 using data generated earlier in the same year.[8] Similarly, a run of papers followed on other major events, such as the 2008 Financial Crisis, the dot-com boom and bust, and the breakup of the Soviet Union. Some of these papers have had lasting impact, but most have not. The trick when writing about the hot topic of the day is to focus on an aspect of it that will still be interest

---

7. From Cochrane's review of this book for Princeton University Press.

8. See, for example, the November 2020 issue of *Review of Corporate Finance Studies*, which is entirely devoted to papers about the Covid-19 crisis.

once the crisis is over and the world's attention is focused on something else.

Everyone has their own approach to picking research areas, but I have found it useful to avoid the moment's "hot" topics in carrying out my own research agenda. I try to find topics that are of fundamental importance, that the literature does not understand well, and that have few people working on them. For example, at the beginning of my career, I thought corporate governance fit this description. It is clearly an important issue, and I was one of the few economists focusing on corporate governance at that time. Since then, however, the number of people working on corporate governance has greatly increased. While I remain interested in the topic, I now focus most of my research efforts elsewhere, although I do still write governance papers when I think I have a new approach to studying the issue. Recently, I have begun to focus my research on private capital markets; they have become incredibly important in the economy, but the academic literature on them is still in its early stages. My bet is that research leading to a better understanding of these markets will yield important insights.

How to Pick Individual Research Projects

Selecting research projects to work on, especially at the beginning of your career, can seem like a daunting task. A new research project has to have the potential to make a major contribution to the literature and to teach the profession something important that it did not previously know. This is a high bar, substantially higher than anything most young academics have previously cleared.

However, getting involved in new research projects can be a lot of fun. Coming up with new research projects to work on involves thinking about the big picture, what we know and what we don't know, and why the answers to particular questions are important. Most academics find it fascinating to think about these kinds of issues—that is why we became academics in the first place.

Unfortunately, the beginning of a research project can also be incredibly frustrating. When you are searching for research ideas in a crowded field, others will be doing the same, so ideas that are obvious or easily executed tend to be competitive. Often you have to drop potential projects that once seemed promising because they have already been done by others. In addition, many ideas that initially made sense turn out, on further investigation, to be infeasible—for example, because they require data that either does not exist or is impossible for you to access.

The best researchers seem to have a knack for finding influential research projects. They usually find questions that others find interesting and that stimulate further work. But if you are not one who effortlessly finds interesting projects to work on (which is most of us), how do you develop a skill for becoming involved in promising research projects? Though there is no magic formula, there are productive ways to approach the search.

A precondition to finding a good research project is a deep knowledge of the literature in which you want to work. A literature can be thought of as a conversation: to contribute productively to it, you need to know what has already been said. Without knowing in detail what came before, it is impossible to gauge the extent to which any potential contribution extends the literature. Specialization and a focus on a particular research program facilitate the acquisition of the knowledge necessary to understand the importance of a particular contribution.

Once you have settled on a particular research agenda, you should take a step back and ask a series of questions. First, ask yourself what big-picture questions the literature tries to address. Make a list of all conceivable questions. Sometimes literatures become obsessed with one particular question when an equally important one (or sometimes an even more important one) remains unaddressed. Next, think about the existing research related to these questions. What do we know now? What don't we know? What techniques have been used so far? Is there room for improvement? What could you add? When answering these questions, you should always remember that the best papers always come about when a scholar does work on an issue that she thinks is important, not when she works on a topic she thinks will impress others.

I recently had a bright doctoral student come to my office with an idea I liked. It was in an interesting and relatively new area, and he had a general approach that might yield new insights. But I thought that the particular question he suggested was not as important as other questions he might ask instead. I suggested that he do what venture capitalists do: make a "market map" of all potential topics in the area. I advised him to list all of the issues that he might research, also list all the papers that have addressed each of them, and then think about what he could add that would be new. I am hopeful that this approach will help him come up with an interesting dissertation topic.

It is important for every researcher to understand the value of her own potential contributions. Does she bring technical skills to a problem? New data? Or simply a more creative approach? Does a student already have a deeper understanding of the literature or the institutions she is studying? The most important thing younger scholars can bring to a research project is often their time and energy, the value of which should not be underestimated: senior faculty, commonly pressed for time, may skip steps or skimp on data work. A younger scholar can sometimes improve existing work by being more thorough and spending more time thinking about its underlying issues.

A scholar should also think about the style of work she is most comfortable doing. Sometimes academics write papers that reexamine others' work by using more advanced techniques. For example, James Heckman, the winner of the 2000 Nobel Prize in Economics, together with Steven Durlauf, published a paper criticizing the analysis in Roland Fryer's well-known study of the effect of racial differences on the use of excessive force by police.[9] Assuming that Durlauf and Heckman are correct, their analysis could materially affect the way we think about racial disparities in policing, which is currently one of the most important and controversial issues facing the United States. Methodological critiques such as Durlauf and Heckman's are an important part of scientific analysis and help to ensure that the profession interprets research correctly.

9. See R. G. Fryer Jr., "An Empirical Analysis of Racial Differences in Police Use of Force," *Journal of Political Economy* 127(2019): 1210–61; and S. N. Durlauf and J. J. Heckman, "Comment on Roland Fryer's 'An Empirical Analysis of Racial Differences in Police Use of Force,'" *Journal of Political Economy* 128 (2020): 3998–4002.

Personally, this approach to research has no attraction for me. I much prefer examining new questions over finding mistakes that others have made. But others love this approach and have made successful careers using it. A scholar has to find an approach to research that works for her and is a good fit for her personality and skills. Otherwise, she will not enjoy doing the research, her heart will not be in it, and the research will tend to be of lower quality.

Finally, in selecting research projects, scholars should always try to ask questions for which the answer actually matters, even if these are often not the cleanest or most straightforward to address. Steve Kaplan, a well-known scholar in my area, often tells his students that if they want to study elephants, then study the whole elephant and not just a pimple on the elephant's skin. What he means is that a researcher should try to understand all aspects of a problem. His metaphor is implicitly critical of scholars who examine only the one aspect of a problem that is easiest to study, while ignoring larger but potentially messier issues. Taking on larger but more complicated issues can lead in the long run to research that is more interesting and useful to readers.

3

Strategic Issues in Constructing Research Portfolios

WHEN I WAS a new assistant professor, I was fascinated by all areas of economics and finance and worked on a lot of different topics, most of which were somewhat related to one another. But I never had a "plan" and never thought very much about my research portfolio—how it fit together and how it was perceived by others. Things have worked out fine for me, but looking back, I see that I would have benefited from thinking a little about optimizing my research portfolio to maximize its impact on both the profession's knowledge and on my career.

This chapter discusses factors that I probably should have thought more about when starting my own career and deciding on which research project to pursue. I begin by describing how research is evaluated and how this evaluation process should affect the way research is conducted. Then I discuss how to think about the costs of a research project and why it is a mistake to start too many projects at once. Finally I provide some guidelines for selecting projects to optimize the impact of your research portfolio, with special attention to issues such as the stages of the projects you should work on at any point in time, the question of when to abandon projects, and your choice of coauthors.

How Research Is Evaluated

Before you can think about how to optimize your research portfolio, it is important to understand how research is evaluated. Both the methods of research and the ways in which it is distributed vary from field to field. In the humanities, a scholar's value is largely determined by the books she publishes. In the sciences and engineering, the amount of money a scholar brings in through research grants is extremely important. And in the social sciences—at least in the economics-based ones—the scholar's refereed journal articles are by far the most important factor when people evaluate her research.

Universities try to maintain at least a pretense of common standards across areas. Consequently, they often claim that they value research in all fields based on its "impact," regardless of whether the research is distributed through journals, books, or conference presentations. The way in which the impact of a scholar's research is determined, however, varies across universities, across departments, and even across individuals evaluating it within a department.

Some departments determine a paper's impact solely by the journal in which it is published. In these departments, junior faculty are often told exactly how many papers they must publish, and in which journals, to achieve tenure. A journal's quality, however, is a very noisy measure of the quality of the papers it publishes. The refereeing process is imperfect and can be political. Sometimes bad papers are published in top-ranked journals, and some important papers can be rejected by more than one journal before they are finally published.

In economics, many seminal papers, some of which led to Nobel Prizes for their authors, were first rejected by at least one journal.[1] Often such a paper was rejected because the referee or editor either did not see its point or was closed-minded about new ideas. Nonetheless,

---

1. For a list of such seminal papers and some interesting discussion about their history and how rudely they were treated, see J. S. Gans and G. B. Shephard, "How Are the Mighty Fallen: Rejected Classic Articles by Leading Economists," *Journal of Economic Perspectives* 8(1, 1994): 165–79. It is a good idea to keep Gans and Shephard's list of rejected papers handy, as it can help keep your spirits up when your own paper is rejected.

all of these papers were eventually published somewhere, and their contributions recognized. We have no way of knowing how many other brilliant papers were never published and their ideas lost.

For this reason, when assessing research quality, higher-ranked departments tend to rely more on citations and careful reads of the papers than on the reputation of the journals in which the work was published. In general, the better the department the less it emphasizes counting papers and weighting by journal quality and the more it tries to measure the paper's impact independently of where it was published. The very best departments regularly deny tenure to scholars who publish many papers in top journals if none of their papers are judged to be sufficiently pathbreaking.

Academics often debate how research quality should be measured, and they usually do not agree on an answer. Nonetheless, it is important for a scholar to have some sense of how research quality and impact are measured at her university and at other universities for which she might someday work.

As economists studying how individuals in the economy respond to incentives, we should always try to respond to the incentives we face ourselves. If your department asks you to write a specified number of papers and to publish them in particular journals, then you should try your best to meet the expectations that the department has laid out. But at the same time, you should always remember that the underlying goal is to produce scholarship that has a lasting influence on the way people think about important issues. Do not let the short-term pressure to publish a certain number of papers in a few specified journals distract you from that goal. If the idea in your paper has "legs" and influences others' thinking, you will eventually be rewarded for writing the paper, regardless of where it is published.

The Impact of Evaluation on the Research Process

To some extent, a young scholar has to cater to the whims of the refereeing process and try to do work that is accepted by the profession. However, I do not mean to imply that your *only* criterion for measuring the quality of a potential research project should be the resulting paper's chances of being published in a journal your university values highly. As discussed in chapter 2, I encourage young scholars to be "hunters" and to set their own research agenda. Sometimes setting your own agenda means doing work a little outside the mainstream. Unfortunately, the most innovative work can be the most difficult to publish.

A scholar's goal should be to do innovative work *and* to publish it in a good place. When you think about starting a new research project, focus on a project that will advance your research agenda and has a strong likelihood of publication in a journal valued by your university. If your approach is somewhat different from the mainstream, it is extra important that you go out of your way to explain exactly why you are using this approach. It is especially important to be clear about the way the paper relates to the mainstream literature and improves on it. A paper cannot have an impact without explaining what is learned from it that we did not know before.

The impact of any paper, and therefore its value to its author, will be determined by the profession's belief about the importance of what is learned from the paper. Often academics complain that these beliefs are subjective and that the process *should* be more objective. I put *should* in italics because it is such a funny word to describe the process of evaluating research. Even though academics often make this complaint, there is almost no way that any evaluation of the importance of a particular research paper could possibly be anything *but* subjective. What is important to one reader will undoubtedly be trivial to another.

The impact of the vast majority of papers will depend crucially on the authors' ability to explain their paper's contribution and why it is important.[2] Sometimes authors themselves do not really understand all the implications of their work and have little sense of whether the profession will find their results interesting. The ability to understand a paper's potential contribution before starting to work on it is an important skill that tends to be learned over time.

---

2. Exceptions are papers like the proof of Fermat's Last Theorem; that contribution was obvious to anyone who read it. If you can write papers like that one, my recommendation is that you stop wasting your time reading this book and get back to working on your research.

An exercise I recommend to authors is to think about their best guess as to what the results of their research project are likely to be before they start working on it. Then they should write a three- to four-page introduction to the paper based on the assumption that the results are as anticipated. The ability to write such an introduction is likely to be related to the author's understanding of the paper's contribution. If she can write an introduction easily and convince her friends that the paper will be interesting, conditional on the results coming out as expected, then the project is probably worth pursuing. If, on the other hand, she has trouble writing an introduction that others find interesting before she does the analysis, she probably will also have difficulty completing the paper after she does the analysis. Even if she does, such a paper is unlikely to end up being influential, since readers are likely to have trouble recognizing the importance of its incremental contribution.

An issue an author should consider when she writes this first draft of an introduction is the extent to which the potential interest in the paper depends on the results. Often the best projects to start—especially for a graduate student trying to write a dissertation—are those that are interesting no matter what the results turn out to be. Papers that provide a "horse race" between alternative theories can be excellent dissertations, since no matter which theory "wins," the paper will make a contribution to the literature. However, some papers are well known precisely because of the way the results turned out. Card and Krueger's 2000 paper is famous because they found that the minimum wage did *not* increase unemployment—a result that is in stark contrast to what is traditionally taught in microeconomics courses. If, instead, Card and Krueger had found an increase in unemployment, the paper would still have made a valuable contribution but would not have had nearly as great an impact.

The Costs of a Potential Research Project

The potential benefits of any research project must be weighed against the associated costs. If the researcher runs a lab and must pay human subjects, or if the project requires data purchased from an outside vendor, these costs can be financial. Most of the time, however, the main cost is the researcher's time. Time is a researcher's most valuable asset, and she must learn to be judicious when allocating it. There are only twenty-four hours in a day, and in addition to doing research, she must sleep, eat, teach classes, have relationships, exercise, and do many other things.

For most scholars, the scarce resource is not *total* time, but *intense research* time. When writing a paper, most people have to be completely focused on it to the exclusion of everything else. Work produced during random hours here and there cannot measure up to the output from distraction-free blocks of time. Blocks of time are precious, and for many scholars the availability of such blocks of time is an important factor affecting their productivity.

Everyone works in different ways, but it is important for every researcher to know the way she works best. Her work habits combine with her other commitments to produce what I call *capacity*, by which I mean the number of research projects that she can productively work on at any one time. This number can vary substantially across people. I have very successful academic friends who can work on ten or fifteen projects at once, and other equally successful ones who can work on only one or two at a time. Scholars' capacities also vary over their careers; my capacity today is actually higher than when I was younger, in large part because my coauthors now usually do the time-consuming data work that I used to do myself.

Every scholar should know her own capacity to work on research projects and not commit to more projects than she can handle. When she commits to work beyond her capacity, work quality tends to suffer, as do her relationships with coauthors, who can feel taken advantage of. A researcher's capacity determines the opportunity cost of any additional research project and should affect which projects she takes. If she is far from reaching capacity, then she should make an effort to find new things to work on, even ideas that are a bit speculative or that depart a little from her main research program. But if she is near or at her capacity, it is important that she be extremely selective about what she commits to work on. A scholar should always find a way to make room for a project that is sufficiently pathbreaking, but she should also stay aware of the costs of overcommitment, which can be substantial.

Structuring Your Research Portfolio

A theme of this book is that much academic work now done haphazardly could be markedly improved with a little thought and planning. Nowhere is this idea more relevant than in the structuring of a research portfolio: a series of research projects that collectively teach readers something important. Ideally, these projects are related to one another and their combined value is greater than the sum of their individual values.

There are a number of issues to consider when constructing a coherent portfolio. Here are some of the important ones:

PROJECTS AT DIFFERENT STAGES. The research process can be long, laborious, and sometimes frustrating. It begins when a scholar and her coauthors have an idea. For a while they probably bounce the idea off of one another to ensure that they understand the issues completely. If the scholar and her coauthors decide to pursue the idea, the analysis itself may be relatively quick or it may take a long time, depending on the nature of the work involved. Then they have to write the paper, circulate it, get feedback, circulate it some more, and present it as many times as possible. At this point, the scholar and her coauthors might be ready to submit the paper to a journal. The review process, which varies from field to field, can be slow. Papers that are accepted usually have gone through a number of rounds of revision, with substantial changes required at each round. In addition, most papers have to be submitted to several journals before they are accepted by one of them, and journals can take a long time between submission and a decision. Finally, if she and her coauthors are fortunate enough to have the paper accepted for publication in a journal, there is usually a substantial time lag prior to publication. The entire process from start to finish usually takes a number of years.

Because the research process is so long and involved, it is often a good idea to stagger projects and to always have some projects at different stages. There are a number of reasons why staggering is a good policy. First, different parts of a project require different skills; for example, initiating a project requires creativity, but perseverance and attention to detail become essential when finishing up the publishing process.

Second, the custom in the economics-oriented fields is to present papers at other universities and conferences in draft or "working paper" form. Once the paper is far along in the publication process, it is less desirable to present the work at conferences or other universities, since any suggestions from discussants or the audience could be difficult for authors to incorporate at that stage. Ideally, a scholar will always have some work at the right stage for presentation: a complete draft that is sufficiently polished to present in public, but not so polished that it is ready for publication. A scholar should avoid being in the position of having to decline speaking opportunities because none of her papers are at the right stage for presentation.

Third, papers at different stages require different kinds of work. A former student recently told me that, as she was revising her job market paper for publication, she could not do the data work required for too long. But she found it possible and enjoyable to complement the data work with reading and thinking about potential new projects.

Finally, it is a good idea to always be starting new projects, or at least thinking about ideas for a new one. When overwhelmed with revisions, many scholars have no capacity to start a new project, and as they avoid thinking about new ideas and new ways of approaching problems, their creativity becomes stale.

KEEP SPARE CAPACITY. When deciding whether to start a new project, it is important to understand the costs associated with the project and take them into account in your decision. Depending on the nature of the research, the project will take time and resources and involve a time commitment to the others involved with the project. In addition, an important but sometimes neglected cost of a new project is that starting a project today could limit your ability to start future projects. It is frustrating when you are so committed to existing projects that you cannot start any new ones. As academics, we should constantly be thinking about new developments in our field, how they relate to our own work, and what extensions are possible. If a new research project limits your ability to act on subsequent ideas because the project takes you close to your capacity, this is a real cost that should be taken into account when making decisions about investing in a new research project.

ABANDON BAD PROJECTS. All of us have some projects that seem very promising when we start them, but that eventually become less interesting than we thought they might be. To preserve research capacity, it is important to reevaluate ongoing projects on a regular basis; if a project is not worth doing *going forward*, then it probably makes sense to abandon it. Once a researcher has put substantial time and effort into a project, she can become subject to the "sunk cost" fallacy: making decisions based on costs that have already been spent and therefore should not be relevant to current decisions. If a project does not appear to justify the *subsequent* time and effort to complete it, continuing it is not likely to be a good idea.

Sometimes, however, it can be difficult to abandon projects, especially when they are coauthored. If a coauthor is subject to the sunk cost bias, or if she does not have a high opportunity cost of time, she may want to continue the project even though you're ready to abandon it (or vice versa). These situations can be difficult, and there are no easy answers. My advice for handling a disagreement between coauthors is to remember the importance of relationships in academia (and elsewhere). Sometimes it is worth making sacrifices to maintain these relationships.

Coauthors

Most work today is coauthored, and finding the right coauthors can in large part determine the success of your research program. I have worked with many more coauthors in my career than most people—fifty-five as of the time of this writing—and each has played an important role in my career. I have been extremely fortunate, as the vast majority of my coauthors have been wonderful—smart, interesting, hardworking, and fun to be with. Equally importantly, I have found a way to work productively with them, and most of the time our skills have proved to be complementary.

How do you find good coauthors? In the absence of hard and fast rules, there are a number of things to consider. First of all, coauthors should have overlapping interests and complementary skills. The project has to be of interest to both scholars and fit into each of their research programs. In addition, each coauthor should be able to bring something to the table for the match to work well. If both coauthors are good at programming but terrible writers, then their paper is likely to be well programmed but poorly written.

Second, compatibility with one another is important on a number of relevant dimensions. Of course, coauthors have to get along personally and have the same worldview about their approach to research. But other factors matter as well. Some people are night owls and work best between midnight and 4:00 a.m. I am more of a morning person, and sometimes have difficulty coordinating with night owls, but sometimes it works great, as the paper can be worked on literally 24/7 since one of us is always awake! In addition, work tempo can affect how well coauthors work together. I am very intense when I work and like to do things immediately. Most coauthors like this aspect of my work habits, but some others prefer to work more slowly and to take a long time to finish things.

Third, it is important to consider a prospective coauthor's age and reputation. Older, more established scholars can be helpful in a number of ways: they often have better perspectives on the state of the literature and possible contributions to it, and they are usually better at navigating the publication process. There are costs, however, to working with more established scholars. They tend to be busier than younger people and less motivated to complete the work in a timely manner. Consequently, they can sometimes take longer to do their part of the work, and sometimes they shirk the work and do not complete it at all. Senior scholars have different incentives regarding the journal submission process: junior faculty's careers depend on publishing in top-ranked journals quickly, while senior faculty would like to publish influential work but are less concerned with the timing. Sometimes conflicts occur because junior faculty want to rush papers to journals too soon while senior faculty want to wait too long.

More importantly (and often unfairly), no matter who does the work, the more senior scholar usually receives disproportionate credit for the research. People tend to assume, often incorrectly, that the senior scholar is the one who had the idea originally. This assumption compounds the especially high cost of working with senior scholars if it is evident that the paper is part of that scholar's research agenda, in which case readers will surmise (perhaps incorrectly) that the senior scholar is the driving force behind the research. It is important for a young scholar to establish her own research identity, and too much work with older and more established scholars can make it difficult to do so.

Fourth, you should consider whether a potential coauthor is good at getting work done and completing projects. Many scholars are smart, nice people with good ideas, but they get bored quickly and move on to other things rather than finishing existing projects. It can be dangerous to start too many projects with people like that. A young scholar's career can become tied to a coauthor's ability and willingness to put in the time to complete projects and to shepherd projects through the often painful publication process. If a senior colleague is a person who enjoys starting papers but hates finishing them, the coauthored work can remain a working paper for a long time, possibly forever. Sometimes young faculty are denied tenure because their senior coauthors decided that they would rather take yoga or mountain climbing more seriously than publishing their coauthored papers.

Fifth, and perhaps most importantly, a scholar's career becomes tied to her coauthors' in a number of ways. Having a coauthor who is sloppy or commits an ethical violation can become a major problem. For example, suppose a coauthor "accidentally" types "2.5" instead of "1.5" as a t-statistic on the variable you are interested in learning about. If this result is deemed sufficiently important, an outsider trying to replicate your "significant" result is likely to fail. You and your coauthor will be equally blamed, even if you had nothing to do with causing the mistake. You still lose if outsiders cannot replicate a result from one of your coauthor's other papers, even if you had nothing to do with that paper. Inferring that if your coauthor is sloppy on one paper, then all of his papers may be equally sloppy, they will suspect that the result in your paper is wrong as well. I sometimes tell students that choosing a coauthor is a little like choosing a spouse, in that you end up suffering for all of the person's failings even if you have nothing to do with them.

Despite these concerns, there is a reason why coauthoring has become the predominant way to do research in many fields. Usually, value can be added by combining forces, as people tend to have different strengths. In addition, it is more fun to do research with someone else. Some of my coauthors are my closest friends, and those friendships had a chance to grow as we went through the research process together.

One thing that has changed in recent years is the ease of working with people who live far away. With the ability to talk via Skype or Zoom and to store files in the cloud using Dropbox, any inconvenience in coauthoring with scholars at other universities is trivial. It wasn't always that way; not that long ago we shared files by mailing floppy disks to one another, by regular US mail (FedEx being too expensive at the time). Today, however, it's sometimes easier to get in touch with my coauthors in Asia or Australia than with my colleagues who live a few minutes from me in Columbus, Ohio. Distance should not be a deterrent to working with other scholars, no matter where they live.

Resist Pressure from Others

An awkward moment sometimes occurs when a friend suggests a potential coauthored project that does not fit into your existing research program. Or when a senior colleague you would like to impress suggests an idea that seems reasonable but does not align well with your work. Or when the idea is a good one but you are close to your research capacity and concerned that committing to a new project could keep you from finishing your ongoing projects. Sometimes you like the idea and also think that the person suggesting it would be an excellent coauthor. It can seem like a great opportunity that you do not want to pass up. However, there are some issues you should think through before you agree to coauthor the paper.

The costs of starting a project with this potential coauthor are the same as those discussed earlier. The project will take valuable time away from your main research agenda, so ask yourself: How wedded am I to my current research program? Am I looking to expand my horizons and move to a different area, or would it be better to concentrate on my main research area? Can these two areas of research be connected by a future research project? How much capital would I gain by coauthoring this work? How much would I lose if I offend a colleague by not agreeing to be a coauthor? How close am I to my research capacity? If you are close to your capacity, then the opportunity cost of starting the project could be quite high. These are some of the issues you should think through before agreeing to start a new project with a friend or colleague.

Some people view coauthorship the same way they view dinner parties—as a way to socialize and to improve (professional) relationships. While there are relationship-building aspects to starting a coauthored paper, they should not be the primary motive for starting a research project. Research is not a social obligation. Research is what we do for a living. Academia is a competitive world, and there are many others searching for ideas related to the ones we are studying.

To compete, you must devote all of your resources to projects that maximize the impact of your research. Usually the best way to do that is to pursue a portfolio of research projects that are related to one another and that develop your reputation in one particular area. Advancing your own research program will be difficult enough absent outside constraints. If a friend's research interests coincide with your own, then it can be wonderful to work with one another. The key is the project: you should never sacrifice the best possible projects just to work with a particular coauthor, even if he is a good friend you really want to work with.

PART II

Writing a Draft

4

An Overview of Writing Academic Research Papers

ONCE YOU pick a topic, then the real work begins. Any research project involves much analysis, whether you are doing an experiment, solving a model, or estimating an equation. In this book, I do not focus on the technical details of economic analysis. There are many books that cover economic theory, econometrics, and so on, far better than I could. My focus is on the craft of putting papers together and writing them in the most effective fashion. Craftsmanship is particularly important when writing papers because a scholar's choices about how to write and present her analysis often spell the difference between a paper being influential and its being ignored.

Many scholars make the common mistake of not taking the "write-up" seriously enough. Academics often say something like: "I've done all the work, now I just have to write it up." If you have made a contribution that is immediately obvious to all readers, such as proving Fermat's Last Theorem, this approach would be sensible. But for the vast majority of scholars, the importance of their research will not be immediately evident to readers. An important part of the job in writing an academic paper is to explain why the research is important and why a reader should care about it.

Writing Research Papers in a Competitive Marketplace for Research

As I discussed in chapter 1, the academic marketplace is becoming more competitive every year. Top journals have acceptance rates under 10 percent, small regional conferences receive 200 to 300 submissions and usually take only eight to ten papers, while large international conferences receive over 2,000 submissions and take 100 to 150 papers. In addition, if you are not yet established and do not have a position at a top-ranked university, it is even harder to get accepted than these numbers would imply.

Editorial decisions at academic journals are usually made through what is known as a "peer review" process, which is discussed in detail in chapter 11. Editors send papers to scholars doing related research, who then write referee reports on the papers. These reviewers are supposed to make a recommendation to the editor and also make suggestions that would help the author improve the paper's quality. The referees are expected to be somewhat antagonistic, and part of their job is to bring up alternative viewpoints. In addition to monitoring the paper's quality, referees help ensure that the author interpreted her results appropriately and acknowledged the paper's limitations.

However, blind reviewing has become a joke in the internet age, when a reviewer can Google the paper's title and immediately see who the authors are. Unfortunately, reviewers sometimes can favor their friends and famous people they respect over people they do not know, even if they are supposed to be reviewing papers blindly. Consequently, if you are not a well-known scholar, it can be particularly difficult to get your papers onto conference programs and published by top journals.[1]

When you submit a paper to a journal or a conference, what can you do to maximize the chance of having your paper accepted? A good place to start is by thinking about the review process from the viewpoint of

---

1. Not everyone agrees with me on this point. In his review of this book, John Cochrane writes: "This is absolutely not true, and you do a disservice passing it on. You leave out an important variable—quality. *Conditional on quality*—of research and of presentation (writing)—it is easier to get on programs if you are nobody from nowhere."

the people making the decisions about your work: the editors, the referees, and the conference organizers. The people running journals and conferences have their own incentives that should be understood by submitters. Editors want to increase the rankings and visibility of their journal, and also their own personal reputation. Consequently, the people running journals have incentives to pick high-quality papers but also to favor higher-profile authors, who bring visibility to the journal and will be cited more often. Conferences work similarly: session organizers want their sessions to be well attended and to have intelligent discussions, so they want to take the best papers. But they also will tend to favor more established scholars to give the conference more visibility and credibility.

Editors and conference organizers often use what might be called a "triage" approach to evaluation. Editors look at a paper quickly and decide whether to desk-reject it. If they send it out for reviewing, they select the referees and send papers they perceive to be of higher quality to better referees. Being reviewed by higher-quality referees benefits the paper's authors because they are likely to provide insightful comments and also are more likely to recommend that the editor request a revision and eventually accept the paper for publication. Conference organizers often quickly go through the papers and eliminate most of the submissions so that they can read the remaining ones more carefully and make the final selections. If a paper does not make it past these initial screenings, it will never be read carefully and given a serious chance.

In this review process, significant decisions about your research are made based on very quick reads of your paper. Therefore, it is extremely important that your paper make a good first impression. No matter what is in the paper, if it does not make a good first impression, it will be rejected a lot. Since the abstract and introduction are the parts of the paper most likely to be read by someone giving it a cursory scan, these parts will have a large impact on the likelihood that your paper will be accepted for conference programs and for publication in a good journal.

A common reaction to this system of cursory reviews is to bemoan the fact that the process is not "fair" and that authors are not all treated equally. Some academics feel that every research paper has some underlying true "quality" and that any process that does not do its very best to uncover that true quality is unfair and evidence of a poorly designed and political system of evaluating research. I am sympathetic to this viewpoint, and we all feel that somehow the system should have a better way of measuring research quality and should treat all authors equally. However, while the peer review system does have problems, there does not seem to be a better one available. As Churchill famously said about democracy, peer review is the worst way to evaluate research— other than all the other ways we could alternatively use to evaluate research.[2] The costs inherent in evaluating research will necessarily make any system of evaluation imperfect. Researchers must accept that the existing system for evaluating research is what it is, and it is not going to change anytime soon. Academics have to learn to navigate the current system of peer review if they are to have a successful career.

Since research is evaluated in an imperfect manner, it is important for a scholar to present her work in a way that is appealing to the decision-makers. Presentation of her work certainly involves writing well, but she should also strive to emphasize what readers are likely to think is interesting, organize the work in a fashion that makes sense, interpret the results appropriately, and cite the prior literature correctly but not excessively. Perhaps most importantly, a successful author must do a good job of highlighting her work's significance and what is learned from it.

How Research Is Written Up

A useful way to approach writing academic papers is not to think about "research" and "write-up" as separate activities. A write-up is the end product of what a researcher does. Rather than saying that "the write-up describes my research," I prefer to say that "the write-up *is* my research."

2. See W. Churchill and R. M. Langworth, *Churchill by Himself: The Life, Times, and Opinions of Winston Churchill in His Own Words* (Ebury, 2008).

Many of the same people who are completely obsessive about their analysis are cavalier about how they write their paper. For example, scholars who prove theorems in their papers are usually incredibly careful to ensure that the theorem is stated correctly, and that the conclusions do in fact follow logically from the assumptions they make. However, many of these same scholars think nothing of describing the results in paragraphs that go on for two pages, using run-on sentences that contain three or four unrelated ideas, and giving little thought to providing a coherent explanation of the results. Or they might not explain the results at all, figuring that any decent scholar would be able to figure out the theorem's importance by himself. This type of scholar, while often very smart, usually feels underappreciated and tends to complain about the review system not treating her fairly.

Scholars should think of their research the way an artist views his art, or a musician his music. An artist cares about not only the subject matter of his painting and the colors and brushstrokes he uses, but also about the framing of the picture and how and where it is hung. An artist will care about these other factors because they affect how people view his creations. Similarly, musicians care about how their music is presented, what the performers wear, and what goes into the music video. A musician cares about these things because they affect people's opinions of his music. The same is true for research: research that is not presented well has little impact because it does not attract attention, does not influence other researchers, and so does not get cited.

A particularly sore point of mine concerns the careless errors commonly referred to as "typos." People often excuse these mistakes by saying that they are "just typos." My view is that typos are errors and should be treated just like any other error. When I was an undergraduate, I submitted a paper I coauthored with one of my professors to a journal. The referee responded that there were enough typos in the paper that he could not be confident the paper was correct given the lack of professionalism exhibited in the write-up. He rejected the paper for this reason (and perhaps others as well). As much as I hate to admit it, the referee was correct to reject our paper. We are professionals, and research is one of the most important things we do. We need to treat the *entire* paper as if it were our life's work, because it really is!

Structuring a Research Paper

When you start writing a paper, you must proceed from the assumption that the work will be read in the manner in which academic articles actually are read, and not how you might like them to be read. Some scholars think that academic papers are read like novels—that readers will take them to the beach and go through them from beginning to end over the course of a week or two. Many novels keep the reader in suspense and only give the reader the outcomes of the important plot twists in the last chapter, or even sometimes not until the very last page.

Such an approach can make for a fun novel, but it is not a good way to write an academic paper. An editor giving a paper written this way an initial screening would not know what the point of the paper is and most likely would desk-reject the paper. In an academic paper, a reader should be able to tell easily what the paper's question is, what the methods are, and what the paper concludes from a quick glance. You should present the central fact and the logic of the paper clearly so that the reader understands easily what you actually did in the paper. You should try to make these points in as transparent a manner as possible, not hiding anything from the reader.

An author's goal should be to get as many people as possible to read her paper as soon she makes it publicly available. To do so, it is important that she write the paper in a way that convinces other scholars to spend their valuable time reading it. With so many new papers always circulating, there is a lot of competition for readers' time. For example, I receive a number of emails every day with listings of new papers, including their titles, authors' names, and abstracts, as well as a link to websites where I can download the papers. I also receive emails from many conferences, including ones I do not attend personally, with links to the papers that will be presented. In addition, because I am old-fashioned, I receive hard copies of the leading journals in my field via regular mail.

Given this deluge of papers I have access to every day, I only have time and energy to read a few of them, aside from the ones that I have to read because they are directly relevant to my own work, they were written by a close friend or student, or I had agreed to review them. Consequently, I scan the emails and journals I receive quickly and then decide which ones I should read more carefully. I download and read only the papers that seem especially interesting. My process is quite similar to the triage approach taken by conference organizers and journal editors: making a first pass through all the submissions tells me which papers seem interesting enough to look at more carefully.

Considering that most academic readers follow this kind of process, the immediate implication is that authors should write their papers so that they seem appealing and accessible after just a cursory glance. Consequently, not all words in a paper are created equally. The words that make it to the email lists and the words that readers will see on a quick read of the paper are far more important than the others. A useful analogy is with land prices in cities. Every city has some areas that are much more valuable than other areas. For example, New York City apartments in the buildings overlooking Central Park in Manhattan are many times more expensive than similar-sized apartments in the poor areas of the outer boroughs. Since apartments overlooking Central Park are desirable and scarce, prices are bid up so high that only movie stars and investment bankers can afford to live there.

Analogously, in an academic paper, space in the abstract and introduction is far more valuable than any other space in the paper. Because of both the way work is evaluated and the way it is read, the abstract and introduction will be read many more times than the body of the paper. For this reason, space in the abstract and introduction is far more valuable than space in the body of the paper, which in turn is more valuable than space in the internet appendices.

Consider the distribution of a typical paper presented in a departmental seminar. A personal goal of mine is to spend at least some time reading every paper that is presented in our weekly seminar. But the amount of time I spend on each paper will vary depending on my initial screening. I always read the abstract and sometimes the introduction right away when it is emailed to the department. If I find the paper interesting and have time, I will read the rest of the paper, or at least the parts of it I think are most important. The amount of time I spend on a given paper ends up being a function of how interesting the paper seems to me on my initial read.

My guess is that most academics follow a practice similar to my own. If they do, then every time a paper is presented in a seminar, most participants will read the abstract and some of the introduction. Some readers will go through the body of the paper and the conclusions, a few will spend time on the technical details of how the authors cleaned their data or provided their theorems, and almost no one will read the appendices. In deciding how to structure their papers, authors should assume that most readers follow this sort of practice.

Another fact to remember is that most readers will not vary the amount of time they spend on a paper as a function of its length. If a sixty-page paper seems interesting, I will try to read some of it, but I probably won't spend that much more time on it than I would on an equally interesting twenty-five-page paper. Perhaps this approach seems odd; after all, any reader spends more time reading a one-thousand-page novel than a two-hundred-page novel. But remember, most readers do not read academic papers completely. They read the abstract and some of the introduction and skim the rest of the paper looking for the interesting parts—perhaps a key table or the author's interpretation of a result they find puzzling. The details in the body of the paper will usually be read only by scholars doing closely related work and doctoral students seeking to learn about the area.

Authors should understand that their paper will be read this way and write it accordingly. They should put the parts of the paper that they want readers to read in the places where they will actually be read. Parts of the paper that are necessary but perhaps not so interesting, such as proofs, details of how data were cleaned, and so on, can go in places where readers do not usually spend time. *An author's goal should be to make the paper as short and readable as possible, subject to the requirement to include all of the information for an outsider to replicate the work.*

·

What Does an Author Hope to Accomplish When Writing a Research Paper?

Authors often sit down to write a paper with dread, especially those who do not like to write. After doing the "fun" part of the research, they now have to "write it up." Not surprisingly, when authors have this attitude, the quality of the resulting paper is often low.

It is helpful to learn to like writing. If you like to write, your papers usually end up being higher-quality. Of course, the causality of this relation is not clear; after all, good writers tend to like to write more than bad writers do. But good writing can be learned, and every academic, regardless of her field, should make an effort to become a better writer.

One way to start writing better is with the right attitude and objective. Instead of setting the goal of "writing it up," have smaller, more manageable goals in mind when writing a paper. Authors of almost all academic papers should achieve the following five goals:

1) To state the point of the paper clearly and convince readers it is interesting and novel
2) To convince readers that the analysis is correct and address alternative explanations
3) To give credit to others
4) To provide details of the research process
5) To draw appropriate conclusions

When you start writing a paper, have these goals in mind. Think about how to accomplish each one in the most interesting and succinct manner. If a paper accomplishes these goals, it is likely to be successful.

1. CLEARLY STATE THE POINT OF THE PAPER AND CONVINCE READERS IT IS INTERESTING AND NOVEL

This goal is perhaps the most important in writing up research, and yet it is sometimes overlooked. An author who spends her life working on a particular topic is normally fascinated with the topic, and the paper's contribution to the literature is likely to be obvious to her. But the reason why a paper is interesting to its author is not necessarily obvious to others, especially readers who do not specialize in the paper's topic. Remember that conference organizers are typically tasked with sorting through two hundred submissions and selecting eight to be presented, and that most research-active faculty receive emails containing forty or fifty different papers every day and download at most one or two of these to read. If a paper's contribution does not stand out immediately, there is a very good chance that it will be overlooked.

The paper's novel contribution should be clearly summarized in the abstract and at the beginning of the introduction. The burden is always on the author to describe exactly what she has done, what the results are, and how she interprets them. She also must explain to the reader why he should care about the paper, not make him figure it out for himself.

In providing this explanation, the author has to make some assumptions about the background of the person who is reading the paper. A reader who is a specialist in the paper's subfield may need no extra motivation to keep reading. However, the more general the anticipated audience for the paper, the more background information an author should include. This background information is often already known by specialists, but an author who wants all potential readers to understand the paper's contribution and why it is interesting might want to include it in the paper anyway.

How should an author decide on how broad an audience to target? There is no easy answer to this question, but a lot depends on which journal the author is hoping will publish the paper. For example, if an author would like to target one of the extremely prestigious general-interest journals in economics, such as *American Economic Review* or *Journal of Political Economy*, she should write her paper in a manner that any professional economist will understand. In contrast, an author who is planning on publishing a paper in a more specialized journal could reasonably omit some background information and assume a higher level of knowledge from readers.

My own practice is to err on the side of providing a little more background information in my papers than is absolutely necessary to ensure that all potential readers understand the paper's contribution and why they should care about it. The cost is relatively low because the additional explanations often take only a few sentences. Being accessible to a wider audience can add to the paper's readership and increase its impact. In the social sciences—and in business schools in particular—we often try to influence practitioners and policymakers in addition to other academics. A surprisingly large number of people are interested in research about the social sciences; if authors make an effort to explain why readers should care about the work and to present the analysis in a clear and understandable manner, the number of people interested in the paper can increase dramatically.

2. CONVINCE READERS THE ANALYSIS IS CORRECT AND ADDRESS ALTERNATIVE EXPLANATIONS

Before an author goes through the details of the analysis, it is important to give the reader a sense of what is coming. The author should explain in as simple a manner as possible why she does what she does, what goes into the analysis, whether she employs any "tricks," and so on. She should also be sure to emphasize exactly what makes the paper unique— such as proprietary data or an interesting experiment—in a manner that all readers will understand even if they don't spend a lot of time going through the paper in detail. In a theoretical paper, the author should clearly explain the key assumptions and the ideas underlying the proofs. This discussion should be sufficient to enable a reader to pretty much tell where the paper is going and what the results are going to be. If the reader stops reading after this discussion for some reason, he should still understand the analysis at a level high enough to have an opinion on the paper and to be able to describe it reasonably well to his friends.

An important part of the discussion at this point is the author's acknowledgment of the "standard" view—that is, what the profession knew prior to her paper. The purpose of a research paper is to change people's priors. This discussion should say exactly how the paper, in the author's opinion, will change reader's priors and why. Part of this explanation should be a discussion of alternative interpretations of the author's evidence and the extent to which these interpretations are valid.

3. GIVE CREDIT TO OTHERS

A surprisingly tricky aspect of writing academic paper is deciding which papers to cite, how to cite them, and where in your paper to cite them. It is incumbent on an author to acknowledge all relevant prior work and to be honest about her paper's novelty relative to prior work. It is neither necessary nor appropriate, however, to spend so much time describing the details of prior work that a reader cannot tell what the paper's own contribution is. Young authors are especially prone to making this error.

Referencing work that you do not completely agree with, or that your results contradict, can be awkward. An author must point out the differences between her work and the prior literature and let readers understand which approaches lead to which results. It is advisable to do so, however, in a polite and scientific way. Authors can be sensitive when their work is criticized; it is their life's work, after all, and a negative critique of their work can have a huge impact on their career. Academics who are normally completely sensible and rational can become extremely emotional and defensive when their work is challenged. Sometimes when discussing prior work, an author has to be extremely careful to elucidate as inoffensively as possible the differences between her paper and prior papers, as well as the reasons why different approaches affect each paper's conclusions.

4. PROVIDE DETAILS OF THE RESEARCH PROCESS

The body of an academic paper describes the research in detail. As a rule, someone who does not know the authors and has nothing but access to the paper and the existing literature should be able to replicate every result in the paper. Every way that the data have been cleaned must be entirely documented, every element of the experimental design should be described, every assumption of a model must be made explicit, all proofs need to be completely explained, and all other relevant details should be included in the discussion. If a doctoral student on the other side of the globe cannot follow the analysis completely and find the same results as those reported in the paper, then the author has not done a sufficiently good job of describing her work.

However, just because a discussion has to be complete does not mean it has to be boring. Sometimes authors feel that there is a trade-off between a readable paper and a complete one that covers all the necessary details. Most of the time, however, it is possible for a paper to be both. The key is to remember that different parts of the paper will be read by different people. Parts that will be read by many people, such as the abstract, introduction, and conclusions, should convey the main ideas but be light on details. The body of the paper should contain as many details as necessary for the paper to be replicated.

The limiting factor on the number of details in the body of the paper is the need to keep it readable. If the body of the paper stops being readable because the problem is extremely complicated, or because aspects of the data collection or algorithms are complicated, a good option is an internet appendix. When using an internet appendix, it often is a good idea to explain the point of the appendix in the text and keep the details in the appendix. So, for example, if a proof has an interesting idea, an author might explain the idea in the text and then refer the reader to the internet appendix for the details. Although the proverbial doctoral student on the other side of the globe must be able to replicate the work using publicly available information, it is okay to require the student to download an internet appendix to supplement the published version of your paper.

Sometimes people are unable to replicate the work because a simple mistake has been made somewhere. Many published papers contain errors. Sometimes published equations are incorrect, but more often an author has forgotten to describe a step she took when constructing the data, accidentally deleted important code, or made some other honest mistake. Alternatively, the person who could not replicate the results could have done something wrong. In any event, it is always important for the author to understand why the paper could not be replicated.

When an author is contacted by scholars who want to understand how she obtained particular results in her paper, she is ethically bound to work with them to help resolve the inconsistency. Helping people replicate her work is not just an ethical issue, however, but a practical one as well. If a scholar tries and fails to replicate her paper, it is in her interest to take the time either to explain what the person is doing wrong or to find the error in the paper herself. Her reputation is likely to suffer if she is rude or unhelpful and the other scholar who cannot replicate her work circulates a paper saying that it is wrong. Being known for producing results that cannot be replicated can be extremely damaging to a scholar's career.

An example of a paper that famously was not replicable was Carmen Reinhart and Kenneth Rogoff's "Growth in a Time of Debt." To address the incredibly important question of whether government debt affects economic growth, this paper presents evidence suggesting that extremely high debt-to-GDP ratios (over 90 percent) do indeed inhibit a country's growth. This paper was highly cited and used in policy debates to highlight the costs of government debt. However, three other scholars, Thomas Herndon, Michael Ash, and Robert Pollin, were unable to replicate the Reinhart-Rogoff findings, and they claimed to have found a number of errors in the original analysis. The incident was highly publicized and embarrassing to the authors of the original paper, who would clearly have been better off had they double-checked their analysis more carefully before publishing their paper.[3]

5. DRAW APPROPRIATE CONCLUSIONS

In some fields, especially mathematics and the sciences, the conclusions the scholar draws from the analysis tend to be factual and indisputable. In the social sciences, however, conclusions are more often subject to interpretation. Some social scientists (like me) enjoy this aspect of our field because we think it makes it more interesting and exciting. But ambiguity can create difficulties when drawing inferences from economic analysis.

3. See C. M. Reinhart and K. S. Rogoff, "Growth in a Time of Debt," *American Economic Review Papers and Proceedings* 100(2010): 573–78; and T. Herndon, M. Ash, and R. Pollin, "Does High Public Debt Consistently Stifle Economic Growth? A Critique of Reinhart and Rogoff," *Cambridge Journal of Economics* 38(2014): 257–79.

Different people can and do interpret the same statistical results in different ways. When drawing conclusions from data that can be interpreted in multiple ways, an author should strive to present all possible interpretations of her data. She should explain the different inferences that could conceivably be drawn from the results, even if she does not, or cannot, distinguish between them in the current paper. However, it is also an author's responsibility to say, if possible, which interpretation she feels is most likely to be true and to explain why. It can be a delicate balancing act to give appropriate credence to all plausible explanations while simultaneously explaining to the reader why she thinks one particular interpretation is the most likely one. An author should always remember that the goal of a paper is to influence readers' priors. If she does not clearly tell readers what she feels the results really mean, then readers' priors are unlikely to change very much.

5

The Title, Abstract, and Introduction

WHEN A paper is posted online, all a potential reader usually sees is the title and abstract. Then, if he looks at the actual paper, he most often reads only the introduction. A paper's title, abstract, and introduction have a large influence on the number of people who read it and therefore can materially affect its ultimate impact on the profession. For this reason, I devote this chapter to discussing the way an author picks a title and writes her abstract and introduction.

The Title

A paper's title is the first thing a reader sees about the paper, and his response to the title often determines whether he will look at any more of the paper. It is the first and most important advertisement for a paper, since a good title can motivate the reader to spend time with the paper. However, coming up with an appropriate title for a research paper can sometimes be tricky.

Several main approaches to choosing a title are available. My preferred approach, and the one most commonly used, is to make the title as descriptive as possible. The idea is for the title to give a reader a pretty good idea about what the paper says. Some descriptive titles are worded in the form of a question, one that will usually be addressed by the analysis, but other titles simply describe the paper's contribution in a few words.

An example of an effective use of a question title is Robert Shiller's famous "excess volatility" paper: "Do Stock Prices Move Too Much to Be Justified by Subsequent Changes in Dividends?"[1] After reading that title, no one could possibly have any doubts as to what is in the paper. (And after reading the title, we all somehow know that Shiller will come to a "yes" answer to his question.) My job market paper used a "short description" title that, in my biased opinion, served its purpose very well. After circulating early versions with several other (longer) titles, I ended up calling the paper "Outside Directors and CEO Turnover."[2] Not surprisingly, after reading the title, most readers correctly assumed that the paper was about the impact of outside directors on CEO turnover. Perhaps in some small part because of the title, the paper has done very well, with over six thousand Google Scholar cites at the time of this writing.

A second approach to deciding on a title is to choose something cute, perhaps an allusion to a saying that readers will recognize. Such a title can sometimes be effective; Leamer's "Let's Take the Con Out of Econometrics" has been an influential paper, probably in part because of the memorable title.[3] My impression, however, is that these titles, while attracting attention, sometimes leave the reader wondering what the paper is actually about. When I tried this approach and made a reference in a title to what I thought was a famous example from Merton Miller's AFA presidential address, it turned out to be one of my less successful titles. In his address, Miller had argued that the costs of financial distress are orders of magnitude smaller than the tax benefits of debt and he quipped that the trade-off between the two "looks suspiciously

---

1. See R. J. Shiller, "Do Stock Prices Move Too Much to Be Justified by Subsequent Changes in Dividends?," *American Economic Review* 71(3, 1981): 421–36.

2. See M. S. Weisbach, "Outside Directors and CEO Turnover," *Journal of Financial Economics* 20(1, 1988): 431–60.

3. See E. E. Leamer, "Let's Take the Con Out of Econometrics," *American Economic Review* 73(1, 1983): 31–43.

like the recipe for the fabled horse and rabbit stew—one horse and one rabbit." When I wrote a paper studying this trade-off, I foolishly suggested that we call it "Horses and Rabbits? Trade-off Theory and Capital Structure." I convinced my coauthors that most readers would see the reference right away. Of course, almost everyone who saw our paper had no idea what the title referred to; instead of perceiving the title as clever, most people thought it was confusing.[4]

Andrei Shleifer likes to use one-word titles, following the practice of Alfred Hitchcock, the great director of suspense movies.[5] This approach works well for Andrei because he is a superstar, and many economists want to know about what he is working on, so the one-word title works as an effective "teaser." When economists see the one-word titles on his papers, they become intrigued, wonder what the paper is about, and then read it to find out. For most of us, however, putting a one-word title on our papers would probably confuse potential readers and lead them to skip over them.

Some of the most successful titles catch a reader's attention in a way that gets him thinking about the issues and wanting to read more. George Akerlof's classic paper developing the idea of adverse selection has a particularly intriguing title: "The Market for 'Lemons': Quality Uncertainty and the Market Mechanism." When a reader sees the paper for the first time, he probably wonders if "lemons" refers to the fruit and does not immediately see why we would care about such a market. Once we start the paper and understand what kind of lemons Akerlof is discussing, most of us start to think about the worst car we ever purchased. We are then fascinated by the resulting analysis of the

4. See M. H. Miller, "Debt and Taxes," *Journal of Finance* 32(2, 1977): 261–75; and N. Ju, R. Parrino, A. M. Poteshman, and M. S. Weisbach, "Horses and Rabbits? Trade-Off Theory and Optimal Capital Structure," *Journal of Financial and Quantitative Analysis* 40(2, 2005): 259–81.

5. See A. Shleifer and R. W. Vishny, "Corruption," *Quarterly Journal of Economics* 108(3, 1993): 599–617; S. Djankov, R. La Porta, F. Lopez-de-Silanes, and A. Shleifer, "Courts," *Quarterly Journal of Economics* 118(2, 2003): 453–517; N. Barberis, A. Shleifer, and J. Wurgler, "Comovement," *Journal of Financial Economics* 75(2, 2005): 283–317; and P. Bordalo, K. Coffman, N. Gennaioli, and A. Shleifer, "Stereotypes," *Quarterly Journal of Economics* 131(4, 2016): 1753–94.

impact of asymmetric information about such a car on used-car markets. A paper as brilliant as this one would have done just fine with a boring title, but the clever one Akerlof used made the paper that much more special.[6]

Different scholars have different philosophies about how to pick titles. One of my coauthors remarked that she really likes short titles (although longer than one word). Another suggested using a catchy title with a more descriptive subtitle, as I tried to do with this book. The important goal when picking a title is to convince readers to read more. It's worth spending time to come up with a title that accomplishes that goal, because a good title can meaningfully change a paper's readership and its eventual impact.

One word of caution: some authors, especially young scholars beginning their career, tend to make their titles a little too cute. It is a bad sign if readers think that a scholar spent more time thinking of a clever title than she did in solving her model or in coming up with the correct econometric specification.

The Abstract

The abstract is a short summary at the beginning of the paper. Historically, abstracts were less important because scholars only read hard copies of papers, so if someone was reading the abstract, he had a copy of the paper in front of him. Today, however, there are many places where a paper's abstract is presented, and its quality affects whether a potential reader downloads the paper and reads it in detail.

For example, the National Bureau of Economic Research (NBER) and the Social Science Research Network (SSRN) send regular emails containing abstracts of new working papers, with links to the actual

---

6. On the other hand, I still find it astonishing that this paper managed to get rejected a few times before the *Quarterly Journal of Economics* accepted it for publication. Could the title have been a culprit? Perhaps a clueless referee thought the paper was somehow about fruit? See G. A. Akerlof, "The Market for 'Lemons': Quality Uncertainty and the Market Mechanism," *Quarterly Journal of Economics* 84(3, 1970): 488–500.

papers. I am probably typical in that I regularly read these emails but download at most one or two papers from them per week. The papers I choose to download are the ones whose abstracts make them sound particularly interesting. So the way authors write abstracts does materially affect the likelihood that I—and undoubtedly other readers as well—will download their papers.

Abstracts can vary in length. Many authors, including myself, have begun to make them longer by adding details about what is in the paper. Some publicly circulated papers have two- or three-paragraph abstracts of more than two hundred words. Writing a longer abstract is fine for an early draft that is being sent for comments and presented in seminars. However, journals usually limit abstracts to about one hundred words, and they can be strict about these limits. Some will not even accept a submission with an abstract of more than one hundred words; the computer counts the words and won't let authors complete the submission unless the abstract is short enough. Given this limit, an author has to be judicious about what she puts in the abstract.

How does an author decide on what to put in the limited space available in an abstract? She should start with the understanding that an abstract is just an advertisement for the paper. Therefore, she should focus her attention on the aspects of the paper that will entice readers to read more of it. The way to interest readers is not by cramming as many facts as possible into the available space, but by getting them interested in the issues the paper raises and persuading them that the paper has something important to say.

I usually start an abstract by explaining the question the paper asks and reminding the reader why it is interesting. For example, an important issue in corporate finance is payout policy. The big puzzle, even after many years of research, is that firms still pay dividends despite the tax disadvantage and even though there are more tax-efficient ways to pay cash out to shareholders, such as stock repurchases. Most readers of a corporate finance paper will understand this issue very well, but some might not, and others might have forgotten about it. So mentioning the tax disadvantage of dividends, or the "dividend puzzle," in the abstract and explaining why firms pay dividends anyway is a good way to remind a reader who doesn't think about dividends regularly that the paper is addressing an interesting issue.

After highlighting such points of interest in your paper, spend the next two or three sentences saying what is "cool" about the paper and its results. If the paper has a clever identification strategy or new, interesting data, say so. Focus on the most important findings and skip over the secondary results, unless they are as important as the main result. In a theoretical paper, describe the idea in a sentence or two, but skip modeling details unless they are the crux of the paper's contribution.

If the methods or data used in a paper are standard, there is no need to waste space in the abstract saying what they are. The same goes for robustness checks. Mention whether a commonly raised alternative explanation can be ruled out because of an interesting test, but do not waste space in the abstract discussing the now-standard set of robustness tests that are in every empirical paper.

Finally, an author should finish the abstract with a sentence or two about what the paper means, and what its main implications are. It is not enough to say that y and x are positively correlated; the author should explicitly state what theories this correlation is consistent with, as well as whether the correlation has any other implications that readers are likely to find interesting. Often, I read abstracts whose authors are so focused on including as many details of the paper as possible in the one-hundred-word space that they forget to tell the reader why he should care about the paper in the first place. Authors always have to remember that they are competing in the market for ideas, and success in that market comes to those whose results change people's priors about important issues. The end of the abstract is a good place for authors to explain to a reader what he might learn if he spends time going through their paper.

Bearing in mind that the abstract is an advertisement for the paper, the author should start with the motivation and the question, present the main results, then spell out what the results mean and why we should care about them. All other details are unnecessary in an abstract and can be left to the paper itself.

The Introduction

Aside from the title and the abstract, an academic paper's introduction is the section that is read far more frequently than the other sections. Reading the introduction is usually sufficient for a researcher who wants to understand the basic results in a paper to decide whether the paper is relevant to her current research, or for a student who wants to know the paper's results for an upcoming exam. While not the most important part of the paper—that would be the details of the paper's contribution described in later sections—it is usually the most difficult to write. The introduction is the part that I and many other authors spend many hours agonizing over before we circulate a paper.

Authors spend so much time on the introduction because, of all the paper's sections, it can make the greatest impression on a reader, and influence the paper's publication and eventual impact the most. I often rewrite a paper's introduction a number of times before I let even my coauthors see it, and then I rewrite it again with my coauthors' help multiple times before the paper is circulated publicly. In the Dropbox folders that I have for my papers, there are many drafts of introductions, with file names like "Intro-Mike-Try 7." Often a draft like this one elicited an email from a coauthor explaining that it was okay, but probably we could do better. So an "Intro-Mike-Try 8" and an "Intro-Mike-Try 9" followed in the next few days. Eventually my coauthors and I reach an agreement on what the introduction should look like, but it usually takes longer and goes through more rounds than any other part of the paper.

Why is the introduction to a research paper so difficult to write, and so important to write well? Introductions have to cover a lot of material, while also being easy to read and to understand. In addition, they have accomplished it in a minimum of space. The introduction and the abstract are the first and often the only parts of the paper that readers look at. They are an author's best shot at getting a potential reader interested in the paper. Consequently, she should try to make the introduction a snapshot of everything that she thinks is important in the paper.

An important principle about writing introductions is that an author should assume that the reader will spend the same amount of time on it regardless of its length. Therefore, everything included in the introduction takes away reading time from something else. The introduction is not meant to be a mini-version of the paper. Not every twist and turn has to appear there.

When writing an introduction, always remember the expression "less is more." Say what is necessary as concisely as possible in a readable and interesting way, while emphasizing what is unique and insightful about your work. Given how much ground an introduction has to cover, it is important to remember that anything other than what needs to be included *should not be there* and should appear only in the body of the paper.

Here is a brief list of the tasks that you should hope to accomplish in your introduction:

1) To grab the reader's attention
2) To state the question you are asking
3) To describe your approach
4) To report the results
5) To provide your interpretation of the results
6) To discuss other implications of the results
7) To provide an outline of the paper, which can be a formal outline or just a brief summary of each of the paper's sections

These seven tasks are a lot to cover in four or five pages—which a typical reader will skim in only a minute or two! Therefore, it is important to leave everything but these seven goals out of the introduction. Including much of anything else usually ensures that readers will miss the point of the paper and fail to appreciate what it has to offer. The two most common elements that are mistakenly included in introductions are long discussions of others' work and detailed presentations of the methods used in the paper.

I will discuss each of the seven parts of an introduction in turn, explaining how an author might accomplish each task in the most effective manner possible.

1. GRAB THE READER'S ATTENTION

This purpose of an introduction is possibly the most important one, yet is sometimes neglected by authors, especially inexperienced ones. Many authors start their paper by saying exactly what they do in their paper, rather than giving the reader a reason for *why* they are doing what they are doing. If it is obvious to potential readers why a contribution is important, then it is fine to ignore the motivation. For example, if your research contains a way to make microprocessors work faster, or a design for a bridge that will hold up better in hurricanes, then you probably do not need to state your motivation because the importance of these contributions is likely to be obvious to most readers. However, as I argued earlier, this type of paper is the exception; in competing for readers' attention, most papers must explain why they are important. In a competitive marketplace for ideas, it is incumbent on the author to give potential readers a reason to spend time on her paper; otherwise, they won't.

The ways in which an author can grab a reader's attention vary from field to field, but ultimately it comes down to persuading the reader of the importance of the issue being discussed. Feedback received from colleagues and seminar participants can help an author know what elements of the paper readers find most interesting, and highlighting these elements in the introduction is likely to pique the interest of new readers. In addition, citing numbers that make the paper's importance evident to readers is a great way to begin a paper. If a potential reader sees that a question addressed by a paper is quantitatively important, he is more likely to spend his valuable time reading it.

One approach that I sometimes find effective is to point out a difference between the assumptions of the academic literature and those of the real world. Recently I coauthored a book chapter on how multinational firms make financial decisions. My coauthors and I started the chapter with some facts about the preponderance of multinational firms in the world today, then noted that despite the large number of multinational firms, most of the academic corporate finance literature has focused on the issues facing domestic rather than multinational firms. In one of my better-known papers on the capital structures of private equity portfolio firms, my coauthors and I began by pointing out that practitioners and academics view the same issues very differently. We used these different approaches to thinking about the issue to construct a model of private equity capital structures.[7]

Another way to grab a reader's attention is to put the issue being discussed in a larger context. A paper documenting that prices are "sticky" is a lot more meaningful to a reader who is aware that the existence of sticky prices underlies much of traditional Keynesian economics. Consequently, documenting that prices are sticky could be an important factor differentiating Keynesian models from New Classical ones. Placing a paper in the context of an important literature sometimes convinces a reader that your paper is worth reading, especially if the reader is a fan of that literature.

Some papers contribute to classic literatures that originated with the "masters" who initiated or revolutionized our fields. If your paper falls into this category, it is worth mentioning the classic work. For example, the question of how a board of directors monitors management dates to a section in Adam Smith's *Wealth of Nations*, and the issue of how corporations manage liquidity was originally raised in John Maynard Keynes's *General Theory*.[8] I have worked in both of these subfields and always make a point to cite the classic works prominently when they are relevant. I do so in part to give credit where credit should go, but also to remind readers of these issues' fundamental importance to debates that have lasted for many years.

Often the key issue that motivated the author to write a research paper, especially in the social sciences, is one that readers think they already understand prior to reading the paper. That author's goal is to

7. See I. Erel, Y. Jang, and M. S. Weisbach, "The Corporate Finance of Multinational Firms," in *Multinational Corporations in a Changing Global Economy*, ed. F. Foley, J. Hines, and D. Wessel (Brookings Institution, forthcoming); and U. Axelson, P. Strömberg, and M. S. Weisbach, "Why Are Buyouts Leveraged? The Financial Structure of Private Equity Firms," *Journal of Finance* 64(August 2009): 1549–82.

8. See A. Smith, *An Inquiry into the Nature and Causes of the Wealth of Nations* (Modern Library, 1776), 700; and J. M. Keynes, *The General Theory of Employment, Interest, and Money* (Palgrave Macmillan, 1936), 196.

begin the introduction by convincing the reader otherwise, explaining that something he thinks he understands is more subtle than he thought, or that the literature has forgotten this important issue, or that there is an important gap in the literature. Once a reader realizes that his understanding of the issue is imperfect, he is much more likely to spend time trying to understand it better by reading your paper.

The attempt to get the reader's attention should be made at the very beginning of the paper. There is no point in getting into the substance of what the paper does before you try to convince the reader that your paper is worth reading. Nevertheless, the "attention-grabbing" part of the introduction should be relatively short. A good approach is to use the first paragraph to explain to the reader why the issue is important. Then start explaining how you address that issue in the second paragraph, and certainly no later than the third paragraph.

2. STATE THE QUESTION YOU ARE ASKING

When I attend seminars or read research papers, I sometimes feel like I am playing the iconic TV game show *Jeopardy*. On this show the host gives the contestants an expression or a name and the contestants have to come up with the correct question that has that answer. In other words, the show's premise is to start with the answer and then quiz contestants on whether they can think of an appropriate question for it. The academic version of *Jeopardy* is a paper whose author looks at some interesting data or does some analysis that somehow seems plausible, but does not tell the reader what the analysis means, or why the reader should be interested in it. The reader or seminar participants feel like they are playing a game of *Jeopardy* in which they have to figure out for themselves what question the author is asking. These papers can be frustrating to read or to referee. When they are presented in seminars, authors often lose control of the room, since everyone in the room thinks the author's goal is something different.

It is important to avoid playing *Jeopardy* with readers in this fashion. Once an author convinces a reader that the overall issue she is studying is interesting, she should narrow that issue to a specific question or two that she will address in the paper. It is usually a good idea to be very explicit about the question your paper is asking. Some authors make the paper's title itself the question that is addressed, while others state the question explicitly in the second or third paragraph. Regardless of how the author raises it, it is important that the reader understand the specific issue or question that will be addressed in the paper. Readers should not have to wait to have the question explained to them; it should be clearly stated as quickly as possible, preferably by the end of the first page.

A benefit of raising the particular question that the paper raises explicitly in the beginning is that the coauthors also become aware of it and can focus their energies on it with no misunderstandings among them. One might think that the question being asked in a paper is so obvious that no reasonable author would ever spend all the time and effort to do a research project without knowing it. In fact, authors proceed with research projects without a specific question in mind all the time. Sometimes authors get so caught up in the details of the modeling or the data work that they forget exactly what they want to learn from the analysis. Other times, coauthors go a year or two before realizing that each of them wants to focus the paper on a different question. Stating the question explicitly in the beginning of the paper lays everything bare and helps to ensure that there are no such misunderstandings.

3. DESCRIBE YOUR APPROACH

Once you have convinced the reader that the overall issue you are studying is interesting and specified for him the question you will be asking, the next step is to explain how you will answer the question. In the introduction, space is extremely valuable, so it is important to think carefully about how much detail to include in this description. The purpose of the description in the introduction is to explain the paper's contribution to a reader who is skimming the introduction quickly. Therefore, details that are necessary to replicating the paper but not to understanding the paper's point should not be included in the introduction. Instead, these details should be deferred to the body of the paper (or to an appendix).

The introduction should focus on whatever makes the paper novel, and why this novelty leads to a unique contribution. Remember that your goal when writing the introduction is to make your paper stand out from the many others that editors and conference organizers will see. When describing your methods, try to do so in a way that will give the reader a sense of what is novel and interesting about your paper's approach. If, for example, you hand-collect novel data or run an experiment with a unique design, then it is worth emphasizing your data collection method. If, on the other hand, you use standard data but in an unusual manner, focus your discussion on your estimation approach or whatever else is different about your paper.

The goal should be to describe your paper so that readers can read and understand it on a quick pass through the paper. The general principle is "less is more." The introduction should contain a paragraph or two that helps a typical reader come away with an understanding of what your paper does and what is special about it. No details that are necessary for replication but not for a general understanding of the paper's contribution should appear in the introduction. For example, in a typical empirical corporate finance paper, it is appropriate to say in the introduction that the sample consists of one thousand publicly traded US companies and covers the period between 2000 and 2010. But including details in the introduction on how these firms were chosen, what filters were applied to the data, or other similar details would waste valuable introduction space that could be used for something else.

4. REPORT THE RESULTS

Once you tell the reader what the question and general approach of the paper are, you should summarize its results. Here it is important to include details selectively, so as to keep the introduction relatively short and readable. A good strategy is to follow the structure of the paper. So, if there is a formal model, explain in a paragraph or two how it works. Then, if you estimate the model, say briefly how you estimate it and what the results are. If the paper consists of a series of related tests that build on each other, at this point in the introduction you should mention the main tests, explain how they work, and discuss the results of each one.

If the paper is empirical, it is important to discuss its most important estimates in some detail. The introduction is a good place to highlight for the reader exactly which results you think are most important and to explain why. Empirical papers often provide estimates of many different variables, so one of your goals when you write the paper is to focus the reader's attention on the ones you think are most relevant. Don't just say whether the estimates are positive or negative. Be sure to give the actual estimates, discuss their magnitudes, and give the reader a sense as to whether the effect is large enough to be meaningful. By discussing these results in the introduction, you are telling the reader where you think he should focus his energies when (if) he reads the rest of the paper.

Readers, however, often don't like to be told what to focus their energies on. It is their prerogative to try to find holes in your analysis. Academics love the give-and-take involved in critiquing new research. A good strategy for authors is to anticipate the objections that will be made and try to respond to them in advance. Almost every paper is subject to at least one or two objections that are raised by the majority of readers or that come up often during presentations. Anticipating these objections, you should think long and hard about the best response and include this response in a prominent place in the paper. If the objection is sufficiently important, you should probably mention it briefly in the introduction and respond to it at greater length in the body of the paper.

Many empirical papers struggle with the notion of causality. It is usually easy to document that two variables constructed from real-world data are correlated with one another. What is much more difficult is to draw inferences that one variable caused the other to move rather than vice versa, and rather than some third unobservable variable causing both of them to move. The difficulty of inferring causality gives rise to many of the objections to empirical papers. Often it behooves the author of this type of paper to discuss in the introduction the extent to which causality can be inferred and the methods she has used to address the issue.

5. PROVIDE YOUR INTERPRETATION OF THE RESULTS

It is important that you discuss not only what you think the results *are* but also what they *mean*. What theories are they consistent with and what theories do they cast doubt on? How robust are the results, and to what extent are there important caveats to your interpretation?

Some authors interpret their results more strongly than is warranted, and sometimes an overly strong interpretation is a deliberate strategic move to attract attention to a paper. In addition, authors sometimes do not accept that there are plausible alternatives to their favored explanation that are also consistent with their results. If an author consistently overinterprets her results, the cost she will pay is that people will not take her papers seriously in the future.

An equally egregious sin that some authors commit is underinterpreting their results. Some authors are so cautious about interpreting the results that their paper becomes a list of facts and statistical findings that gives the reader little sense of what the results mean. Readers tend to get bored with this kind of paper and find it hard to understand why they should be interested in it.

It is sometimes hard to know exactly how hard to push your results as you search for that fine line between overinterpretation and underinterpretation. A good rule is to make it clear what you think the results mean, even if you add a number of caveats and discuss plausible alternative interpretations. However, you also need to avoid overselling your work and to be honest about the extent to which the results distinguish your favored interpretation from the alternatives.

6. DISCUSS OTHER IMPLICATIONS OF THE RESULTS

The author's task in the introduction is to provide a short summary of what is in the paper, as well as what she thinks the results mean and what they add to our knowledge. The goal should be to persuade readers, and especially reviewers, that the paper is worth spending time on. After reading the introduction, the reader should want to learn more details about the analysis by reading the rest of the paper. Therefore, you want to point out any ancillary predictions of the model you present or implications of your empirical work other than the ones you focus on. Some readers will be less interested in your central questions than in the additional ideas you present. If you raise these additional ideas in the introduction, these readers might value the paper more highly. Alternatively, if you wait until the end of the paper to make these points, these readers may never see them, as they may never get that far.

7. PROVIDE AN OUTLINE OF THE PAPER, EITHER A FORMAL OUTLINE OR A SUMMARY OF THE RESULTS

It has become traditional to end the introduction with a paragraph that starts with a sentence that begins: "The remainder of the paper proceeds as follows: . . ." This sentence is followed by one-sentence descriptions of each section of the paper. Some journals require such paragraphs, while others discourage them. Some of my papers have been almost accepted when the editor told me to add a paragraph along these lines, and other papers at the same stage included such a paragraph until a different editor told me to take it out.

This type of paragraph is almost never read and rarely adds anything of value to the paper. If you have a choice in the matter, it is usually a good idea to skip it. A better solution is to structure your introduction around the paper's organization and integrate the outline of the paper into the discussion of its content. So, for example, when discussing the formal model, one could say something like: "In section 3, I present a model of . . . in which agents are risk-averse but principals are risk-neutral." Then, when discussing the next section, start with a similar sentence. By the time you reach the end of the introduction, the "outline" paragraph will have become superfluous.

Common Mistakes in Writing an Introduction

The introduction of your paper should be a summary written in a way that encourages potential readers to read the entire paper. The focus should be on *your paper* and its contribution; anything that distracts from that discussion should be minimized. Authors have a tendency to confuse readers by including extraneous information in the introduction in two ways: (1) providing too much technical detail about their paper that is not necessary to understand the paper's point, and (2) spending too much time discussing other scholars' papers before explaining the point of their own.

PROVIDING TOO MUCH TECHNICAL DETAIL

Many authors are justifiably proud of the effort they put into their papers. They have understood up-to-date methods and perhaps modified these methods to suit the question they are asking. These authors sometimes go into laborious detail in the introduction on how they did all the work in their paper. However, authors who use elaborate and novel approaches can use far too much space in their introduction discussing their methods.

If the paper asks an applied question and the paper's methods are a means to an end rather than an end in themselves, you can confuse readers about the paper's point if you provide too many details in the introduction. If, on the other hand, the point of the paper is developing new methods rather than using them in an application, then the methods should be the focus of the introduction. Authors should shy away from including too many equations and formalisms in the introduction; it is usually better to explain in words how the method works. The formal discussion can come later. Space in the introduction is precious, and it should not be wasted on details that can be covered in depth later on.

SPENDING TOO MUCH TIME DISCUSSING OTHERS' PAPERS

It is always tricky to know how and where to cite the work of other scholars. Academics are always required to give credit to those who did related work. Citing the relevant literature is a service to readers who do not know it well and also an appropriate courtesy to the authors of those other papers.

A common error is to cite the previous literature in too much detail and too early in your own paper. I often read papers on areas I'm interested in but haven't worked in myself, and the authors start these papers with a discussion of this interesting-sounding work. By the time I get to page 3 or 4, however, I have seen some ideas I like, but I can't quite understand the point of the paper I'm reading. Too often the author has not told me by page 3 or 4 what the point of her own paper is because she is spending so much time describing others' work. Sometimes I never figure out the paper's point and come away from it thinking more about its literature than about the paper itself.

An author's primary goal in her introduction is to explain the point of her own paper, and she should provide this explanation right away. Doing so usually means deferring discussion of others' work until later. But what if your paper builds on the work of others? Do you ignore those other papers? Before you discuss your own work, how do you explain your paper to a reader who needs to know the background necessary to understand it, but without confusing another reader who already has too much information about others' work?

One way is to explain the ideas and main results of the prior literature quickly and clearly. The details of which author did what can be left to the body of the paper. Alternatively, it is useful to provide lists of relevant papers in a footnote, perhaps sorted into categories for different types of papers. In general, however, avoid citing others' work in too much detail before getting into your own paper's idea and results.

There are exceptions to this rule. Sometimes a paper is an extension of a particular paper, or a response to a paper whose authors made an error or misinterpreted something. In this case, the author should start the paper with a discussion of the other paper and the issues about it that she wishes to address. The example of a well-written introduction that I use in my doctoral class is Andrei Shleifer and Robert Vishny's "Large Shareholders and Corporate Control." This paper builds on Sanford Grossman and Oliver Hart's "Takeover Bids, the Free-Rider Problem, and the Theory of the Corporation," so it begins by briefly describing the Grossman and Hart model. The paper's introduction then provides a lucid discussion of the important role of large shareholders in the economy, before describing the model developed in the paper: how large shareholders can affect takeover markets.[9]

If a paper extends a long literature, the author should focus on the source of the literature and leave the details for later. For example, if the paper is about whether firms should maximize profits to the exclusion of other factors, such as concerns about the environment or the firm's workers, then it would be almost a requirement to start the discussion with Milton Friedman's classic arguments.[10] But if the author discusses every paper related to this question before she explains the point of her paper, she will probably confuse many readers and distract them from understanding the point of *her* paper.

In summary, there are many issues to consider when writing an introduction, which serves as both a summary of the paper and an advertisement for it. Perhaps the most important and neglected role of the introduction is to explain to readers why they should care about the issues discussed in the paper and the particular question that it addresses. The author has to work hard to make the introduction short and readable, while explaining the paper's important points clearly. To ensure that the introduction sufficiently summarizes the paper but is also short and readable, the author must defer much important information, such as literature surveys and technical details, to the body of the paper.

9. See A. Shleifer and R. W. Vishny, "Large Shareholders and Corporate Control," *Journal of Political Economy* 94(3, part 1, 1986): 461–88; and S. J. Grossman and O. D. Hart, "Takeover Bids, the Free-Rider Problem, and the Theory of the Corporation," *Bell Journal of Economics* 11(1, 1980): 42–64.

10. See M. Friedman, "The Social Responsibility of Business Is to Increase Its Profits," *New York Times Magazine*, September 13, 1970.

6

The Body of the Paper

THE LITERATURE REVIEW, THEORY, DATA DESCRIPTION, AND CONCLUSION SECTIONS

MOST ACADEMIC writing is far too formulaic for my taste. In almost every academic paper, the first section is called "Introduction," followed by the obligatory "Literature Review" in the second section. The next section is "Theory" in a paper with a formal model and "Hypothesis Development" in an empirical paper. After that comes "Data Description," then "Empirical Specification," "Results," and finally "Conclusion."

I don't object to this way of organizing a paper. My problem is with authors using it without thinking about whether this way of organizing a paper rather than an alternative is appropriate for the paper they are writing. Before writing a draft, an author should ask herself the following kinds of questions: Is the formal model really necessary? If so, could it appear in the appendix? How much literature is there to review? Could it be integrated into the rest of the text, or does it require a separate section? Should the results be organized into one section or two? Should the empirical specification be its own section appearing prior to the results, or should it be integrated into the discussion of the results?

One easy way to deviate slightly from this formulaic model and make things a bit easier on readers is to give the paper's sections more descriptive titles. For example, in a recent working paper, instead of calling a section "Literature Review," I call it "Prior Work Measuring Risk and Return of Private Equity Funds." Instead of giving a section the title "Results," an author could call it something like "Estimates of the Effects of Minimum Wage Laws on Employment," to cite one example.

Authors should always try to think of ways to make their papers more thoughtful and user-friendly, including how they organize it into sections and how they word section titles. A young scholar, thinking the organization of a paper is fairly unimportant relative to the paper's contribution, may not think much about these issues and simply follow the standard approach outlined earlier. But an author should always remember that a paper is the sum of many seemingly unimportant things. When she pays attention to each of them, her paper will become more readable and ultimately become more influential.

Since academic papers are organized into sections and each section contains issues for authors to be concerned about, I will discuss each in turn. The issues involved with the presentation of empirical results are sufficiently important that I will skip them in this chapter and devote all of chapter 7 to discussing them.

Literature Review

One of the most misunderstood sections of an academic paper is the literature review section. A description of the prior literature is important because it places a paper in the context of what is already known and its position vis-à-vis the questions that the literature has historically tried to address. However, authors frequently do not put enough time and effort into this part of the paper. As a result, the literature review is often boring and badly written, and consequently skipped over by readers (other than to see if they themselves are cited). Authors who don't put sufficient effort into making the literature review readable, interesting, and informative are missing an opportunity to increase the impact of their paper.

The literature review section has two goals: First, it has to bring a reader up to speed on what has been done already so that he can better understand the paper's contribution. Sometimes it is effective if the author explains how her paper fits into this literature and exactly what it adds that is new. Second, the literature review gives credit to other authors for the work that they have done and acknowledges their contributions. Giving appropriate credit to others is part of the scientific process, and regularly failing to do so can damage a scholar's reputation.

With these two goals in mind, an author should spend some time thinking about how to make the literature review as useful as possible to the reader. Many authors, thinking that it is always better to cite more papers, devote one or two sentences to any paper that is conceivably related to their paper. When written this way, literature review sections tend not to have much structure and do not connect the papers to one another or to the author's paper. This type of literature review often seems motivated by a wish to appear thorough rather than to explain to a reader where the paper's contribution fits into the existing literature.

Before starting a literature review, you should ask yourself some questions about the nature of the prior literature and its relation to your paper. A key assumption when writing up results for the first time in a scientific paper is that you are writing for professionals in your field, not for undergraduates or the general public.[1] Given that the target reader is a professional, it may not even be necessary to review the literature at all. But if you do decide to include a literature review, what papers should you cover, and in what depth? How should you organize the discussion? And where should it go in the paper? Does the literature review require a separate section, or could the discussion be integrated into another part of the paper? Often the relevant literature can be sufficiently surveyed at the end of the introduction or in another section, and a separate section surveying the literature is not necessary.

If you decide to include a literature review section, your goal should be to make it a self-contained document that can be read as background reading by a scholar wishing to learn about a subspecialty. Instead of just

---

1. I don't mean to imply that you *shouldn't* write up your results for different audiences. I am a big fan of writing about research so that nonspecialists can understand it. Rather, I am saying that when you write an article for publication in an academic journal, you should assume that readers are professionals in the field.

writing a perfunctory background section before getting to the results, think about the literature review as interesting and important in its own right. If a reader is not that interested in the results you present in your paper, the literature review you write might nevertheless be useful if he wants to learn about the subfield in which you are working.

Many authors seem to be trying when they write the literature review to give equal time to all papers in order not to offend anyone. I think a better way to approach the section is to start by explaining the main issues and questions that the literature has addressed. How has the literature addressed these issues? What are the main results the literature has found? What are the pitfalls it has had to overcome along the way? What are the main questions left to be addressed? How does the current paper fit into all of this, and how is it different from the most related extant work?

In other words, your literature review section should be organized around the *issues* in the literature rather than the *papers*. Of course, you still need to discuss all the relevant papers, but you should do so in the context of the issues they address. One useful approach is to group prior work based on the approach they adopt. For example: "Some authors obtain identification using weather as an instrument (see xxx). These papers typically find that. . . . Other authors have obtained their identification through regulatory changes adopted in xxxx (see xxx)." This way of discussing the literature can be helpful to a reader because it provides a perspective on the reasons why authors adopted particular approaches, the effect of different approaches on results, and which work could be most relevant for understanding the current paper. Another useful approach is to group prior work based on their findings; for example, "Some papers find that A is positively correlated with B (see xxx), while others come to the opposite conclusion (see xxx)."

Perhaps the most difficult issue an author faces when writing a literature survey is deciding what to cite, what to leave out, and how much to write about each. There are no hard and fast rules. But you must remember that not all papers are created equal. Make sure you discuss the seminal papers that started the literature in much more detail than you give to the later, more marginal contributions. A reader should be able to get a sense of the main issues in a literature without being overwhelmed by references to too many papers.

Authors do get offended if they are not cited and think they should have been. When deciding whether to cite a paper, try to put yourself in the shoes of the paper's author and ask yourself if you would be offended if it were your paper not being cited. If it's a close call, a good idea is to give the benefit of the doubt to authors and add a citation. However, don't take this practice too far. Sometimes authors cite every paper that is even tangentially related to their own, making their papers cumbersome and difficult to read. If there are a lot of related (but not too related) papers, one strategy is to add a footnote with a list of somewhat related papers that does not describe any of them in detail. Such a footnote acknowledges the contributions of related papers without affecting the readability of your paper.

It is important to be professional when deciding which papers to cite and how to cite them. Self-citations are appropriate in many circumstances, since a scholar's work often builds on her prior work. But many authors go overboard and cite themselves to an extreme, sometimes to the exclusion of others' equally relevant work. Such a practice comes across as self-serving and unprofessional, and it can create unnecessary tension with the authors of the other papers, who are likely to end up refereeing the paper or discussing it at conferences. In addition, authors are more likely to cite the work of established senior scholars to the exclusion of work by younger, less well known scholars. Young scholars, especially those who are not "well connected," justifiably complain that their papers are not cited nearly as often as they would be if they were written by a more famous and influential author.

Scholars also tend to overcite work by their friends, their advisers, and the editors of the journals in which they wish to publish their paper—a practice that can make an author look petty and unserious. As a thesis adviser, I often tell my students to drop some of the references to my work that they include in their papers. When I was a journal editor, I did the same. While it can seem like a good idea to add references to the work of people you wish to impress, it is obvious to readers what you are doing, and it makes a bad impression on them. In general, the best policy is to make all citation decisions based on the work itself and to ignore the identities of its authors.

Theory

The best way to write the theory section of a paper is determined by the paper's purpose and by what the author hopes to accomplish with the theory section. The purpose of some papers is to convey a new idea, and that can be done through a formal model or through verbal arguments. In mainly empirical papers, the model is included to provide a formal structure through which a reader can better understand the empirical work. In papers that are a combination of the two, the model is presented and calibrated, or the model parameters are estimated structurally. The way an author writes the theory section should vary substantially depending on the type of paper she is writing.

If the purpose of the paper is to convey a new idea or modeling approach, then the theory section is the paper's key section. Much more detail about the theory should be included in the text of this section if the author thinks of the paper as a theory paper than if it is mainly an empirical paper with a theory presented to pull together the empirics. Even if the paper is pure theory, it is nonetheless important to think carefully about which details to include, which to omit, and how to describe the analysis to a reader.

Sometimes the main goal of a paper is to prove a hard theorem, derive an asymptotic distribution of an estimator, or suggest an easier or more straightforward proof to a well-known theorem. In this case, the proof itself would of course be the focus of the body of the paper. For more applied papers, however, the main point of the paper is not normally the proofs. Readers want to know that all the propositions are true, but they usually do not care a lot about how the proofs work. In other words, the proofs are essential for the theory to be correct, but not something that needs to be highlighted in the text. Often it is best to present the proofs in an appendix, either at the end of the paper or online. In an appendix, proofs won't distract the majority of readers from the paper's main message but are still available for the minority of readers interested in seeing them. An advantage of online appendices over ones published in journals is the absence of length restrictions. If the proofs are in an online appendix, the author can provide interested readers with every detail, without skipping any steps.

If your reason for writing the paper is more applied, then I would encourage you to minimize the quantity of technical details of the theory you provide in the main text. Remember the general principle that most readers will spend the same amount of time on a paper that they spend on other papers, regardless of its length. If a faculty member has a free half-hour before a paper is presented in a seminar, then that is all the time he will spend on the paper. If he spends that time wading through technical details, then he won't spend as much time understanding what you want him to learn from the paper's analysis. The point to remember is that you should always structure your paper so that readers will spend their time where you want them to spend it.

When writing a theory section, I recommend starting simple and adding complications later on. It is great if you can start with a real-world example that illustrates your model's idea. If the behavior of a real firm follows the behavior of the model, then the model will appear to be more relevant to readers. Starting off by explaining what happened to a particular firm allows readers to relate to the model and understand that the model is not just algebra, but a characterization of an important phenomenon.

Authors often think that presenting the most complicated version of their model will impress readers, but in fact it is more likely to confuse them. Most models are built on one idea, and then complications to this idea are added. So, when describing a model, start with the main idea, which often can be fairly simple when explained by itself but confusing in the context of a complicated model. Once you explain the main idea and the mechanics of what drives the model's action, readers will be much more willing to delve into the model's details—even details that would seem byzantine in the absence of an understanding of the model's idea.

Data Description

A necessary part of any empirical paper is a discussion of the data used in it. Many authors treat the write-up of the data description as just that: simply a necessary part of the paper that they have to write. Not surprisingly, many data sections read as if the author thought them to be unimportant. Readers of such data sections can easily tell that the author put minimal effort into writing it. Since so many data sections are written without much care, readers tend to assume that the data description will not be important or interesting, and often skip over this section when they read a paper.

One way to improve the impact of your paper is to make all of its sections as interesting and innovative as possible, and the data section is no exception. By putting some thought and effort into it, you can make the description of your data a positive element of your paper that provides value to readers.

The best way to write a data description depends a lot on the nature of the data. If you are using standard data that all your readers will know about, then the data section can be shorter and you can focus on letting readers know exactly how you structured the database. Which observations are included and which are omitted (and why)? How did you construct the variables? What are the main patterns in the data? How are your data different from data presented by other authors?

In many fields, new, very large data sets are now available, often because of the revolution in information technology. For example, some interesting recent work has been based on Amazon website reviews and on job histories posted on LinkedIn. These data can be interesting in their own right. But are they credible? To what extent are they subject to self-selection? Over time, these types of databases will become increasingly important in the social sciences; describing them and their limitations will make data sections less formulaic and hopefully more innovative in the future.

If your data are new and different from what is in the literature, your data section can take on an importance of its own. Academic papers tend to be written around tests of hypotheses coming from theoretical arguments. Readers are sometimes not particularly interested in the hypotheses themselves, however, but instead are interested in the paper's topic. They want to learn more about the topic and might be interested in doing their own related work. For these readers, the data section could be the most important section in your paper. Your paper can be useful to them if it makes the facts they want to know accessible to them, even if they are not particularly interested in the hypotheses you happen to be testing.

For example, my dissertation was about boards of directors and their role in corporate governance. The three published papers I wrote that came out of the dissertation were some of the earliest papers in the economics and finance literature on the topic.[2] When I was writing the dissertation, I was most interested in the hypotheses I was testing: which directors monitor the most, how directors are chosen, and their effect on corporate performance. But when I was writing the papers, I was advised to do a good job of covering the basic facts about boards. How large are boards? What is their composition in terms of "insiders" and "outsiders"? What are the backgrounds of the directors? How long do directors and CEOs serve? How often do CEOs and directors have prior relationships? Many of the citations of these papers have come from authors interested in these facts rather than the hypotheses I tested. The data descriptions in my papers apparently have been very useful for readers—and consequently ended up helping my career greatly.

In addition to its own inherent interest, the data description plays an important role in the scientific process. A thorough description allows others to know exactly what you did in your analysis. The rules of academic research are that all data must be described in sufficient detail for a stranger with nothing but your paper and knowledge of the field to be able to replicate your work. Consequently, it is important to describe every step you take in detail, even those that are "standard" in your subfield.

---

2. See Weisbach, "Outside Directors and CEO Turnover"; Hermalin and Weisbach, "The Determinants of Board Composition"; and Hermalin and Weisbach, "The Effects of Board Composition and Direct Incentives on Firm Performance."

An author should write the data section for a potential reader who is a graduate student on the other side of the world and wishes to replicate her analysis. If the writing isn't clear, or if details are left out, this graduate student will email the author, usually long after she has forgotten exactly how the data were constructed. In the event that you get such an email (and you will if your paper becomes well known), it is extremely helpful to have a detailed documentation in a data appendix that can clear up misunderstandings.

A common problem is that authors can be insufficiently clear when they describe the data cleaning process. For example, authors sometimes forget to describe how they dealt with the observations that they think are likely to be data entry errors because they are such outliers. Were potentially faulty observations dropped, or were they winsorized? How did the author decide which observations were likely to be errors? There is often not a single "correct" procedure for dealing with these kinds of issues, but an author has to make clear to any reader exactly how and why she chose the procedure she used.

Efforts to replicate papers fail surprisingly often.[3] Scholars who try to replicate well-known papers frequently find different results from those reported by the authors. Usually there is an innocent explanation for the discrepancy. Perhaps the author forgot to document something she did, or the database changed between the time when the author wrote the original paper and the time when the replicator downloaded it, or the replicator made a mistake in his analysis. Nonetheless, when an outsider is unable to replicate published results, it casts doubt on the paper and is embarrassing and professionally costly to the paper's author.

---

3. Campbell Harvey has an excellent discussion of the issues involved with replication in his presidential address to the American Finance Association. An example of a well-known area of work for which many results could not be replicated is a huge literature in finance documenting "anomalies." Anomalies are patterns in the data that, if true, could point to profitable trading strategies that are inconsistent with the efficient markets hypothesis. See C. R. Harvey, "The Scientific Outlook in Financial Economics," *Journal of Finance* 72(4, 2017): 1399–1440; and K. Hou, C. Xue and L. Zhang, "Replicating Anomalies," *Review of Financial Studies* 33(5, 2018): 2019–2133.

Authors should always remember that it is in their own interest for anyone who tries to replicate their study to be able to do it. If someone tries and fails to replicate your study, it becomes your problem, *even if the reason why they failed to replicate is their own mistake.* People talk, and your paper will become "suspect." In the age of the internet, once someone posts that something is wrong with your paper, it is there forever.

Therefore, it is in your interest to make sure that your data description is 100 percent accurate. When possible, you should post the data online; if you are not allowed to post the raw data, then post the code; journals are starting to require authors to do so anyway. Even if it is not required, it is in your interest to be as transparent as possible to avoid misunderstandings. Taking a little extra care in describing your data cleaning when writing the paper can save you much heartache later on.

A discussion of the empirical methods and results normally follows the description of the data. Here I am skipping, however, to a discussion of the conclusion section because I have devoted the entire next chapter to the issue of reporting empirical results.

The Conclusion

At the end of a paper, authors sometimes don't know what to say. They have made their main points relatively quickly in the introduction and in more detail in the body of the paper. By the time they get to the end, it can seem a bit silly to repeat everything a third time. So what should authors put in the conclusion section?

The answer to the question of what goes into a conclusion depends a lot on the author, and whether she has anything more to say. The principle of "less is more" applies here; if the author does not have anything else to say, it is perfectly fine to just take two or three paragraphs to briefly summarize the paper. In that case, I would recommend calling the last section "Summary" rather than "Conclusion," since "Conclusion" implies, at least to me, that the author has some broader message to convey beyond merely repeating what she has said earlier.

I have ended papers with a short "summary" section, and no one has ever objected. But I prefer to use the last section of the paper to think about broader issues related to those the paper addresses. For example, I propose in a recent paper a way for firms to use machine learning tools to aid in their corporate governance—in particular the way they select directors.[4] At the end of the paper, my coauthors and I decided to discuss the paper's relation to the broader literature about how and why algorithms can sometimes do better than humans at making decisions. We felt that finishing the paper this way would give readers a sense that our findings were not so much a curiosity as an application of a larger and important idea.

The conclusion section is the place where you can be a bit speculative. You can tell readers what you really think the results mean, subject to appropriate caveats. You can talk about ways to apply the ideas in the paper to other questions. It doesn't really matter whether or not you have completely fleshed out these thoughts. Readers like to finish papers with some additional ideas that they can think about and are inclined to give authors more leeway for presenting speculative ideas in the conclusion than for allowing the main ideas developed in the body of the paper to be too speculative.

I like to end the conclusion with a paragraph about future research ideas. The purpose of an academic paper is to extend our knowledge, and any given paper is only one step in the learning process. By discussing subsequent work, you can remind readers that your paper is part of a growing and exciting literature. Although they can rarely act on your suggestions for future research, readers do appreciate hearing them. Such suggestions, even if they are somewhat speculative, can be a positive and forward-looking way to end by highlighting the importance of your paper's contribution.

4. See I. Erel, L. Stern, C. Tan, and M. S. Weisbach, "Selecting Directors Using Machine Learning," *Review of Financial Studies* (forthcoming).

7

Reporting Empirical Work

MUCH RESEARCH in the social sciences involves analysis of data. These data are often collected from the real world, but they also come sometimes from experiments or simulations. In a typical research project, the scholar looks at many numbers, does all kinds of tests, shows the results to friends, and then does more tests. When she finally gets around to writing the paper, she has many more results than she could possibly include in one paper. She must decide which numbers to report, which to omit, how to report them, where to report them, and how to describe them in the text. Many publicly circulated papers report too many results while also managing to omit the ones that the reader most often wants to see. These papers can be infuriating to read, since the author, instead of reporting information the reader would like to know, goes on and on about things he doesn't care about.

Sometimes the fault lies not with the author but with the editorial process. Referees and editors can make the paper *less* reader-friendly and useful by forcing authors to include many pointless robustness checks and caveats in the interpretation of the results. It can be incredibly frustrating when referees and editors force you to include so many additional tests that your paper becomes overly long and hard for a reader to wade through. Editors and referees think they are being diligent and thorough in asking for many additional tests, but too often they actually add little to the analysis. In doing so, these editors and referees manage to make papers less readable and influential while driving the author crazy at the same time.

The decisions an author makes about how to report results can play a large part in determining a paper's impact. However, the way to go about making these decisions is rarely discussed in classes. We do spend a lot of time in our doctoral programs teaching about appropriate statistical techniques for analyzing data, and our journals regularly publish new methodological advances related to these techniques. In seminars we argue endlessly about issues such as the clustering of standard errors and the validity of instruments. Yet papers with valid instruments and appropriately clustered standard error estimates are rejected all the time because the authors report their results in ways that readers do not find useful.

A Paper's History and How It Is Written

A misleading aspect of journal articles can be the author's description of the process by which the research was done. Journal articles tend to give the impression that the work was done in the order presented, that the results presented in the published paper were *all* of the results achieved, and that the research process followed the logic discussed in the paper. The author starts with a question, details the three or four main steps she took in the analysis, and then presents the results. This framework can make the research process sound quite simple, leading students who read nothing but the paper to think that doing research is far easier than it actually is.

Most of the time, the research process is much more haphazard than published papers make it out to be. Authors normally do far more work on any research project than is ultimately reported in the published paper, and drafts are usually rewritten and restructured a number of times prior to becoming publicly available. After circulating a paper and getting feedback, an author rewrites it, often making major changes, prior to submitting it for publication in a journal. Then the review process often leads to even more changes. I've received (and written) referee reports saying something like: "Tables 1 through 4 are terrible, but tables 5 and 6 could be interesting if the analysis were completely redone. Perhaps the journals could think about publishing a paper oriented around the results in tables 5 and 6 with the following focus. . . ." If the resubmitted paper follows the approach laid out in the report, it may be almost a completely new paper. However, a reader will never know the history of how it was developed and might in fact think that the published version is similar to the author's first draft.

I discuss the review process in detail in chapter 11, but the point here is that, even though a paper's history can be long and sometimes convoluted, the author does not need to tell the entire history of how the research progressed. One of my coauthors once remarked to me that the paper we finally published after a number of rejections had been "three different papers" along the way.[1] In various drafts, we had changed the emphasis of the writing, the data we used, the hypotheses we tested, and the methods we used; we even added a coauthor along the way.

When we wrote the final draft of that paper, we did *not* say anything about the paper's history, the tests we performed in the prior drafts, and the interpretations and implications of those tests. A scholar reading the published version of the paper would have no way of knowing about the multiple drafts, what the earlier versions said, or which results did not make it into the final version. My coauthors and I tried to present the results in the order in which they made sense intellectually; the order in which we actually did the tests was not relevant to this decision.

When writing a draft of a paper, every author should take a step back, think about the most coherent way to present her analysis, and write it that way. Whether that presentation coincides with the history of how she actually did the analysis is not relevant and should not affect how she presents her results in the final version of the paper.

How to Write Up Empirical Results

Suppose you have finished the analysis on your research project, and it is time to write a draft. You try to write the introduction but get stuck when it comes to describing the empirical results because you aren't quite sure what they will look like. Which results should you report?

1. If you don't believe me, take a look at the original version, which is still available online as a working paper, and compare it to the published version. See B. Julio, W. Kim and M. Weisbach, "What Determines the Structure of Corporate Debt Issues?," Working Paper 13706 (National Bureau of Economic Research, 2007), with I. Erel, B. Julio, W. Kim, and M. S. Weisbach, "Macroeconomic Conditions and Capital Raising," *Review of Financial Studies* 25(2, 2012): 341–76.

Where do you present them, and how do you organize the paper? How do you optimally make use of tables or figures, and how should you structure them to greatest effect? Sometimes it is obvious how to organize a paper's results. Other times authors can go through multiple revisions before finding a structure that they are happy with.

In most research projects, the author has a fair amount of discretion over which results to report. Since she cannot publish every single test she has done, she must decide which ones to include in the draft and which ones to omit. Often it is not obvious exactly how to make these choices.

Suppose an author is writing a paper about a hypothesis that comes from a theoretical model and her research consists of a test of that hypothesis. For example, perhaps she has studied a model in which political factors related to uncertainty about the current or next government affect the cost of capital of particular kinds of firms. She gathered a sample of firms and found a setting in which she could measure both the political uncertainty and the cost of capital for that particular set of firms. She came up with a way to identify the relation causally and then did the estimation. Through this process, she made several choices, including what sample to use, how to measure the variables of interest, and how to do the estimation. At the end of the day, she now wants to come to some conclusions about what the data are telling her about the validity of the theory she has tested.

As she decides what to include in the empirical section of her paper, her goal should always be to give a fair assessment of the empirical findings and what they mean. The results she does report should be selected with the goal of persuading a skeptical reader that the empirical results are robust and the inferences she draws from them are appropriate. However, these inferences are conditional on the choices the author has made throughout the research process. Readers will wonder whether the paper's conclusions are sensitive to those choices, and it is the author's job to persuade them that she has given an honest accounting of what she did, the factors that were likely to influence the interpretation she made, and the extent to which her choices in her experimental design mattered for the paper's conclusions.

With these objectives in mind, an author should spend some time thinking about the optimal way to report her results. Any project is likely to offer any number of possible results to report. Some of them are absolutely necessary, some are optional, and others are to be avoided altogether. I will discuss each type in turn.

What Does an Author Have to Report?

In the "absolutely necessary" category are all the results needed to satisfy two particularly important concerns in to almost every empirical paper in any field: replication and robustness. A write-up must include sufficient detail for another scholar to replicate the analysis using only the information provided by the author. Replication is an important part of the scientific process, and there has recently been much controversy in the social sciences about papers that cannot be replicated. When other scholars try to replicate published work, they often end up with different results, usually because of careless reporting in the original paper. The authors did not say (and sometimes cannot remember) exactly what they did.

Nowadays, since coding is such an important component of data analysis, a number of journals are requiring authors to share their code publicly. This practice is a good one, and I encourage authors to post their code publicly regardless of whether doing so is required by a journal. When sharing code, authors should make efforts to keep their code "clean" and well documented so that an outsider can easily understand it and more easily replicate their results. Providing user-friendly code is in the interest of authors, as the consequences they face if others try and fail to replicate their findings can be substantial.

The second crucial element in a professional reporting of empirical results is a serious discussion of their robustness. An author has to make many choices when conducting an empirical study—how to construct the sample, how to treat outliers, what the empirical specification will be, and which results will be reported. Readers naturally wonder how these choices affect the paper's conclusions. When going through any empirical paper, skeptical readers are likely to have the following sorts of questions: Had the author used a different approach, would she have gotten a different answer? When the author eliminated observations that she thought were typographic errors in the database, did she actually do something more sinister (maybe by accident) and create a spurious relation in the data? Is the paper's conclusion a location- or period-specific result, or is it more general? Is the statistical approach appropriate, and would alternative ways of doing the estimation have led to different implications?

The author's job is to convince a reader that she has addressed all these issues and given a fair accounting of them in the write-up. Sometimes it is a good idea to err on the side of being a bit too thorough with robustness checks, so as to leave no doubt in the reader's mind. It is important to be careful when writing up these tests to emphasize what is really going on in the data, but to do so in a way that a reader who is not interested in the robustness checks can easily skip them.

What Does an Author Want to Report?

Ensuring replicability and robustness is part of convincing a reader that there is nothing wrong with your analysis. But a good paper has to be more than correct. It has to offer something interesting and unique enough to attract attention from potential readers.

An author should start from the assumption that most readers will spend a fixed and relatively short amount of time on the paper, and so she should try to structure the write-up to maximize their interest. The way to do so is to focus the most prominent parts of the paper around the issues that the target reader will find most interesting. Other less interesting but necessary elements, such as robustness checks and proofs, should be put in less prominent parts of the paper, in either separate sections or appendices.

Often a paper will contain much more useful information than is relevant for testing the specific hypotheses considered by the paper. A good empirical paper can provide institutional background and background facts that will be useful to others. For example, private capital markets have become extremely important in the economy, yet they have just become a major area of academic research in the last few years. Academics have been relatively slow to understand these markets because data on private markets are usually private and unavailable to academics for research purposes. In addition, these markets function by using institutions that are different from those traditionally studied in academia. Consequently, the early scholars studying these markets, such as Paul Gompers, Josh Lerner, and Steve Kaplan, have written a number of influential papers whose impact derives in part from their lucid explanations of the institutional environment of this market and also from their inclusion of many facts about it that others found useful.

These authors went out of their way to provide the facts that would be useful to readers regardless of whether those facts were relevant for the hypotheses they were testing in the paper. For example, in Kaplan's job market paper examining the hypothesis that firms increase in value when they undergo a leveraged buyout, he provides numerous facts about leveraged buyouts, such as their ownership structures pre- and post-buyout, their capital structures, and the incentives that are pro-vided to managers in a buyout.[2] While these facts are not necessarily crucial for testing his main hypotheses, they are interesting by them-selves, and his paper is often cited because it includes these facts. Kaplan was able to make his paper more influential by using his space wisely and reporting as many novel facts as possible that were of interest to readers.

What Does an Author Not Want to Report?

With most research projects, certain steps are more or less standard in the literature. Readers have seen something similar to these steps many times and are likely to have gone through them in their own work. For example, in finance we often estimate what we call "beta," which is a

2. See S. Kaplan, "The Effect of Management Buyouts on Operating Performance and Value," *Journal of Financial Economics* 24(2, 1989): 217–54.

commonly used measure of a security's risk. If a finance professor estimates beta in a standard fashion, she must document exactly how she did the estimation so that an outsider can replicate her results. However, there is no need to spend much time discussing the estimation in her paper because most readers are likely to find such a discussion a little boring and will tend to skip over it.

There is a substantial opportunity cost to everything an author discusses in detail in her paper. If she steers a reader's attention toward something mundane that he has seen before, he not only will be bored but will spend less time on the material the author wants him to focus on. An author's goal is to have her paper be known for the parts of it that are novel and interesting. Any space spent on well-known things will distract readers' attention from those parts. Papers are sometimes rejected because reviewers never get to the interesting part of the paper. Even papers that do get published can see their impact diminished if their new contribution is not clearly evident to readers.

Where to Report Results

When an author is thinking about reporting empirical results, the goal is to maximize the usefulness of the paper to each potential reader. What makes this process complicated is that there are likely to be many different types of readers to whom the author wishes to cater. The vast majority of readers are casual readers who will glance through the abstract and introduction prior to the paper's seminar presentation or when it comes out in a journal or an online blog. These readers might look at a table or two but will not spend more than five or ten minutes on the paper, regardless of how long it is. Other readers are willing to dive into the details of the paper, perhaps because they want to learn the paper's literature or are thinking about working in the area in the future. Finally, there will (hopefully) be a few readers who read the paper extremely carefully and go through every table in detail. These readers may want to understand everything in the paper because they are doing related work. The challenge an author faces is to write her paper in a manner that appeals to each of these readers.

How does an author balance the interests of different kinds of readers and make her paper interesting to all of them? It is a bit of an art, and authors do not always get the balance right. Some papers I read go on and on, plodding through so many details that I have trouble finding the important and interesting sections. Other papers skip over so much that a reader working on a related paper has to contact the author to find out what exactly she did. Sometimes the author will fail to report, or will hide, obvious robustness tests, leading others to question the paper's conclusions. Reaching a "happy medium" is sometimes difficult.

One way to help readers sort through a paper to the degree they wish is to organize it carefully and transparently. Most empirical papers have a main finding, and sometimes two or three of them. The rest of the empirical tests are designed to convince readers that this result is correct and not spurious for one reason or another. For such a paper, I think that a sensible approach is to separate the main results from the robustness tests, get to the main table quickly, and make it as easy to understand as possible.

After the author presents the main result, perhaps in a separate subsection, she can go through the litany of potential objections to it. Specialized results that are likely to be of little interest to most readers can go in an online appendix. A casual reader is likely to read the section about the main result and skip some of the robustness tests, while a more interested reader will probably read the discussions of all of them. The key thing to do is to make it easy for both kinds of readers to figure out what is the main test and what is robustness.

An author has an important decision to make in choosing which results to present, and in what order. For most papers, an author has estimated a number of alternative approaches but can include only a small fraction of them in the paper. Should she present the estimates in levels, or in first differences? Which control variables should she include? Which sample period? For most empirical papers, the number of potential variants in specification can go on and on, and there is usually no correct answer to all of these questions. Instead, the author should try to give the reader a sense of the factors to which the result is robust and the factors that can change it.

One approach to organizing a paper that authors sometimes use is what I call the "mystery novel" form of organization. In a mystery novel paper, the author presents results using a seemingly plausible approach. She then explains to the reader what is wrong with this approach. Over the course of the paper, she changes the specification, adds and subtracts variables from the equation, and presents alternative models. By the end of the paper, the "mystery" is solved when the author presents what she argues to be the correct specification, usually in one or two of the later tables.

Some people like this kind of paper, but I personally find it infuriating to read. When I read an academic paper, I want to know quickly what the paper's arguments are and what its conclusions are. For example, if the author thinks fixed effects belong in a specification, then she should say why they belong up-front and put them in the main specification. Some authors, however, present results without fixed effects first, and then go on for several pages about why the first set of results are not correct because the fixed effects should in fact be included. These authors do eventually get around to reporting the results with fixed effects, but a reader who is pressed for time can easily miss the main point of the paper and look at the wrong table when trying to understand the results.

How to Report Results

In addition to *what* results to report, and *where* to report them, an author has to decide *how* she wants to report her results. Should the results be presented in a table or a figure, and how should each be constructed? The basic challenge is to present data to a reader in the best way to convey the author's message in the most compelling manner. Unfortunately, authors often use an overly formulaic approach to presenting data. In economics, the most common approach is to construct a table or two of means and medians, followed by regressions with the dependent variable at the top and the independent variables listed in the far left-hand column. While there is nothing wrong with this way of presenting data—I often do it this way myself—authors often use it out of laziness rather than from any belief that it is the optimal approach.

Real-world data is usually complicated and multidimensional. To perform statistical analysis on these data, a researcher must collapse them to a manageable level, usually focusing on one or two variables that can be analyzed statistically. In doing so, much interesting information can be lost. Statistics sometimes does a good job of conveying the data's basic message, but does so at the cost of losing some of its texture. When presenting results, authors should attempt to structure their presentations to ensure that they convey as much of what is interesting to readers as is possible. Often graphical analyses can convey such information in the most convenient manner.

A classic book that describes innovative ways of displaying data is *The Visual Display of Quantitative Information* by Edward Tufte.[3] I would encourage all scholars to read this book carefully and to think seriously about adding it to their library. Tufte's book contains numerous examples of graphs and charts that have been structured to fit data and display its texture in ways that could not be done using standard formulaic approaches.

The graph that Tufte claims was "the best statistical graphic ever drawn" is the illustration that tells the story of Napoleon's 1812 invasion of Russia, which was created by the French civil engineer Charles Minard in 1869. See figure 7.1 for an English translation of the graph.

For those of you who do not know the story of Napoleon's invasion of Russia, please stop working on your papers for a few days and read either *War and Peace* or a history of the Napoleonic Wars. This invasion is one of the great tales in recorded history, and every educated person should know the story.[4] On June 24, 1812, Napoleon invaded Russia with 422,000 men (and 180,000 horses). After fighting a number of battles through the summer, including a particularly large and bloody battle at Borodino, he was able to enter Moscow on September 14. Finding the city without food and other resources, Napoleon and his troops retreated back to France, fighting the particularly cold winter and the Russians along the way. Of the original force, only 10,000 soldiers, less than

3. See E. R. Tufte, *The Visual Display of Quantitative Information* (Graphics Press, 2001).

4. A good source is Andrew Roberts's biography, *Napoleon: A Life* (Penguin Books, 2014). It is not surprising that Roberts uses the Minard graph as part of his discussion of the 1812 invasion of Russia.

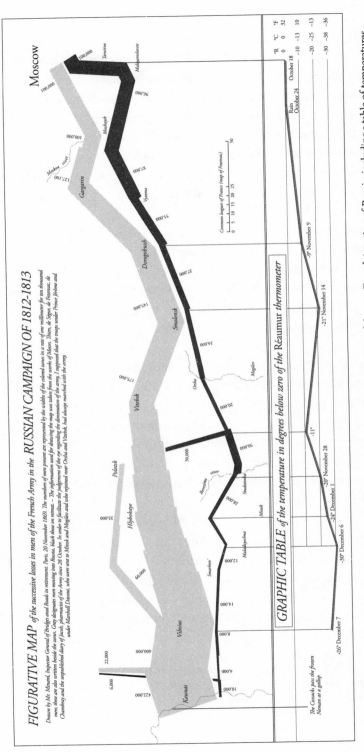

FIGURE 7.1. Modern redrawing and translation of Charles Joseph Minard's figurative map of the 1812 French invasion of Russia, including a table of temperatures converting degrees Réaumur to degrees Fahrenheit and Celsius. Adapted from DkEgy/https://commons.wikimedia.org/wiki/File:Minard_Update.png

5 percent of the army's original force, were able to make it out of Russia.

Minard's graph illustrates, in one picture, many aspects of the story, including major cities and battles (Smolensk, Moscow). The graph is superimposed on a map of Russia, so it is possible to see the routes Napoleon took both in and out of Russia. The gray line (tan in the original illustration) shows the route he took to Moscow, while the black line represents the more southerly route he and his troops took back to France. The width of the line is proportional to the number of men Napoleon had at any point in time; decreases in the lines' width mark points where Napoleon lost men. For example, the black line gets noticeably thinner where a number of French soldiers died while (barely) crossing the Berezina River under fire. Finally, and perhaps most illustratively, Minard includes at the bottom of the graph the temperatures Napoleon faced while retreating, a feature that highlights the extreme cold faced by the troops during the Russian winter.

The Minard graph is still celebrated today because it does an extraordinarily good job of illustrating so many aspects of Napoleon's disastrous campaign in one picture. The graph is special in part because Minard designed it to fit what he wanted to illustrate. As such, he was able to capture the geography of the campaign, the enormous troop losses, and the locations of the losses, as well as the extreme temperatures faced by the troops. I find it telling that this graph was made in 1869, many years prior to the invention of Excel. Perhaps because he was unable to rely on standard packages, Minard invented something far superior to what most people would have done today!

Although most researchers will not come up with something as innovative as Minard's graph, they can improve their papers substantially by thinking carefully about the problem they are trying to address, then structuring their presentation of the empirical analysis accordingly. Sometimes sophisticated graphs are unnecessary and detailed verbal descriptions can play that role instead.

For example, my former colleagues Harry and Linda DeAngelo, when they are working with relatively small samples, are very good at supplementing their papers with appendices that contain short case studies describing each observation in their sample.[5] Their appendices provide texture about exactly who owns the company's securities and their relationship with the company, as well as the timing and specifics of the union negotiations. I always found the appendices to their papers to be particularly interesting reading, much more so than most academic papers. Although probably not a requirement for publication, the extra flavor the DeAngelos bring to their work through these extra descriptions makes it more meaningful to me, and probably to others as well.

Interpreting Results

Finally, after an author presents her work, she must provide an interpretation for the readers. What do the results mean? What are their implications for important theories? Are there other potential implications of the work—for example, for public policy?

Authors normally begin their analysis in an empirical paper with a question, often one arising from a set of alternative theoretical possibilities that the empirical work can help distinguish. After reporting the results, an author should go back to that original question and explain to readers what the analysis has taught them about it. Ideally, she should be able to tell a "story" about what she thinks the data are trying to say through the lens of the paper's statistical tests. An author should be honest about the extent to which her results rule out alternative stories, and the extent to which readers should think of them as suggestive rather than conclusive.

A common mistake that authors make when interpreting results is focusing too much on statistical significance and not enough on the magnitudes of their estimates. Empirical papers often are written as if the authors think that when a coefficient has a p-value of .05, it is almost definitely different from zero, but if the p-value is .06, then the

5. See, for example, H. DeAngelo and L. DeAngelo, "Managerial Ownership of Voting Rights: A Study of Corporations with Dual Classes of Common Stock," *Journal of Financial Economics* 14(1, 1985): 33–69; and "Union Negotiations and Corporate Policy: A Study of Labor Concessions in the Domestic Steel Industry in the 1980s," *Journal of Financial Economics* 30(1, 1991): 3–43.

coefficient is almost definitely not different from zero. In each of these two cases, however, the appropriate interpretation is that it is more likely than not that the coefficient is not zero, but there is some small chance that the coefficient equals zero. Much too much is made in research in the applied social sciences about the difference between "significant" and "insignificant" results.[6]

When I read papers, I try to focus on the coefficients themselves rather than their statistical significance level. What are the actual estimates? Are they large enough to matter? If we change the independent variable by a reasonable amount, say one standard deviation, how much do the estimates imply about the change in the dependent variable? These are the questions that the authors of the vast majority of empirical papers should be focusing on and readers should think about. Instead, academics tend to obsess about whether the coefficients are statistically significantly different from zero, ignoring the more interesting and important issue of the size of the coefficients, as well as what they imply about the issue that the paper is addressing.

In my mind (but not everyone's), it is even perfectly fine to discuss the magnitude of statistically *insignificant* coefficients while at the same time ignoring significant ones. In a well-specified equation, every estimate represents an unbiased estimate of a coefficient. Suppose the best estimate of a coefficient you are interested in is 2.0 and it has a *t*-statistic of 1. Even though we cannot reject the hypothesis that the coefficient equals zero at conventional statistical levels, it is still more likely to be 2 than 0, and certainly more likely to be 2 than −2. Why not say so in the paper if this coefficient is one number that readers are likely to be interested in? It is incredibly misleading and almost dishonest to act as if it is more "conservative" and "scholarly" to ignore the information contained in estimates that are not statistically significant at conventional levels.

Authors differ in their approaches to interpreting results. Some who are fairly aggressive when they interpret results like to draw strong

6. In addition, there is always a lot of noise when measuring standard errors, so reported *p*-values are often misleading.

conclusions from it about major theories. These authors tend to be particularly aggressive in their interpretations when the results confirm their own prior view. Others are more conservative and interpret the results more narrowly. These more conservative authors like to give credence to all potential theories, sometimes even ones that are a priori implausible to most readers.

A famous example of two papers using differing approaches to interpretation dates from the early 1980s. In 1981, Stephen LeRoy and Richard Porter published a paper that developed what are known as "variance bounds" tests; the same year Robert Shiller published a paper on the same topic (which I mentioned in the previous chapter).[7] The idea that these papers test, the "efficient markets" theory, is one of the important theories in finance and economics. In lay terms, it states that the movement of stocks and other securities is only a function of rational expectations of future payoffs, which for stocks come in the form of dividends. The alternative to the efficient markets theory was most famously posited by Keynes, who argued that investor psychology, or what he called "animal spirits," can determine stock prices in addition to fundamentals.

The Leroy-Porter and Shiller papers present similar statistical tests that document that the variance of observed stock prices is too large to be justified by subsequent changes in dividends, as would be predicted by the simplest form of efficient markets theory. But the papers differ in their interpretations: Leroy and Porter are relatively cautious: they focus on the statistical analysis and do not draw strong conclusions about the implications of their work for the theory of efficient markets. In contrast, Shiller views his tests as important evidence against efficient markets theory.

Economists like to argue about which paper interprets these tests appropriately. Many have criticized Shiller for overinterpreting his results and ignoring other possible explanations. For example, variation

7. See S. LeRoy and R. Porter, "The Present Value Relation: Tests Based on Implied Variance Bounds," *Econometrica* 49(3, 1981): 555–574; and Shiller, "Do Stock Prices Move Too Much to be Justified by Subsequent Changes in Dividends?"

over the sample used in Shiller's paper in *expected* returns could have created patterns similar to the ones he documented, even if the efficient markets theory were true. The literature, sparked in large part by these two papers, has gone back and forth in its interpretation of the patterns these papers document.

There sometimes is a payoff to authors in interpreting their results aggressively. In part because he interpreted his results this way, Shiller was able to build a persuasive case not just of the statistical correctness of his tests but also of the important big-picture implications of his results for how capital markets work. Today not all academics agree with Shiller's interpretation of his results. Nonetheless, in 2013 he was awarded the Nobel Prize in Economics for this paper and for his follow-up work questioning the efficient markets hypothesis and emphasizing the importance of investor psychology in capital markets.

Academics argue constantly over the appropriate way to interpret results with multiple possible explanations. Authors often are asked to "tone down" their interpretations by referees and editors, who want papers to come across more scientifically and less argumentatively. My own view is somewhere in the middle. I think it is important that any author give credence to all possible explanations of her results. However, I also feel that an author's responsibility is to let the reader know what she thinks the results really mean and what the most plausible explanation for them is.

8

Writing Prose for Academic Articles

AS I DISCUSSED EARLIER, academia can be thought of as a market-place in which researchers compete over ideas, primarily through articles and seminar presentations. Scholars introduce new ideas that compete with the accepted ideas, and the scholar whose ideas turn out to be the most influential is rewarded with high status in the profession. In most fields, this competition is conducted in English, so the more facile a researcher is with the English language, the more successful she is likely to be. It is not a coincidence that the most successful academics tend to be excellent writers, public speakers, and teachers, regardless of their field.[1]

Sometimes scholars take the view that, as academics, our work should speak for itself and there should be no need to explain it. In this view—which is often loudly expressed when academics complain about their work not being appreciated, often at bars late at night or on internet message boards—smart readers should understand research without much need for explanation. Can scholarship be judged "apolitically,"

---

1. There are exceptions. One Nobel Prize–winning economist is completely incoherent when speaking publicly. I have attended three or four of his seminars over the years, and each time regretted being there after the first five minutes of the talk. This economist can get away with being such a poor speaker because his contributions have been so important that they have become celebrated in spite of his poor presentation skills.

based solely on its merits? To what extent does writing matter, and can it be separated from the contributions it describes?

A very succinct illustration that sometimes writing does not matter is a paper by John Conway and Alexander Soifer, supposedly the shortest mathematics paper ever written.[2] The original submission was entitled: "Can $n^2 + 1$ Unit Equilateral Triangles Cover an Equilateral Triangle of Side $> n$, Say $n + \varepsilon$?" The body of the paper consisted only of the words "$n^2 + 2$ can," together with two diagrams presenting the way in which the example was constructed. However, without the consent of the authors, the editors of the *American Mathematical Monthly* moved the authors' suggested title to the body of the paper and added a different title, making the published version slightly longer than the authors intended. Nonetheless, the authors' point remains clear: to answer the question they raise, the picture speaks for itself and no explanation is necessary.

As it happens, the Conway and Soifer paper is not the shortest academic paper ever published. In 1974, the *Journal of Applied Behavioral Analysis* published a paper by Dennis Upper entitled "The Unsuccessful Self-Treatment of a Case of 'Writer's Block.'" The body of the paper contains no words, but a humorous note from a referee appears at the bottom of the page:

> I have studied this manuscript very carefully with lemon juice and X-rays and have not detected a single flaw in either design or writing style. I suggest it be published without revision. Clearly it is the most concise manuscript I have ever seen—yet contains sufficient detail for other investigators to replicate Dr. Upper's failure. In comparison with other manuscripts I get from you containing all that complicated detail, this one was a pleasure to examine. Surely we can find a place for this paper in the Journal—perhaps on the edge of a blank page.[3]

2. See J. H. Conway and A. Soifer, "Covering a Triangle with Triangles," *American Mathematical Monthly* 112(1, 2005): 78. For an entertaining discussion of this paper and related issues, see A. Soifer, "Building a Bridge III: From Problems of Mathematical Olympiads to Open Problems of Mathematics," *Mathematics Competitions* 23(1, 2010): 27–38.

3. D. Upper, "The Unsuccessful Self-Treatment of a Case of 'Writer's Block,'" *Journal of Applied Behavioral Analysis* 7(3, 1974): 497.

The Importance of Language in Academic Articles

These amusing examples aside, the impact of the vast majority of academic articles depends crucially on how well they are written. It goes without saying that the English in a paper must be "correct." When I review papers, my tolerance for grammatical mistakes and typos has declined over the years, and I now consider too many typographic mistakes to be grounds for rejection, regardless of the paper's content. While some would disagree and say that papers should be judged on their "merits" rather than their presentation, most editors are happy when referees reject badly written papers, even if the papers have other desirable qualities. Authors are presumed to be professionals; grammatical mistakes and typos indicate a lack of professionalism and care about their work that is probably indicative of other aspects of the paper.

There is much more to a well-written paper than simply correct grammar and an absence of typos. A well-written paper has to explain why the question it asks is interesting, what the paper's contribution is, why a reader should care about this contribution, and what its implications are for our understanding of larger issues. And the paper should accomplish these tasks in a style that makes it easily readable.

I learned the importance of writing papers that are easy to read and that explain their point carefully when I was a graduate student. One of the most popular papers among MIT economics students in the 1980s was an *Econometrica* paper by Jerry Hausman, a professor of ours who developed a new kind of specification test.[4] This test is a way of examining the underlying assumptions of a model (such as whether independent

4. Yes, at MIT papers were popular or unpopular among the students, and we spent endless hours discussing the merits and faults of different research papers. It says something about the mentality of MIT economics students, a number of whom would become world-renowned economists, that we could take such a liking to a paper whose contribution was as dry as a chi-squared test that evaluated the fit of a model. Of course, its "popularity" might have had something to do with our (probably incorrect) belief that including such a test was a necessary requirement for earning a high grade on an econometrics paper. See J. A. Hausman, "Specification Tests in Econometrics," *Econometrica* 46(6, 1978): 1251–71.

variables are correlated with residuals) by comparing the coefficients estimated under the assumption of no misspecification to those of an estimator that is consistent regardless of this assumption.

As graduate students, we were amused to discover that in 1973, five years prior to the publication of Hausman's paper, another paper, also published in *Econometrica*, had proposed essentially the same test as Hausman's.[5] We did not understand why this paper, by an econometrician named Wu, did not scoop Hausman's. Given that Wu's paper was published five years before Hausman's, why was Hausman's paper considered so important? Why was it even published at all?

One day, perplexed by this issue, I sat down and read Wu's paper. The contrast between the two papers could not have been more evident. Hausman's paper is beautifully written (by the standards of statistics papers, which are never Shakespearean). Hausman's paper explains why specification tests are important and lays out the details of the test as simply as possible. Wu's paper, on the other hand, presents a lot of equations without really saying what they mean. As a nonspecialist in econometrics, I'm sure if I read Wu's paper without first knowing about Hausman's, I would not have grasped its importance.

Despite the fact that Wu's paper was published five years earlier, Hausman's paper has had much more impact. At the time of this writing, Hausman's paper has 18,342 cites on Google scholar while Wu's paper has 1,173.[6] In addition, a number of the cites to Wu's paper were from people like me who know about Wu's paper only because of Hausman's. Consequently, if Hausman had never written his paper, Wu's would have had even less impact than it actually did. Today the test is commonly referred to as a "Hausman-Wu" test, or sometimes a "Wu-Hausman" test. It is likely that Wu's paper benefited from the publication of Hausman's, even though at the time he probably felt that his work should have precluded the publication of such a similar paper.

---

5. See D.-M. Wu, "Alternative Tests of Independence between Stochastic Regressors and Disturbances," *Econometrica* 41(4, 1973): 733–50.

6. The difference in citations could also reflect that Hausman is a famous MIT professor and Wu taught at Kansas. No one ever said that academia is fair.

How to Improve Your Writing

A reader might be thinking at this point that she already knows that writing is important, but what she does not know is how to make her writing better. Unfortunately, there is no magic formula for improving your writing. Writing is one of those skills that do not come naturally to everyone. It can improve with effort, however, and it is a good idea for scholars in all fields to put effort into continually improving their writing skills. Most universities have writing centers designed to help students write better, and there are many books devoted to writing improvement. I encourage young scholars to seek help in improving their writing from the many sources they are likely to have available to them.

I frequently observe that people who write poorly often think of it as a chore that they hate to do, while people who write well tend to like writing, at least in part because people usually like to do things they are good at. But it is also true that people who like to write spend more time on their prose. They tend to reread their papers many times to ensure that the text is as readable as possible. Good writers often think that it's as important to find the best way to explain an issue in a paper as it is to choose the best way to do the statistical analysis or accomplish any other major component of the research project.

Academics who dread writing papers commonly refer to the writing of their papers as the "write-up." This dread is especially common among scholars for whom writing academic papers is doubly difficult because English is not their native language. In fact, the use of the phrase "write-up" undermines the importance of the writing of the paper. It makes it sound perfunctory rather than an essential part of the research process.

Academics who do not like to write often think of research as separate from the write-up. Only when they have finished much of the analysis do they force themselves to write a draft. They also tend not to proofread the draft as carefully as they should. They almost never put in the effort to revise their prose to make it as readable as possible. As can be seen with the Wu-Hausman example, ensuring that your prose is easy to read rather than merely "correct" can make a huge difference in your paper's impact.

I think that instead of viewing the research and the write-up as separate tasks, it is more productive to view the write-up as part of the research itself. A scholar who prides herself on doing the very best job she can in structuring her experiment and performing the statistical work should also take pride in putting together the most coherent draft. Putting together a draft that is easy to read is every bit as much a part of the research process as anything else that a researcher does.

When I was a doctoral student, my adviser, Jim Poterba, suggested that I spend some time studying the work of scholars whose writing I liked and whose papers I wanted to emulate. Jim suggested I start with Marty Feldstein and Larry Summers, two very prominent economists who write well. So I read some of their papers. Then I read my own job market paper. Then I read theirs again. Not surprisingly, there was a huge difference in the quality of the writing, both in terms of the papers' structure and the quality of the prose. This exercise made clear to me exactly where my writing was lacking and how it could be improved. In the end, my job market paper, as well as my subsequent papers, got much better through this exercise.

I often suggest to my students that they do something similar. I encourage them to consider the work of a prominent scholar who does research somewhat related to their own. They should pick someone who they think communicates well and also does interesting research. I urge them to read some of this scholar's papers carefully, read their own papers again, then repeat the process until they have read both sets of papers a few more times. The differences between their papers and the prominent scholar's are almost always obvious to the students. They notice the differences in the writing quality, but also in the depth of the analysis and the importance of the issues being discussed. The exercise can be painful, but it usually helps students produce much better papers.

Another way to write better papers is to read a lot outside of your own field, especially high-quality writing by non-academics. We all get stimuli from the world around us and unconsciously copy things that we are exposed to. Writing works in a similar manner. We tend to mimic the stylistic patterns of what we read. So if you make an effort to read well-written non-academic books, you will be more likely to write well yourself.

Academic writing tends to be overly dry and full of jargon. If all you read is the writing of other academics, your writing will tend to become similar to it—formulaic and not particularly exciting to read. Reading non-academic writing can inspire you to write more interesting prose that nonspecialists can understand and specialists can enjoy.

There are many places to look for interesting non-academic reading that will help you improve your writing skills. While some of your reading should be articles about politics or current events, a significant portion of what you read should be serious, well-written books on subjects in which you are interested. Fiction and nonfiction work equally well.

I enjoy reading books about history and find that doing so helps my academic writing. There are many non-academic historians who write well about fascinating topics. Since both economics and history study human interactions, I find well-written history to be a natural place to find inspiration for economics research. When I become frustrated with my own writing, I sometimes reread books by Bruce Catton, my favorite writer about the American Civil War. I find that Catton has an entertaining yet elegant way of describing dramatic events and a skill for turning a phrase that we all wish we could emulate.[7] After reading a Catton book, I feel that my prose improves, although perhaps that is an illusion.[8]

There are also many very readable books about economics written by non-academics. These books can provide interesting perspectives on our field and show us how to write about it effectively. One author who writes particularly well about economics is Sylvia Nasar. Her biography of John Nash, *A Beautiful Mind*, is a classic and was made into a popular

7. For example: "A certain combination of incompetence and indifference can cause almost as much suffering as the most acute malevolence." Bruce Catton, *A Stillness at Appomattox*, 277. Or: "His soldiers and the country might have been better off if Burnside had been more of a quitter, but that was one defect which he lacked." Bruce Catton, *Glory Road*, 77.

8. There are of course a great many other historical writers whose books would inspire anyone writing about the social sciences, including, to cite only a few, Barbara Tuchman, David McCullough, Ron Chernow, Stephen Ambrose, and Winston Churchill.

movie. Another of her books, *Grand Pursuit: The Story of Economic Genius*, tells the reader about both the personal lives and the contributions of some of the most important economists over the past two hundred years. Both books provide excellent examples of how to write about economics in a clear and entertaining fashion.[9]

A graduate student should invest in her writing skills just as she would in her skills in math, computer programming, data, modeling, and institutional knowledge. Whenever she reads an academic paper, in addition to understanding its scientific contribution, she should think about what makes the paper easier to read, or more difficult, and what aspects of its writing and presentation make it a more or less valuable contribution to the literature.

Many books and articles are available that discuss how to write better, and graduate students should certainly take the time to read least some of them. A few particularly good sources for young economists are John Cochrane's *Writing Tips for PhD students*, William Zinsser's *On Writing Well*, William Strunk and E. B. White's *The Elements of Style*, and Deirdre McCloskey's *The Rhetoric of Economics*.[10]

What Style of Writing Should Be Used in an Academic Article?

Before you write anything, you have to decide on the *style* of writing to use. By style I mean the way you structure your sentences and paragraphs, the way you organize the paper, the language you use, and so on. Note that I'm using the word "style" differently from the way it is typically used by English teachers. If you Google "style of writing," you see writing styles classified into four categories: expository, persuasive, descriptive, and narrative. Apparently, the standard view is that academic writing falls into the "persuasive" category, which seems completely

---

9. S. Nasar, *A Beautiful Mind* (Simon & Schuster, 1998); S. Nasar, *Grand Pursuit: The Story of Economic Genius* (Simon & Schuster, 2011).

10. Cochrane, "Writing Tips for PhD students" (2005); Zinsser, *On Writing Well* (Harper Perennial, 2016); W. Strunk and E. B. White, *The Elements of Style* (Allyn & Bacon, 1999); McCloskey, *The Rhetoric of Economics* (University of Wisconsin Press, 1998).

wrong to me. Academic research is not intended to persuade the reader of anything; its goal is to evaluate data honestly and draw reasonable inferences from it.

An academic article should have a certain degree of formality to it. For example, I would never use a contraction in an academic article, even though I use them all the time when I speak (and when writing this book). But even though an academic article is a formal document, an author has a large degree of discretion over the style of writing she can use. To see why, take a look at some of the papers that have been presented in your seminar series lately. Probably some of them are relatively "stuffy" and formal, with a lot of big, flowery words, long sentences, and paragraphs that go on forever. Others might be mostly equations without too many words explaining what the equations mean. Many of the papers are likely to be full of jargon and references to unexplained prior papers that readers are presumed by the author to know well but that only a specialist in a particular subfield really understands.

As a reader can probably tell, I'm not a big fan of any of these writing styles. I think that an author should try to write her paper in as reader-friendly a manner as possible. Most readers find that papers are easier to read if they are well organized, if they use simple, short sentences and paragraphs, and if they make their point as succinctly and clearly as possible. It is wonderful if the author has exceptional command of the English language and can use elegant and entertaining prose, as Bruce Catton and Sylvia Nasar do. Most successful academics, however, do not have such flair, yet they can still produce papers that are well written and easy to understand.

One economist who wrote with incredible elegance was Adam Smith. Not only did he start the field of economics with his *Inquiry into the Nature and Causes of the Wealth of Nations*, but he did it with a literary flair equaled by few economists since. For example, I love his characterization of how corporations are governed:

The Directors of [joint stock] companies, however, being the managers of other people's money rather than their own, it cannot be expected that they should watch over it with the same anxious

vigilance [as owners would]. . . . Negligence and profusion, therefore, must always prevail, more or less, in the management of the
affairs of such a company.[11]

These sentences of *Wealth of Nations* are famous because they are the
origin of the economics literatures on agency theory and corporate governance, as well as of the expression "other people's money." They are
also beautifully written in language that we don't see in academic papers
today. I always make a point of reading these passages aloud in class and
facetiously tell the students that anyone who uses the expression "negligence and profusion" in one of their papers will automatically get an "A."[12]

Beginning to Write a Paper

A simple way to think about the discussion of ideas and empirical results is to ask yourself: "How would I like to have the issues presented
to me if I were a nonspecialist interested in the topic?" Most nonspecialists would appreciate a paper written with a minimum of jargon, simple,
not fancy language, short sentences and paragraphs, and clear explanations of what the author does, why she does it, and what the results
mean. It also helps if the author minimizes the number of footnotes,
making sure they are really ancillary and not essential to understanding
the paper, and avoids fancy-sounding but content-free expressions like
"to wit" as much as possible.[13]

After I write a few pages, I always go back and reread my prose carefully, usually at least two or three times. I ask myself if any of my sentences can be split into two. If one sentence can be made into two sentences, it is usually a good idea to do so. The same goes for paragraphs.
Each paragraph should contain only one main idea. If you can divide a
paragraph into two smaller paragraphs, each with a coherent idea, then

11. Smith, *An Inquiry into the Nature and Causes of the Wealth of Nations*, p. 700.

12. No student has ever taken me up on that challenge.

13. I sometimes fight with some of my coauthors who insist on using the phrase "to wit" in
our papers. Alas, I don't always win these fights, and the phrase can be found in a few places in
some of my work. I still don't know what the expression means.

it is usually preferable to do so. Academics love to repeat themselves; try to eliminate as much repetition as possible, and make the paper as streamlined and as straightforward as possible. Shortening and simplifying your text can make your paper easier to read and understand to a surprising extent.

Think about who your target reader is and exactly how much he knows. Did you use acronyms that he might not understand? It is easy to forget that others are just thinking for the first time about a subject in which you specialize, and they might miss an acronym or two you use. Does the target reader have enough background to understand your analysis? If you are in doubt about how much background to provide, try to err on the side of providing a little extra explanation. Specialized readers who see a few extra sentences of background usually don't mind going through things that they already know. But a reader who is a bit less specialized can be turned off if you assume background knowledge he doesn't have. Remember that such a reader is a possible reviewer of your paper for a journal or grant. The last thing you want to do is to turn off a reviewer who might, in frustration, recommend that the paper be sent to a more specialized journal.

The most important factor in deciding on the style of writing to use is accessibility: you want to make the paper accessible to the largest number of readers. Some authors seem to think that by presuming a lot of background information that some readers do not have, they are making their article more "elite." I find this attitude to be naive. Presuming too much knowledge and not explaining what you are doing in detail is a good way to get your paper rejected, or to lower its ultimate impact if it does happen to get published.

Common Mistakes in Academic Prose

Having read many papers in my thirty-plus years as an academic, I have developed a sense of what I like and what I don't like in academic prose. Among the corrections that I'm inclined to make in students' and colleagues' papers are stylistic choices that are not necessarily incorrect but do make a paper less reader-friendly. Here are some of my favorites:

ACTIVE VERSUS PASSIVE VOICE. Every American teenager is taught in high school English to use the active rather than the passive voice. A sentence written in the active voice has both a subject and an object, while a sentence cast in the passive voice leaves out the subject and describes what has been done to the object without saying who or what did it. For example, the sentence "I drove the car to the office" is in the active voice, while "The car was driven to the office" is in the passive voice. The active voice is generally preferable, because it is more descriptive; in this example, it makes clear who is driving the car. Sentences written in the active voice usually have a sharper and livelier feel to them than those written in the passive voice.

However, many academics who learn this lesson in high school immediately forget it when they write academic papers. So they write, "The data were gathered," not "I gathered the data," or "The following interpretations are evaluated" rather than "I evaluate the following interpretations." Some people think that the passive voice sounds more scientific and formal. Perhaps it does, but it also makes prose more difficult to read and gives it a clumsy and sterile feel. It also is less descriptive. A paper that says "Equation (1) was estimated" rather than "We estimated Equation (1)" is leaving it a mystery as to who did the estimation. The reader can usually assume the authors did the estimation, but perhaps not; sometimes equations are estimated by other people and then reported by the authors. Why leave doubt in anyone's mind about who did the work?

The passive voice is not incorrect per se, and it is okay to use it from time to time. But if you make an effort to use the active voice as much as possible, your papers will generally be easier on the readers you're trying to attract.

"THIS." One of my pet peeves about writing is the use of the word "this" to refer to a general idea, an argument, or virtually anything else the author has in mind but isn't specifying. I constantly correct students and coauthors who use "this" in this manner, sometimes multiple times in the same paragraph. My view is that using "this" to refer to an idea you have just described is symptomatic of laziness. The author couldn't quite think of what to say when describing his idea, so he says "this." It doesn't require any thought and the reader can usually (but not always) figure out what the author means.

Simply put, the pronoun "this" is a modifier, So do not use it as a kind of place-holder noun, no matter how many other people do. To keep it simple, make sure that whenever you use the word "this," there is a noun after it. If you tempted to use "this" as a noun, think about what you are actually referring to as "this" and use that word or term instead. Try to treat this rule as a hard and fast one, and if you don't allow yourself to violate it, your writing will improve.

SENTENCE FRAGMENTS AND RUN-ON SENTENCES. A sentence fragment is a collection of words that together do not form a complete sentence. Authors should avoid using them, and the appearance of a sentence fragment in a paper indicates to me that the author did not care enough to proofread her paper. When readers see that an author has not proofread her paper, her life's work, they wonder: what else has she messed up in her analysis?

Most writers are aware that they should avoid sentence fragments, but I do see them surprisingly often in papers that have been publicly circulated. Sentence fragments, often involving subordinate clauses, are a sign of careless writing. For example, I too often read passages like: "I cluster the standard errors. Because I was concerned that the errors could not be independent." In this example, the second "sentence" is actually a sentence fragment, not a full sentence. The two parts should be combined into one sentence: "I cluster the standard errors because I was concerned that the errors could not be independent." The existence of sentence fragments in publicly circulated, and sometimes published, papers highlights the importance of proofreading papers carefully and paying attention to mistakes pointed out electronically by programs like Microsoft Word and Grammarly.

Run-on sentences are more difficult to identify. While English teachers have standard definitions of run-on sentences, I prefer to classify them in more practical terms. Each sentence should make one and only one point. Because academics love to describe complicated ideas, many of them try to cram as much as possible into their sentences, which become long and complicated. Such a sentence is hard to read, for a reader will forget what the author was saying at the beginning of it. It is much easier for a reader if the author splits the long sentence into two or three smaller sentences.

Sometimes authors write run-on sentences when they separate ideas by commas (which is called a "comma splice"). This practice can lead to long, confusing sentences. It is usually better to separate two related ideas into clauses that are separated by a semicolon, but I think the best practice is just to separate the ideas into separate sentences. Readers usually find paragraphs easier to read and understand if the points are made in short, easily digestible chunks and sentences take up at most one or two lines of text.

PRESENT TENSE. A somewhat awkward decision you must make when writing a paper concerns the verb tense you should use. In other words, should you use the present tense ("I *estimate* the following equation") or the past tense ("I *estimated* the following equation")? By the time you write a draft, you have already estimated the equation, so it might seem natural to use the past tense. What you are really trying to say, however, is that anyone who estimates that equation, no matter when they do it, will get the results you report. In other words, the results you are reporting are, you hope, timeless. For timeless results, the present tense is appropriate.

For this reason, I was taught to use the present tense when writing academic articles. I always teach students to use the present tense, and I use it in my own papers. But if you prefer using the past tense, there is nothing wrong with that approach. The key thing is to be consistent throughout the paper. Some authors unintentionally switch back and forth between past and present tense, which can be very annoying to their readers.

Advice for Non-Native Speakers

English has become the official language of academia. All the important journals I know of are published in English, major conferences are almost always conducted in English, and many universities in non-English-speaking countries teach in English. It is efficient to have all work in one language, so that everyone can read everything that is written in a field. However, having everything in English does impose the additional requirement on non-native speakers that they conduct their professional business in a foreign language.

Being able to conduct professional business in a foreign language goes well beyond fluency. Almost all foreign students who come to the United States to study are fluent. I can almost always figure out what they are saying, and they seem to understand me without any problems. I find the fact that all our international students speak English so well to be incredibly impressive, since I personally am completely hopeless in any foreign language other than FORTRAN. But merely being able to be understood in English, while certainly sufficient to live in an English-speaking country, is not good enough for an academic.

The standards for academic writing do not vary with the nationality of the author. A reader should not be able to tell whether an author is a native speaker by reading her paper. Regardless of whether a scholar is French, German, Korean, Chinese, or Turkish, she is expected to write English as well as anyone from the United States or Great Britain who has had their whole life to learn to write well in English. Therefore, if English is not a scholar's native language, she has to work extremely hard on her English writing skills to meet this expectation.

Writing English is probably more difficult than speaking English for non-native English speakers. A listener trying to figure out what a non-native speaker is saying will often give him the benefit of the doubt if his English is not perfect, and sometimes certain mistakes can even come off as charming when spoken. However, written English is expected to be correct, and readers have little tolerance for grammatical errors. Nonetheless, it is possible for non-native speakers to become excellent writers in English. Non-native speakers have always been prominent in the academic world and currently make up the majority of scholars in many fields.

If you are a non-native speaker, it is important to remember that you can't let yourself be afraid to write in English. Some international students have told me that they are so afraid to circulate a paper in English that they procrastinate until the very last minute to begin writing. Waiting so long, however, leaves no time for them to revise their papers as much as needed. When these scholars finally circulate their papers, too many of them are insufficiently polished and fail to impress readers. If you are unsure about your ability to write in English, then it is crucial that you start writing early, go through many drafts, and continually improve your work.

A good practice for non-native speakers who wish to have an academic career is to read non-academic, high-quality English writing as much as possible. Non-native speakers should try to spend their free time talking in English, preferably with native speakers. English should not just be a language to know as a scholar, but also a language to be as comfortable writing and speaking as their native language.

It is a good idea for all young scholars, especially those whose native language is not English, to seek out as much help as possible. A good practice is to find people within their field who they get along with and to spend time reading each other's work carefully, paying special attention to the writing. Often native speakers can be talked into helping with language-related issues.

But beyond getting help from one's friends, it is a good idea to consult a professional editor. Producing research is what a scholar has chosen to do for her career. If she can make her research better with an investment in a professional editor, then hiring the editor is likely to be well worth its cost.

PART III

Once a Draft Is Complete

PRESENTATIONS, DISTRIBUTION, AND PUBLICATION

9

Making Presentations

OUR WORK as academics involves communicating research results, which we do most often by presenting papers to audiences. Many of the people a scholar is trying to influence with her work will not read her paper but instead will see her or one of her coauthors present it in a seminar or a conference. These presentations can have a large impact on people's impression of papers, and also of their authors. Consequently, it is crucial that a scholar learn how to present her work in a way that communicates her motivation, methods, and conclusions in a persuasive and entertaining manner.

Unlike in other fields in which a research seminar can cover an entire topic, the custom in the economics-based disciplines is to focus a seminar entirely on one of the presenter's papers. However, the best way for a scholar to structure a seminar presentation is not necessarily to create an oral version of the paper. Some authors insist that, no matter what, they will discuss every result in the paper in the same order as in the text. These authors sometimes essentially read their paper when presenting it. Not surprisingly, these presentations often do not do a good job of conveying the paper's message to the audience.

Papers and presentations are fundamentally different, and they are designed for different tasks. A paper is a formal characterization of the research. It must motivate and explain the analysis and also contain sufficient detail that a stranger can replicate the results. Once published, the paper will be online for eternity and will constitute the public record of the research.

In contrast, a presentation is more like an extended advertisement for the paper. It is a onetime event that can and should change when an author presents her work to different audiences. During the talk, an author has a fixed amount of time to present her work. She can be interrupted with questions that can lead to lively discussions that sometimes veer far from the questions addressed by the paper while cutting into the time she has to explain her research.

People attending a paper presentation realize that the speaker faces these time constraints. Consequently, the expectations they bring to a presentation are different from those they bring to the paper itself. When attending a presentation, a scholar's goal is to understand the main point of the paper and its implications, and to form an opinion on whether the paper is correct and important. An attendee does not expect to see every detail of the paper, and he knows that he can always look at the paper itself for documentation of the steps the author went through to reach the conclusions discussed in the presentation.

Planning a Presentation

An author has a number of goals that she hopes to accomplish in a presentation. She has to convince the audience that they should care about the issues the paper raises and pay attention during the rest of the talk. Most research papers are part of a larger literature that some in the audience will be familiar with, but others will not. The author must give enough background so that attendees who are not familiar with the literature can appreciate what she has done and how it contributes to ongoing debates. In addition, she must explain how she did the work and address any methodological issues raised by people in the audience. Finally, the author must explain why she interprets the results the way she does and discuss other interesting implications of her analysis. And she has to do all of these things in an entertaining manner and finish in the allotted amount of time.

Accomplishing these tasks in front of a skeptical and sometimes hostile audience can be more difficult than many young scholars expect it to be. If an author does little planning for the presentation beyond following the paper, she can sometimes get in trouble and not do a good job of conveying the paper's message to the audience. Instead, an author should plan the presentation separately from the paper. Sometimes the presentation can directly follow the paper, but other times it should take on a life of its own. Some reasons to deviate from the paper are time limitations, complications in the analysis that can be simplified or omitted in the presentation (but not in the paper), and a desire to focus on something different in the presentation than in the paper.

When an author presents a paper at another university, she should consider her presentation an opportunity to have a conversation with the local faculty, remembering that her presentation is not just a one-sided, one-size-fits-all show. The goal of a presenter is not (only) to wow the audience but to get real feedback on the paper that will help improve the analysis. To increase the likelihood of receiving useful suggestions, it can be a good idea to open up the presentation to issues on which local faculty are experts.

Time Management

Presentations are almost always scheduled for a fixed time period. In economics and finance, seminars customarily last about an hour and a half, lunch talks take an hour, and presentations at conferences are usually given only fifteen or twenty minutes. Seminar participants can interrupt speakers with questions, while conference attendees usually have to wait until the speaker is finished to ask questions.

It is important to keep time considerations in mind when planning a talk. Authors should try to adjust the amount of material they cover in a presentation for the amount of time allotted to them. Some authors, when given a twenty-minute time window at a conference, attempt to use the same presentation they would deliver at a ninety-minute seminar and just talk faster. This strategy is almost always a bad idea; a better approach is to focus the talk on the main results and to cut material that is not absolutely essential.

Just as the space in written papers is not uniformly valuable, an author's time during a presentation varies in importance. The most important period is the first five or ten minutes of the talk. During this relatively short period of time, the author needs to explain to the audience why they should care about the paper, what the paper's approach is, and what can be learned from the analysis. If the author does not do a good job convincing the audience that her research is worthwhile at the beginning of the talk, as Jesse Shapiro puts it, "the talk is over, and you just don't know it."[1]

An author should go into a talk with an expectation about the amount of time she would like to spend on each part of her presentation. Before the talk, she should write down the approximate time she hopes to be at when finishing each part. For example, if the talk is scheduled for an hour and a half, probably twenty to twenty-five minutes would be a good amount of time to spend on the motivation for the research and a summary of results. Then the author should plan approximately how long she wants to spend on each subsequent section.

When I give a talk, I decide in advance which results are most important and which can be skipped. If the talk is going according to plan, then I can present all the prepared slides. However, if it is taking longer than expected to cover the material in the early part of the talk because of a large number of questions, then I can skip all but the most important results to ensure that I spend sufficient time on each of them.

No matter how much a speaker is delayed by discussion in the early part of the seminar, it is important to get through all the important results before the last few minutes of the talk. By the end of the talk, people have stopped paying attention and started thinking about lunch, their next meeting, the class they have coming up later in the day, or any number of other things. If the main results are presented in the last five minutes of the talk, seminar participants will not have time to understand the issues in the paper. And even if they are still paying attention by that time, they won't be able to ask the author questions about things they do not understand about the findings. If a seminar speaker does

---

1. See Jesse Shapiro, "How to Give an Applied Micro Talk: Unauthoritative Notes," https://www.brown.edu/Research/Shapiro/pdfs/applied_micro_slides.pdf.

not get to the most important results in the paper early enough, the seminar is likely to be received poorly, even by scholars who are predisposed to like the paper.

Motivating a Presentation

When preparing a presentation, it is useful to approach the issue from the perspective of a listener. As scholars, we attend many presentations, whether from outside speakers, our colleagues, or our students. My department is similar to most in that all faculty and doctoral students are expected to go to departmental seminars regardless of whether we are interested in the topic. In addition to departmental seminars, all faculty listen to many student presentations, attend seminars in other departments, and participate in a number of conferences. Some of the time we go because we want to hear what the speaker has to say, but often we attend because we have to. Our minds will tend to wander if the speaker does not give us a reason to pay attention, especially if the talk is in an area far from our own interests.

Most people subconsciously decide in the first few minutes of a presentation whether they should pay attention for the remainder of the talk. If a listener is really interested in a talk, he can become very engaged, trying to follow everything the speaker says and getting as much out of it as possible. However, listeners often "tune out." They become bored in the beginning of the talk, miss something important the speaker says early on, and then spend the rest of the time watching the clock, sneaking peeks at their smartphone, and thinking about anything but what the speaker is talking about. Occasionally these bored participants will ask a question or two, but mostly they count the minutes until the talk ends.

A scholar should approach her presentations with the hope of keeping as many listeners engaged as possible and minimizing the number who tune out. The key is the beginning of the talk: it is incredibly important to get the audience interested during the first few minutes. The way to pique the audience's interest is by convincing them that you have something interesting and important to say. What is important to academics varies from field to field, so a scholar should know what is valued in her field sufficiently to make her paper appealing.

Since my work is in applied economics, I usually try to convince listeners that my research is not just interesting to academics but also potentially useful to our understanding of an important real-world issue. If I convince the audience that a particular issue is really important to our understanding of the real economy but not that extensively studied, then academic economists usually come to the conclusion that they should pay attention to what I am going to say. Numbers help a lot: often scholars outside a particular field have not realized the quantitative importance of a topic until the speaker provides them with evidence. For example, to interest an audience of nonspecialists at a talk about private capital markets, I tell them of the enormous amount of capital currently in these markets and its importance in the economy, which almost always does a good job of getting them to pay attention.

A second option is to relate your results to classic literatures in the field. In economics, a good idea is to start with Adam Smith, John Maynard Keynes, or Milton Friedman, then explain how your research builds on a question one of them originally raised. The audience will most probably appreciate the reference and realize that you are talking about an important issue.

A third way of generating interest in your talk is to point out a gap in an important literature and to explain how your paper fills that gap. If listeners care about that literature, they are likely to pay attention. If not, they are likely to go back to their phones and check their email or read about whether their favorite team won or lost last night.

Know the Audience

A number of considerations related to the specific circumstances of the talk can affect the planning of your presentation. Who will be in the audience? Will it be a seminar, a conference presentation, or a PhD class? Are you being considered for a job? What is the audience's background and level of technical sophistication? Will there be a discussant? Will the audience ask questions along the way or will you be able to present the paper uninterrupted? What kinds of issues do you expect the audience or discussant to raise?

The audience's background will affect the amount of background material you have to cover and the way you can discuss issues raised in the paper. The general rule is that the more specialized an audience, the less background information is necessary. The National Bureau of Economic Research puts on prestigious conferences in most subspecialties of economics where the participants are top scholars working in the area; at these conferences, authors have little need to pique the interest of the audience and can get right into the meat of their talk. Departmental seminars are attended by people from all subfields, so it is important to include enough background information so that nonspecialists can appreciate the work's importance. In a classroom situation, it is sometimes necessary to include very basic material before getting to the more sophisticated and interesting parts of the research. In finance and some other fields, we sometimes have the opportunity to explain our research to practitioners doing work related to our research, and so we don't normally need to provide much institutional background information in these talks. However, with practitioners, it is usually a good idea to explain some things that academics could be assumed to know well (like how to interpret regression coefficients).

A presentation that is a "job talk" has a somewhat different audience than a regular seminar presentation. Faculty who are not interested in the subject will feel like they should show up and try to understand the paper. Sometimes deans and faculty from other departments attend the talk as well. These faculty will be as interested in the speaker's presentation skills and personality as they will be in the research she is presenting. When a job is on the line, faculty are concerned about how the speaker would perform as a teacher and colleague if they hired her. Consequently, in job talks it is particularly important to keep nonspecialists in mind in making your presentation and to make sure it comes across as both professional and entertaining.

The Role of Slides

Central to any presentation today is a set of slides (sometimes called a "deck"). An author will plan her presentation around the slides she uses and follow them throughout the talk. A high-quality slide deck can improve a presentation and serve as a valuable aid in a number of ways.

The most important role of a slide deck is to provide a visual aid for the talk. A speaker can put equations, summaries of results, figures, and other elements of the research on her slides, so that the audience can see them easily. In addition, an author can include bullet points containing logical arguments, or even cartoons or pictures that will entertain the audience. If the audience does not follow everything the speaker is saying, often the slides can help them understand her points. Slides can also remind the seminar participants where the author is in the presentation, and they can contain basic information the audience should be aware of. If it is a theoretical paper, the slides can contain the equations being discussed together with variable definitions and any other information that will help the audience understand the model. In an empirical paper, it is a good idea for the slides to contain details about the sample period, sample size, estimation procedure, and so on. Putting this information on the screen can help the speaker avoid questions about basic information that interrupt the flow of the presentation, thus leaving more time for substantive issues.

A good slide deck can help the speaker keep the audience's attention on the topics she wishes to discuss. The slide being presented, by telling the audience what they should be focusing on at that moment, can help a speaker maintain control of the discussion. Keeping control in an academic seminar can be more difficult than you might think. Discussions of academic work can move far from the issues that the speaker wants to focus on, or even the paper she is presenting. A trick that can help a speaker maintain control of the room during a seminar is to look to the slides during a break in the discussion and move on to the next one. The audience is likely to look at the board, see the next slide, and move its focus to whatever is said on it. Which is exactly where the speaker wants their attention to be!

A speaker should construct the slides with the goal of keeping the audience's attention on the issues she wishes to emphasize in the talk and not on tangential issues that might come up. For example, it is common in economics to estimate equations including many explanatory variables, often too many to show clearly on any one slide. Scholars should present the complete equations, including all variables and their coefficients, in the paper. In the slide deck, however, it can be a good idea to include only the main variables of interest that are relevant to the hypothesis the author is interested in testing. This way, the speaker can focus the audience's attention on the issues she wants to emphasize and keep it from wandering to other variables that are not relevant to her hypothesis.

A slide deck can also provide a useful takeaway from the presentation. Like most faculty, I distribute my slides to students for all the classes I teach. The slides provide a guide for the students, telling them what aspects of the material I think are most important and will cover in class. With research papers, slide decks can be useful documents; a practitioner who works in one of my research areas has told me that he much prefers learning about my research by reading my slides than by reading the papers themselves. Some faculty even post presentations of their papers online, since the slides provide an easy-to-read summary of what the author wants to say.

Constructing a Slide Deck

An author should construct a slide deck with these goals in mind: to display the paper's results; to provide guidance for the audience; to focus people's attention on the issues the author wants to cover; and to serve as a document that people can take away from the presentation that covers the author's main points in a straightforward manner. These objectives should be what an author focuses on when she constructs her slide deck.

However, many authors try to do too much with their slides. One common mistake authors make is to use the slides as a way of demonstrating their skill at PowerPoint, or whatever program they are using.

We have all been to presentations where pictures and graphs went flying across the screen in all different ways and have come away amazed by the author's PowerPoint skills. These presentations can be quite entertaining. The problem with them, however, is that afterwards the people who attended the presentation often end up talking about the slides, not the content of the talk. If the audience focuses their attention on the slides themselves rather than the subject being discussed, then the slides have become too much of a distraction. Slides are supposed to help the audience understand the author's ideas, not become themselves the subject of the audience's attention.

Another common problem is that authors try to cover too much material on each slide. Too much material on each slide leads the audience to spend too much time reading the slides rather than listening to what the speaker has to say. Or worse, the audience could struggle to read what is on the slide because the author used too small a font. If the audience cannot read a slide, they will interrupt the speaker to ask what the slide says, disrupting the flow of her presentation. In this case, a slide deck intended to keep the audience focused where the speaker wants the focus to be instead becomes a distraction that causes the audience's attention to wander.

The small-font-size problem might sound trivial, but in fact it is extremely common that people in the back of the room cannot read the presenter's slides, especially tables that have been copied directly onto them. If you are unsure about a slide deck, take it to an empty classroom and put it on the screen. Go to the back of the room and see how small the words and numbers are. If it is at all difficult to read them, then you have a problem. It is important to make the font larger and the slide more readable, if necessary by deleting some of the numbers from the table and getting rid of some of the text. Making slides easy to read is a notion that no one would disagree with, but not everyone actually bothers to make sure that *their own* slides are readable.

Another common problem in presentations is the number of slides an author tries to cover in a single talk. As I discussed in chapter 7, most papers have several main results and other, more ancillary results that deal with potential objections or special cases. In that chapter, I encouraged authors to focus their writing on the main results and to move as much of the other material as possible to appendices. In presentations, the same principle applies, but even more so. Presenters have only a fixed amount of time and have to allocate it wisely to communicate their material effectively. Since almost every paper contains far more results than could be effectively discussed in a short period of time, it is important to focus on presenting only the most important ones.

The objections that are commonly made to the results should be addressed head on, but ones that come up occasionally can usually be omitted and discussed only if someone in the audience raises them. Some scholars include links in the presentation that will take them to optional slides that address less commonly raised objections, so the author can use them if the issues happen to come up during the talk. I think this practice is a good idea, but one done more for the presenter's peace of mind than anything else—it is extremely rare that presenters actually have to click on those links during a presentation.

One issue that scholars, especially young ones, worry about too much is the software package used to create the slides. As I write this paragraph, the most fashionable package is called Latex, although in a few years it will probably be something else. It is fine if a scholar prefers Latex—it is a very good package, especially for equations. The point, however, is that a scholar shouldn't feel that she *has* to use Latex rather than PowerPoint or any other program that she is comfortable with. The purpose of slides is to help the speaker convince people that her research is interesting and important, not to be something of independent interest. The goal should be to keep the slides simple and use them to support the talk, not to have them become a topic of discussion themselves.

The Keys to a Good Presentation: Answering Questions and Keeping Control

The quality of an author's slides is only one of many factors that determine how well a presentation goes. The largest factor, of course, is the quality of the underlying analysis. But by the time the author is getting ready for the presentation, the paper is what it is. She has to think about what would make the best impression given the strengths or weaknesses of the paper she is going to present.

There are some things that an author should think about when preparing and delivering her presentation. She should talk clearly, loudly, and to the audience. Acoustics are surprisingly bad in some seminar rooms; our department unfortunately has a fan that can make it difficult to hear the speaker and questions from the other side of the room. If the speaker talks in a quiet voice and the audience has to try hard to understand what she is saying, it becomes easier for them to tune out. In addition, some speakers, especially when they are nervous, give boring, lifeless talks because they tend to read from their slides rather than talk to the audience. A presenter should make an effort to talk directly to the audience, make eye contact with them, and explain the issues in clear, easy-to-understand words.

Even if the speaker is an outsider, or a scholar much younger and less well known than some senior faculty in the audience, she should do whatever she can to let them know she is in charge. One easy thing a speaker can do is to erase the blackboard and close the doors to ensure there is no extraneous noise from the hallway. I have attended many seminars at various universities where the board contained advertisements for the finance club or even calculus problems from the last time the classroom was used. In many of those cases, the speakers felt like a guest and didn't think it appropriate to erase the blackboard, but leaving extraneous material on the board distracted the audience when they wanted the audience's attention on their paper. When a speaker visits another university, she is a guest for the majority of the trip. But during the seminar, it is her show, and she should work hard to remain in charge throughout the duration of her talk.

A good idea is to start the talk with a brief remark about something personal, something light, a small planned joke. A funny joke can relax an audience. When I'm visiting another university, I like to talk about the place and the hospitality they have shown me, or even tell a funny (but not too embarrassing) story about one of their faculty.

A scholar's talks, like many things, improve with practice. The first time a scholar presents a seminar, she is usually nervous and can be somewhat robotic in her answers. Over time she will get more comfortable in front of a seminar room, and better at explaining things to an audience and answering their questions well. Therefore, it is a good idea for all of us, especially young scholars who are new to the profession, to give as many talks in front of as many different audiences as possible.

A number of excellent speaking coaches are available for hire. For a young scholar who is too timid in front of an audience, or who feels that she needs help for any reason, hiring a coach can be a valuable investment. The ability to talk comfortably in front of an audience is one of the most important skills an academic can have; investments in improving this skill are usually worthwhile.

It is important that a speaker use her time in a presentation wisely, since time is always limited and audiences can tune out quickly if she does not get to the point quickly. A common mistake is to waste time on literature surveys, especially in the beginning of a talk, when time is most valuable. Sometimes it is necessary to spend some time on the prior literature, since part of the paper's motivation could come from someone else's research. But the speaker must still be careful to focus the discussion on her own work, not on the earlier papers. Seminars can go off-track quickly if they devolve into discussions of a controversial paper that someone else wrote a few years ago. These discussions distract from the author's message and make it extremely difficult for her to get the audience to focus on her contribution rather than the controversial paper.

One of the key metrics by which academics rate seminar presentations is the way in which speakers answer questions. A speaker's answers can convey the depth of her knowledge, the way she thinks about problems, and the extent to which the research is robust to reasonable alternative assumptions or research designs. Her answers also convey much about the speaker herself: how open-minded she is, what kind of colleague she might be, and how she would do in front of a classroom.

If the speaker does not know the answer to a question, it is fine for her to say so. The key thing is to appear thoughtful; the audience will want to hear that the speaker has thought deeply about the issues in her paper even if she does not know the answer to every question asked about it. Sometimes speakers come across as arrogant because they don't appear to be taking questions seriously. By not answering questions respectfully and clearly, a speaker can turn a successful presentation into an unsuccessful one.

In any research project, there are many choices that a scholar must make along the way. By the time she is presenting her work, she will have made many such choices. People will question the choices she made, sometimes aggressively. She will hopefully have thought about most of the methodological issues people raise, and in much more detail than the people asking about them. So when they do ask these questions, she should clearly explain why she approached the issue in the manner she did. There is no need to be bashful or defensive. By the time an author is presenting the work, she should have thought about various possible specifications and decided on the appropriate one. Most of the time, it is fairly straightforward to explain to the audience why she made the choices she made throughout the research process.

A good way to answer a question about a possible alternative methodological choice would be to discuss what the results would have been using the alternative approach, how sensitive those results might have been to the choices she made during the research process, and why she thought the approach she took was superior to the alternative. Giving these answers in a confident, scholarly tone can show her questioners that she is on top of the issues they raised.

One common problem that speakers have in answering questions comes from not listening carefully enough to the question. Sometimes when someone asks a simple explanatory question, the author does not understand exactly what is being asked, assumes it's the one question she dreaded, and gives an overly defensive answer. If a speaker is not sure exactly what is being asked, it is perfectly fine to ask the person to repeat or rephrase the question. A good practice after answering a difficult question is for the speaker to ask the questioner if she actually answered the question he asked. Another good practice is to defer questions that are more appropriate for later in the presentation. But if the speaker does that, she has to be sure to answer the question at some point; otherwise, the questioner could feel that she is ignoring him.

When I defer a question, I always make a point of answering it eventually. When I answer, I also try to direct my answer at the person who asked it, looking at him to be sure he realizes that I am answering his earlier question.

Sometimes in seminar presentations an audience member tries to dominate the discussion and asks a series of aggressive questions. The person could feel offended by something in the paper, or just have a different point of view from the author's. Regardless of the reason, it can be trying for a speaker to be continually interrupted by a belligerent questioner. One approach is to say, "I only have x minutes left, I'd really love to discuss this issue with you. Maybe we can continue this conversation after the talk." Or, "That is definitely an important and interesting topic. But let me try to move on with my talk and show you the model. Hopefully, the answer to your question will become clearer as I explain what I am doing in more detail."

The important thing is to keep control of the talk. The goal should always be to avoid turning the seminar into a fight. Therefore, the speaker should answer questions calmly and politely, no matter how aggressive a questioner's tone. If possible, she should defer questions and suggest that she and the questioner talk privately about the troublesome issue after the talk. However, regardless of what the speaker does, some academics are just obnoxious and like to take out their frustrations on seminar speakers.

In any academic's career, there are always a number of memorable seminars, often ones that involved questionable behavior by audience participants. One of my friends managed to offend his dean in his second year as an assistant professor, and the dean responded by being rude and insulting to my friend. The dean didn't really listen to anything my friend said and seemed to get much joy out of tormenting a new assistant professor. My friend, despite an excellent research record, ended up leaving that school and had a successful career elsewhere.

I once presented in front of a famous faculty member who is a friend of mine, but who is also well known for liking to hear himself talk. He went on and on about various things during the talk, making it difficult for me to get in a word edgewise during my own seminar. I don't think he had any particular problems with my paper—he just was in the mood to talk, and I'm sure he didn't think he was going out of his way to cause me difficulties. That is just the way he always is. Even though he wasn't trying to be difficult, however, he made the afternoon unpleasant for me, and his colleagues probably got less out of my paper than they otherwise would have.

Discussing Other People's Papers at Conferences

At conferences, paper presentations are often followed by a discussant giving her perspective on the paper, typically for a period of ten or fifteen minutes. Young scholars often do not know what to say in their discussion the first few times they are asked to discuss a paper at a conference. Discussing a paper in a high-profile conference is often not an easy task: the discussant must try to give a fair assessment of the paper while not offending the author too much and entertaining the audience at the same time. How should you go about preparing such a discussion?

When given a few minutes to discuss a paper in a public forum, a scholar should have a few goals in mind. She is supposed to be an expert in the field who has spent time studying the paper. The audience looks to her to help understand whether the paper is correct, what can be learned from it, and where it fits into the larger literature. In addition, she should try to help the author make the paper better and frame her criticisms in a way that does not belittle or embarrass the author.

A common approach is what I refer to as a "formulaic discussion." In this kind of discussion, the discussant spends a few slides summarizing the paper's findings. Then she tells the audience it is a "great paper" and suggests that they all read it.[2] The discussant concludes the discussion by pointing out some suggestions for the author, usually minor things the audience doesn't care about. For example, the discussant might

---

2. Sometimes the scholar who serves as the discussant will subsequently referee the paper for a journal. It is not unheard of for the same person who proclaimed the paper to be "great" in public to later tell the editor privately that it is kind of stupid and to recommend rejection.

suggest that the author use three-stage least squares instead of two-stage least squares, or that she cluster the standard errors differently.

As a reader can probably tell, I'm not a fan of formulaic discussions. The summary of the paper, which can take half of the discussant's time, is usually a waste of the audience's time because it repeats what the author just said in her presentation. Discussants' compliments for authors often come across as phony, and their suggestions, while sometimes helpful to the author, are often of no interest to anyone else in the room.

Rather than following a formula, I recommend that discussants try to give a short talk that the audience will be interested in. They should present their view on the issues addressed by the paper, explain how the paper fits into the larger literature, and give an honest assessment of the paper's incremental contribution. An approach that works well for me is to spend the first few minutes of the discussion talking about the issue the paper addresses. I start as if I am teaching a class or explaining to a student what the literature is about. Then I discuss the paper's results, what they contribute that is new, and what confirms what others have already found. There is no need to present the paper again; the authors almost always do a decent job explaining what they did. Instead, I focus my discussion on what I think we learn from the paper, what it adds to the literature, where it falls short, and what its implications are. The important thing is to give the audience my own perspective on the issues in the paper, not just repeat what the author said.

I was recently asked to discuss a paper on private equity infrastructure funds. Before I talked at all about the paper, I explained what these funds are, gave a few real-world examples of how they have been invested, and explained how they work. I told the audience what my friend who used to run an infrastructure fund said about the way they worked. Then I brought up the paper's results and compared the paper's perspective to my friend's. The discussion went very well, as the audience seemed to appreciate what I said and told me they learned something from the discussion.

Discussants often wonder about how critical they should be of a paper they do not like. If a discussant is negative, most of the audience will forget about the discussion relatively quickly, but the author will remember it for the rest of her life. A paper's faults are often obvious to the audience, however, and a discussant who fails to point them out can look foolish. A sensible strategy is to point out the paper's drawbacks, but to do so in as nice a way as possible. If there is something the author can salvage from the paper, try to give her a gentle push in the appropriate direction. The goal when discussing a bad paper is to point out its flaws to the audience in a way that does not embarrass the author or get her too upset with you.

After the discussant makes her points, the author has a chance to respond. Authors often use this opportunity to give a long, detailed diatribe about why the discussant is wrong. The author might in fact be correct and the discussant wrong, but it doesn't matter. By this point no one is listening. The attendees have made up their mind about the paper and are anxious to go to coffee break or to hear the next paper. Anyone would want to fight back after a negative discussion, but the problem is that the audience is rarely listening after the discussant is finished. For this reason, I think authors should always thank the discussant, quickly point out any errors that the discussant made, and leave whatever time remains for audience suggestions, which sometimes can be very useful.

However, the most important response to any discussion, especially a negative one, is to spend time digesting the discussant's comments and revising the paper based on them. If the discussant was negative, there is usually a reason why. Perhaps he didn't understand what the author did or ignored a key element of her analysis. If so, then it is likely that the author didn't explain what she did very clearly, or put the explanation in a part of the paper where the discussant didn't notice it. Or it could be that the discussant's objections are more serious than the author presumed. No matter what the discussant's reaction is, an author should always make an effort to understand the reason for his reaction, and to revise the paper with the goal of receiving a better response the next time she presents it.

10

Distributing, Revising, and Publicizing Research

ONCE AN AUTHOR HAS completed an initial draft of a paper, she must decide what comes next. How should she distribute the paper? To whom should she give it? In what order? When should she present it to her colleagues? When should she put the paper online? When should she submit to conferences and journals? And which conferences and which journals, in what order?

The answers to these questions are often not obvious to young scholars, who tend to disseminate their work somewhat haphazardly. But the process of distributing a paper to the public can materially affect its impact, because it determines who reads the paper first and the particular version that is read by each reader. The distribution process also affects the feedback an author receives throughout the process of revising the paper. Ultimately, this feedback can be a major factor affecting the quality of the paper that is eventually published. The way research is circulated, like everything else in the research process, should be thought through and done in a systematic fashion.

Soliciting Feedback on New Papers

Many papers end up being very different when they are published from what they were when first written. The changes, which usually (but not always) improve a paper, typically stem from feedback the author received from friends and colleagues. Most successful academics are good at utilizing the suggestions they receive to improve their analysis and heighten the impact of their paper. If a scholar is to take advantage of feedback on her papers, however, she first has to receive it—hopefully at a stage when the feedback is most useful.

When thinking about the comments she can expect to receive on a paper, an author should remember that there are a number of different types of readers. Hopefully, a few people will be available to provide detailed thoughts on her paper if the author asks them nicely. These people most often are close friends, colleagues, or students, as well as scholars who work on related topics.

Most people who read her paper, however, will do so only once. While a few will provide the author with detailed feedback, most are likely to give her only a general reaction. The vast majority of readers will just look over the paper and try to understand the paper's goals, general approach, and results. Therefore, people who are willing to give an author useful feedback on a paper are a valuable resource and should be treated as such.

An author should also remember that readers' opinions about a paper tend to be correlated with one another. As authors, we try to anticipate people's reactions: what we think they will be interested in, what they might be bored with, what potential problems readers will think are serious, and which ones they will think are not a big deal. Sometimes these predictions turn out to be correct, but often they are not. Invariably, there are one or two issues with any paper I write that I didn't think were that important when I wrote the first draft but that almost every reader brings up. Usually, these are concerns about my analysis, although occasionally they tell me what they like about my paper and think I should emphasize more.

When an author distributes a paper, her goal is to learn what the common reaction is to the paper without exhausting all of the feedback she is likely to get. It is inefficient to send a paper to everyone you know and have all of your friends make the same suggestions to you. Instead, it is preferable to send a paper out sequentially. Send it first to one or two close friends who are likely to read it and give comments. After making revisions that address the important issues they raise, send it to a few more people. Continue the process, addressing each set of comments as you receive them, and keep sending the paper to other people until you finally have sent it to everyone who might be interested. This approach takes longer than sending the paper out all at once, but it helps you make much more efficient use of the feedback you are likely to receive.

I recently read an interesting paper that I had been given a copy of early in the paper's life, prior to the authors receiving much feedback from others. The paper had two major sets of results. The ones that the authors reported first seemed fine to me: I thought they were undoubtedly correct but not particularly surprising. The results in the second set, however, were quite novel: they used a new technique to address questions that the literature had not previously addressed. I wrote an email to the authors to let them know my reaction to the paper. In it, I encouraged them to deemphasize the first set of results and focus more on the second set. If the authors agreed with me, they should try to make this change before sending it to too many others. That way, their next set of comments will likely address different issues from the ones I raised. Those comments will be more valuable to the authors than if the next person to read the paper merely repeats what I have already told them.

Because of examples like this one, I always encourage my coauthors to send our papers out for feedback sequentially. Before we let anyone else see the paper, my coauthors and I usually go back and forth about how to write the paper. We normally argue a little about how to structure the paper but ultimately converge to a version that we think is as good as we can make it. After my coauthors and I agree, I usually ask my research assistant to give the paper a careful read. At Ohio State, we are fortunate to have excellent doctoral students assigned as research assistants; my research assistant normally not only finds typos and awkward sentences but makes substantive comments that sometimes lead my coauthors and me to rethink some of our analysis. When my coauthors and I have digested these comments, I try to give the paper to one or two friends of mine who I think are likely to read the paper carefully. My coauthors and I incorporate those comments, and then repeat this process as often as seems useful. I feel that it is important that our paper go through several rounds of revision before I am willing to present it in a public forum, let alone put it online to make it easily available to anyone in the world.

The cost of this sequential distribution process is the extra time that it takes. Authors generally want to distribute papers as quickly as possible, for a number of reasons. First of all, research is a competitive marketplace, so the sooner your paper gets out, the better claim you have that the paper is the first to do what it does. Second, authors often have human capital reasons to speed up the research process as much as possible. Doctoral students' job market prospects are improved if they have established research that appears likely to be published soon, junior faculty come up for tenure at prespecified points in time, and even senior faculty have reviews that depend on their ability to produce important research in a timely manner. Third, and perhaps most important, our research is something we put time and energy into and hopefully are proud of. We all enjoy sharing our research with friends and discussing it with them as soon as we can.

These reasons to speed up the distribution process are important. But authors should remember that most readers will read the paper only once. If there are mistakes in the version of the paper that is distributed, if it emphasizes the wrong thing, if the writing is mediocre, or if it does not contain some interesting results that will be in subsequent versions, then the author risks not making her best impression. A consequence of circulating the paper too soon is that the author risks having readers think less of the paper than they would if she had waited a little longer to circulate it.

This discussion highlights the importance of having a network of friends and colleagues who are willing to give you honest, constructive, and fast feedback on your papers. You should work throughout your career to develop these relationships. One way to develop working relationships with scholars in the same area is to reciprocate by providing useful feedback to others on their papers. When given a paper to read, you should make a serious effort to give the author detailed, constructive comments whenever possible. This effort is likely to be more than a nice gesture to a friend—it is an investment that can yield huge benefits when the friend responds by helping you make your own work better.

Presenting Papers

After an author circulates her paper privately among her friends and uses the suggestions she receives to make the paper as strong as possible, she should try to publicize her paper more broadly. By this point, there should be no logical errors in the analysis, the writing should be high-quality, the reasons for presenting the paper should be obvious, and obvious alternative explanations should have been addressed. The paper should be something that the author is proud of and wants to share with the entire profession. Hopefully, the profession will appreciate it and recognize its brilliance!

There are a number of reasons why an author should spend time and effort publicizing her work. First, the way that research has an impact is through its influence on others. If the profession does not know about a paper, it is hard for the paper to become influential. Second, a strong paper will enhance people's impression of the author herself, helping her reputation in the profession. Finally, when more people see the work, the author will receive more feedback and have still more chances to improve the paper.

When publicizing her work outside her close circle of friends, the author should continue to use the sequential process discussed here. She should first present the paper to groups that are most likely to give useful feedback. Then she should revise the paper, incorporating the feedback, and continue to present the paper as often as possible. In addition, she should make other efforts through social media and personal contacts to draw attention to her work.

Most departments have a weekly "brown bag" workshop over lunch, mostly for internal speakers.[1] These tend to be informal events at which

---

1. The term "brown bag" comes from the days when participants would bring their own lunches, usually in a brown paper bag. I haven't seen an actual brown bag at a "brown bag"

people present relatively early versions of their papers. When I revise my own papers, I have found brown bag workshops to be extremely useful. Regardless of what people say about the paper during the talk, I find that spending time with the paper beforehand preparing my remarks is particularly valuable. Thinking about the structure of a presentation, what is important, what to emphasize, and what are likely to be objections, leads me to rethink a paper in ways I hadn't thought of while I was writing it. In addition, my colleagues can be counted on to bring up the toughest objections to any paper I show them. After addressing my colleagues' concerns, the ones I hear at other universities and from referees usually seem easy. Because my papers tend to improve so much after discussing them during brown bag workshops, I always try to present new papers in one before taking them on the road.

After discussing my paper in an internal workshop, I try to visit other universities and present it in their seminars. I am fairly well known in the profession, so I usually have more invitations than I have time to accept. For people just starting their career, arranging outside talks can be more difficult, but there are ways for a less established scholar to generate opportunities to present her work at other universities. Keeping in contact with a network of close friends helps, and letting these friends know when you have a paper to present can generate invitations. If you arrange to be in the city of an outside university for some other reason, that school will often invite you to present in their seminar series, since the school will incur no costs by hosting you. One strategy for scheduling presentations, therefore, is to visit universities for other reasons and then try to arrange talks while you're there.

Internationally, invitations tend to go to people who have visited the area before. For example, Chinese universities are much more likely to invite someone who is a regular visitor to Asia than someone who does not travel internationally very often. When you begin to travel overseas

workshop in many years; in my department, we serve pizza at these events. I'm sure our doctoral students have no idea where this strange term comes from.

and meet international scholars in their home country, subsequent opportunities to visit again often materialize fairly quickly.

Another place where scholars present their research is at conferences. In recent years, the number of conferences held in most fields has greatly increased. Unfortunately, despite the increase in the number of conferences, it has also become more difficult to get on programs at high-quality conferences because the number of submissions for each conference has grown even more rapidly than the number of conferences. For example, in finance, large conferences run by the major associations have acceptance rates of around 10 percent or lower. Even smaller conferences run by individual departments get at least two or three hundred submissions and take only eight to ten papers. Given that conference organizers usually prefer having papers from well-known scholars and people they know personally, getting on programs can be particularly difficult for someone who is not established and does not know the conference organizers.

I encourage young scholars to submit their papers to conferences regularly despite the long odds. A sensible strategy is to send papers to a number of different conferences with the hope that they make it on to one or two programs. Getting a paper accepted for a more specialized conference can be a bit easier, since submissions are limited to papers on the specific topic of the conference. Conferences focused on one topic can be more valuable to authors than general-interest ones anyway, since the papers are usually related to one another and their authors are better able to give valuable feedback on each other's papers.

A good policy is to attend the major conferences in your field whenever possible, even if one of your papers is not on the program. Conferences are a good way to make connections and hear interesting papers. However, some people go overboard and attend too many conferences. These events can take a lot of time and be expensive. It is important to remember that, as a scholar, your most valuable resource is time. Some young scholars forget to guard their time sufficiently and spend too much of it traveling to too many conferences.

Mass-Mailing Research

An easy way to publicize your research is to send copies of your papers to people who work in the area. Even before I post a paper and make it publicly available, I email a copy to the people whose work is most closely related to mine. I include a short note that summarizes the paper's contribution and let recipients know that I would appreciate hearing any reactions they have to the paper. After sending papers out this way, I am likely to receive suggestions on how to improve my paper. The people to whom I send my paper also will be more likely to remember it when they revise their own papers and to invite me to present it if they organize a conference related to the paper's topic.

I am sufficiently established that I usually know the people to whom I send my papers fairly well. But it is a good idea to write to scholars who are doing related work even if you are just starting out in the profession and do not know them personally. An author should not be shy about making sure that the leading scholars in her area know about her work. If a young scholar explains who she is and what her paper does, people doing related work will most likely appreciate hearing about the paper. In the worst case, they won't care about your paper and will delete it quickly, but even then nothing is lost by having emailed it to them.

Remember these two key things: First, do not send a paper out until you are absolutely sure it is ready. And second, when the paper is ready, do not be bashful about approaching people and telling them about the paper.

Publicizing Research Online

When you present a paper at another university, the faculty and students at that university can certainly see the paper, but until you post the paper online, its exposure is still somewhat limited. If major issues come up in the seminar and you want to revise the paper substantially, it is unlikely that copies of the earlier version containing the mistake will appear a few years later. Even after public presentations at universities, a paper is not *that* public until it appears online.

After you post a paper online, however, it becomes completely public. People from everywhere in the world can download copies and keep the pdf files. If there are mistakes in the analysis, or if you later change your mind about the appropriate interpretation of the results and rewrite that part of the paper, copies of the original version can pop up in the future. These versions can haunt you if, as sometimes happens, readers bring up a problem in the older version that you have by that time addressed.

Another risk of posting a paper online is that others working in related areas can steal some of the ideas in the paper and include them in their own papers. I personally have never had this problem, but I have heard stories of it happening to other faculty. A number of faculty are reluctant to post their papers online until they are almost published for fear that someone will steal their ideas.

Sometimes when a paper is online an author receives feedback that can be unpleasant. For example, a reader could write to an author claiming that he could not replicate the results that were posted online, or that there was a mistake in a derivation or the data work. If the criticism is correct, then it is extremely important for the author to fix the mistakes and repost a new version of the paper as soon as possible. However, such criticism is often misplaced and stems from a misunderstanding or an error on the part of the person writing to the author.

Regardless of whether the author thinks the criticism is correct, it is important for her to engage with the person who contacted her. That person *believes* he is correct and will not be happy if the author does not appear to take him seriously. Therefore, any author who is contacted about a potential mistake in her paper must immediately decide whether the criticism is correct and then explain what is going on to the person who contacted her. If she ignores the issue, the person could go public with the criticism, which would likely be embarrassing to the author and damaging to her reputation.

For these reasons, an author should think hard about when she will be ready to allow her paper to appear online. I usually wait until the second or third draft before I am willing to post my papers publicly. If I present an early draft at another university, I often request that the department distribute the paper to their faculty via email rather than post it publicly on their website, to limit the extent to which my paper will be publicly circulated before it's ready. Some faculty go further than I do and insist that early versions of the papers they present in seminars be distributed as hard copies rather than by email, to ensure that no one forwards them outside the university.

After I present a paper a few times and am confident that it won't change much in the near future, I do post it online. And when I post it, I go all out and try to make it available in as many places as possible. Our department has its own working paper series, which contains copies of new papers from our faculty. I always enter my papers into this series when they are sufficiently mature to be online. The papers in our departmental working paper series are automatically posted on the public website Social Science Research Network, which is a widely used network of working papers from all areas of the social sciences. In addition, since I am a research associate at the National Bureau of Economic Research, I enter my papers into the NBER working paper series as well.

Other Ways to Publicize Research

In addition to posting online, authors should take advantage of other opportunities to publicize their research. One such opportunity presents itself when visitors come through a scholar's university. Most departments have seminar series, and faculty are normally given the chance to meet with the speakers while they are on campus. Faculty, especially the younger ones, should always take advantage of these meetings and, if possible, use them to solicit feedback on their work.

Another way to publicize research, and also to network, is through social media. I do not have a Twitter account or a blog, but some of my colleagues post their papers as well as discussions of them on these media. I am active on Facebook, and I am amazed by the connections I have made with faculty at other universities by reading their posts every day. A number of faculty post regularly on Twitter and have been able to use this platform to publicize their research as well as to network with other scholars around the globe. Social media is becoming increasingly important in all aspects of our lives, and I strongly encourage young faculty to make an investment in it to increase their visibility and connections within the profession.

One place where you should *not* publicize your papers (at least not too much) is during someone else's seminar, or when discussing someone else's papers at a conference. It is extremely annoying to speakers, and to other audience members, when someone asks a long question in a seminar that is basically a summary of their own most recent paper, or when a discussant more or less ignores the paper he is supposed to discuss and presents his own paper. During someone else's talk, the time belongs to them, and it is rude to distract from their work unless the issue you bring up is extremely pertinent.

Maintaining an Up-to-Date Website

One place where I immediately post any paper mature enough to be online is my own website. I *always* keep my website up to date with the most recent versions of my papers. When I revise a paper and am ready to post the new version publicly, I update the website very quickly. No more than five or ten minutes after the update is finished, the new version will be online and the old version will not be downloadable anymore. Why should I let people download old versions of my papers when there are new versions available?

Websites have become a necessity for all academics in the twenty-first century, including both faculty and graduate students. I do not understand why some people do not have one, or why they let their website become out of date. Once a website is up and running, it takes no time to update it. Academics regularly look at each other's websites, and there is no excuse for letting them see outdated information when it is so easy to keep the information up to date.

Not having an up-to-date website can be costly. A few years ago, we had an unfilled position in my department. I brought up the name of someone I thought would be a good person for us to hire. This person probably would have accepted an offer from us and would have loved the job. But when my colleagues Googled her name, they didn't find a website. The discussion then moved on to other scholars, and we ended up hiring one of them for the position.

When to Submit a Paper to a Journal

One issue that young scholars often wonder about is the appropriate time to submit a paper to a journal. Some submit early drafts before the paper has been sufficiently polished. Usually, these submissions are quickly rejected. Others wait so long to submit that by the time the editor receives it, their paper is no longer novel and is rejected for that reason. How do you decide on the correct time to submit a paper to a journal?

The issue is complicated by the custom in most fields of not submitting a paper to two journals at the same time, and also of not resubmitting a rejected paper to the same journal again.[2] In addition, in most fields there are only a small number of journals that are considered top-tier, and among these top-tier journals, not all are appropriate for a given paper. For example, one of the top journals in economics, *Econometrica*, historically has mostly published papers that break new methodological ground. So if an author writes an applied paper that is not methodologically sophisticated, she probably would not want to waste her time submitting to *Econometrica*.

An author should approach a submission as a continuation of the revision process. When she writes a new manuscript, she first sends it out to close friends, then revises it based on their comments. When the paper is as good as she can make it, she presents it in an internal workshop, then revises it again. Next, she presents the paper at outside workshops and revises it afterwards based on the comments received there. Along the way, she sends the paper to other scholars working in the area and receives even more comments from them. At every step, she revises the paper to be as good as she can make it. Eventually, she runs out of

---

2. An exception to this rule is law, a field whose journals are usually student-run law reviews. For law review submissions (but not submissions to peer-reviewed law journals), simultaneous submission to multiple journals is allowed.

useful suggestions. Only when she reaches this point is the paper ready for submission to a journal.

There are some factors that can speed up or slow down this process. For instance, how crowded and competitive is the scholar's area of focus? When there are others working on similar questions, she should do whatever she can to speed up the revision process, since the first paper to be submitted usually has a higher likelihood of being accepted for publication than the ones submitted later on. Of course, if the author speeds up the revision too much and the paper looks "early" to editors and reviewers, it could be rejected for that reason. Some academics working in competitive fields tend to submit papers too soon and get upset when reviewers are not sympathetic.

There are also career-related reasons to try to speed up the submission process. Scholars coming up for tenure soon naturally want to submit their work as quickly as possible. However, they should remember that editors will not take their tenure decision into account when handling their papers. So these scholars could be hurt in the long run if they rush the revision process, submit too soon, and have a paper rejected that might have had a better chance if they had polished it more prior to the initial submission.

Journal Submission Strategies

Once a paper is ready for submission, a scholar has to decide on the journal to which she should submit it. This choice is actually more difficult than you might think. Journals differ on a number of dimensions. Within a large field like economics, some journals are general interest (*American Economic Review*), and others focus on a particular subject (*Journal of Labor Economics*). While all are refereed, the review process they use can vary. Some use a more bureaucratic process involving multiple referees and associate editors, while others rely almost solely on the opinions of one referee. Some editors read papers carefully, give detailed comments to authors, and overrule referees with whom they disagree. Others simply forward the referee reports to authors and follow the referees' suggestions, regardless of what they are.

Authors can thus have very different experiences dealing with different journals. Some experiences, such as having to satisfy just one referee, are relatively straightforward. Others are complicated by having to placate multiple referees and editors, who sometimes disagree with one another.

There are a number of factors to weigh in choosing a journal. First and foremost is the journal's prestige. In every field, a small number of journals are considered top-tier. These are almost always the journals that usually publish the best-known papers and have the highest "impact factors."[3] They are also valued extremely highly by universities when making promotion decisions. Many departments (including my own) focus promotion decisions mainly on a faculty member's publications in journals they consider to be top-tier.

However, not every paper belongs in a top-tier journal. Top-tier journals try to publish general-interest papers that are interesting to the majority of the profession. Some specialized papers, even if they are well executed and add meaningfully to our knowledge, ask questions that are too narrow for the top-tier journals. Submitting a very specialized paper to a general-interest journal usually leads to a rejection and wastes everyone's time: the author's, the editor's, and the referees'.

The time element can also be significant. Some economics journals can take over a year to respond to authors. Waiting a year to get a response from a journal can be costly, especially if the odds are low that the journal will request a revision. During that year, others may be writing competitive papers, the author can get interested in other topics, and the tenure clock keeps ticking away. A number of my classmates from graduate school sent their dissertations to extremely prestigious general-interest economics journals like *Journal of Political Economy* or *Econometrica*. While some had their papers accepted, more ended up losing a year or more before submitting their paper to the more specialized journal that ultimately accepted it. Some of my classmates had

---

3. The impact factor of an academic journal—a commonly used measure of a journal's quality—is an index that reflects the yearly average number of citations received by articles it has published in the last two years.

written papers that had some appeal for general-interest journals, so it made sense for them to try those journals. But those who had written high-quality but specialized dissertations should probably have submitted their papers to more appropriate outlets. In part because they submitted to a higher-ranked journal and consequently lost valuable time, some of the papers from my classmates' dissertations were never published.

The most significant cost of a submission is the time it takes.[4] The cost of delaying publication by waiting for a journal to respond is meaningful and should not be underestimated. If a paper is rejected after a long time, the author then has to spend time revising it rather than working on new research. In addition, there is an emotional cost to getting rejected after a year of waiting. It is true that you will never be published in a top-tier journal if you do not submit your work to them from time to time. But I recommend submitting only papers that you feel have a real shot at getting accepted because the cost of waiting a long time for a rejection can be substantial.

It is important to consider the fit of the journal to a paper when deciding where to submit it. Has the journal recently published papers of a similar style to yours? Given that editorial boards change, do the *current* editors of a particular journal like the style of the paper you are considering submitting? For example, many economists have historically been hostile toward behavioral research. Fortunately, this attitude is changing, but for a long time it was pointless to submit a behavioral paper to a journal with anti-behavioral editors who would not take the paper seriously. Having an editor who takes an interest in a paper and guides the paper through the review process is wonderful. Sometimes having an editor like that makes it worth submitting to a slightly less prestigious journal.

---

4. Most journals do have submission fees, but the majority of these fees are relatively low. The journal that has historically had the highest submission fees is the *Journal of Financial Economics*, which at the time of this writing has a fee of $1,000 for nonsubscribers. While this fee sounds high, the editors of that journal have always argued that compared to the impact of a publication in *JFE* on a scholar's human capital, their relatively high fees are trivial.

Finally, an author should remember that the journal submission process can be her last chance to improve a paper. The revision process can be stressful and tiring, but at the end of it, most papers end up better. Even if a paper is rejected, the suggestions an author receives from one journal can help her improve her paper so that it has a better chance at being published in another journal.

When a paper finally is ready, there is no reason to waste time: the author should submit it to a journal quickly. Then she should incorporate whatever feedback she receives into the draft as soon as possible, regardless of whether that journal is interested in publishing it. If the paper keeps improving throughout the revision process, it should eventually be published in a good outlet.

11

The Journal Review Process

IF YOU wander around at a cocktail party full of academics and listen to random conversations, it is likely that sooner or later you will over-hear some discussion of the review process at a journal. Invariably, the journal will be referred to by its initials (*JPE, AER*, etc.), and the discus-sion will be concerned with some outrageously unfair thing that the editor (and referees) did. In the opinion of the people you're overhear-ing, the editor probably either played favorites and accepted a mediocre paper by someone they don't like or rejected a wonderful paper by one of the people talking. However, no matter how much people complain about the review process, it usually works reasonably well. Most of the time referee reports are reasonable assessments of a paper's quality and editors' decisions usually make sense given the quality and objectives of the journal.

Academics are obsessed with the way journals review papers, the procedures journals use, the politics involved, and perhaps most impor-tantly, which of their friends' papers have been accepted by the top jour-nals. And they have good reason to be so concerned. The opaque, some-times inefficient system used by journals to decide which papers to publish is an incredibly important element of academics' professional lives. The ability to navigate the review process well has always been a necessary ingredient of a successful academic career.

Every academic puts an inordinate amount of effort into the review process in one way or another. Much of their career is spent preparing their papers for submission, revising them in response to referees' comments, and writing reports on other people's papers. Together, these activities take up a large fraction of academics' time outside the classroom. Often a scholar's "reward" for a successful career is to be asked to be an editor herself, a job that entails overseeing the review process, hearing appeals, and, often, handling the journal's management tasks, such as choosing associate editors or determining journal policies. Even aside from the amount of time spent on their own papers, interacting with journals in one way or another can take at least a few days of every *month* for an active researcher.

Consequently, it makes sense to think a bit about the review process, and how journal submissions are evaluated. Understanding how the review process works can aid a young scholar in maximizing her chances of having her work published in the best possible journals.

In this chapter, I discuss the way a submission works from beginning to end, trying to emphasize differences between the practices of different journals. At each step I try to advise authors on what they can do to improve their chances of getting their papers accepted.[1]

Preparing the Paper

As emphasized in the last chapter, a paper submitted to a journal should have gone through many revisions and be at the point where the author cannot think of anything substantive to do that would improve it. However, some scholars can take revising too far. I know assistant professors who waste incredible amounts of time making meaningless changes to papers because they are nervous about submitting them to journals. For example, some spend valuable time programming the computer so that whenever they submit a paper to a journal, it reformats the paper to look like an article in that journal, with the same fonts, paginations, and so on. This type of effort does nothing to improve the paper's analysis or likelihood of acceptance.

---

1. My colleague René Stulz has written a very good set of "Tips for Authors," which is available at: http://jfe.rochester.edu/tips.htm.

Other authors rerun every test five times, then make a small change and rerun them again a few more times. Although it is good to redo the analysis from time to time to ensure there are no mistakes, after a while an author hits a point at which the return from redoing things one more time is outweighed by the cost in time and delay. Before submitting a paper, she must make sure that the analysis is correct, but making minor changes solely for the sake of making changes accomplishes nothing useful and is unlikely to affect the opinions of editors and referees.

There are some things that do matter and can substantially affect the response an author receives from a journal. The writing, especially in the abstract and introduction, is incredibly important. The author should make sure that anyone reading the first few pages knows exactly what the paper does, why it matters, and what the results and objections to them are. As I stressed in chapter 5, the introduction is the most important part of the paper since that is the only part of the paper that many who see the paper will actually read. Referees, although they are supposed to go through the entire paper carefully, sometimes do not make it past the introduction, especially if they are not impressed by it. Therefore, an author, especially an inexperienced one, should spend a lot of time polishing a paper's introduction before submitting it to a journal.

The other thing an author should think a lot about before submitting to a journal is the paper's length. It is *much* easier to publish a paper with twenty-five pages of text and seven tables than one with forty pages of text and fourteen tables (appendices don't count). Editors often claim that they prefer short papers because journal space is scarce, but I'm not sure that is correct. When I was an editor at *Review of Financial Studies*, the publisher, Oxford University Press, placed no limitations on the number of pages in each issue. I think the truth was that Oxford University Press actually liked to have longer issues for the journal's readers.

I have no idea whether other journals actually have page limits or just say they do. My theory on why it is so much more difficult to publish longer papers is that they tend to be more painful to review than shorter papers, so referees are more likely to respond negatively. Editors, too, prefer shorter papers since their job is easier if papers are shorter and readers tend to find them easier to go through.

Regardless of the reason, it is definitely easier to publish shorter papers than longer ones. Therefore, prior to submission, an author should go through the paper and chop anything that isn't essential, such as tests of alternative hypotheses that most readers don't really care about, generalizations of models that add complications but no new ideas, and redundancies in the paper's prose. Much of this non-essential material can be described in the text and moved to an appendix, possibly an online one. The key factor in determining whether material should be included in the main text or in an appendix is whether a typical reader would find it interesting or superfluous. If a finding in a paper does not advance its key points and is likely to be considered non-essential by most readers, then the author should think about moving it to an appendix. If the referee turns out to be one of the few people who really care about the finding, the author can always move it back into the main text.

A few years ago, one of my students had a job market paper that I really loved.[2] When her job market process was over, she spent some time incorporating the feedback she received from the schools she visited, then tried to publish it. I was sure that referees would think the paper was very good and that it would be accepted by one of the top three finance journals. Unfortunately, and to my surprise, her paper was rejected by all three. After these rejections, my student asked me to look at the paper again and to help her decide what to do next. When I read the version she had been submitting, I realized that she had diligently incorporated every suggestion she received from her job market seminars, like students all over the world are taught to do. But in doing so, her paper grew from thirty readable and interesting pages to forty-five boring ones, which was probably why the referees at the top journals recommended rejection. I helped her chop whatever was not absolutely necessary from the paper and shorten it to under thirty pages. Her paper was accepted at the next journal she submitted it to.

This story highlights the importance of taking advice from one's adviser, even after finishing the PhD. I wish my former student had asked

2. I still do. I teach it in my doctoral class every year.

me to look at her paper prior to her initial submissions. The fact that the paper was unnecessarily long is the sort of thing that is obvious to someone who has been rejected many times over the years but not so obvious to a newly minted PhD. It is usually a good idea to consult with a thesis adviser or other experienced scholars when making decisions about journal submissions, including when to submit, where to submit, and how to revise papers prior to submission.

Forming a Submission Strategy

The rule in most fields of academia is that a paper can be submitted to only one journal at a time. The review process is very costly in terms of editors' and referees' time, so journals will not pay these costs unless they have the option to publish the paper if they like it.[3] In addition, the paper cannot be resubmitted to that journal if it is rejected. Some authors try to make small changes to the paper, call it a new paper, and try the same journal again. This strategy is almost always a bad one, since editors usually notice such submissions, reject them quickly, and end up thinking less of the authors.

Given that an author can submit to only one journal at a time, how does she decide which journal to try first? Why not always start with the best journal in the field? In many circumstances, it does make sense to try the top journals first. There is no stigma to getting a rejection, so long as the paper is reasonably well executed. The major cost to such a submission, aside from the emotional cost of rejection, is the time it takes to get a response.

As mentioned earlier, many scholars substantially underestimate the value of that time. While a journal takes as much as a year to provide an editorial response to an author, others' continuing work on competitive papers may reduce the novelty of her paper, as well as her capacity to do new work. She may waste her own valuable time thinking about changes

---

3. Since law reviews are edited by students, the opportunity cost of reviewers' time is low. Perhaps for this reason, law reviews are willing to consider manuscripts for publication even if they are also being considered by other law reviews. If their paper is accepted by more than one law review, the authors can choose the journal in which the paper is published.

she could make to the paper, what the referees' reactions are likely to be, and so on.

I think that an author should try to form a realistic expectation of whether a paper has a substantial chance at getting accepted before submitting it to a journal. Forming this expectation can be difficult because it requires accepting the limitations of her paper. If an author thinks her paper has broad appeal and she has received positive feedback on it in presentations and from advisers and colleagues, then she should probably try a top-tier journal. Having a publication in a top journal is very valuable, especially for junior faculty who will be up for tenure soon. But all authors should be aware of the time and energy involved in the submission process. If a paper is having problems at the top journals and a lower-ranked journal is likely to take it without too much effort on the author's part, then it might make sense to publish it there and move on to the next paper.

The Initial Submission

Most journals today use a program called Editorial Express or some similar software that enables the submitter to upload the paper and other relevant information directly to the journal's website. This kind of program makes the journal's job easier, as it computerizes all the information they require and includes a link to a payment system that processes the submission fee.

The one important decision an author must sometimes make at the time of the initial submission is choosing an editor to handle the paper, since some journals let authors suggest an editor at that time. These journals do not guarantee the author's choice of editor, but my experience is that well over half the time the suggested editor does handle the paper.[4] Most journals have multiple editors with different tastes in

---

4. Journals sometimes do not use the editor the author suggests because the managing editor wants to even out the workload among editors, or because there is a conflict that prevents the requested editor from handling the submission.

research, so the choice of the editor who will handle the paper is extremely important.

When given the chance to suggest an editor, an author should suggest the editor she believes will be sympathetic to the paper and its message. This person is usually the editor whose own research is closest to the research underlying the paper. However, when an author is concerned that the editor whose research is closest to hers could be predisposed against the paper—perhaps because the editor has well-known views contrary to those expressed in the paper, or has a student with a paper competing with the author's, or for any number of other reasons—that editor should be avoided. Another reason for not choosing such an editor is that a different editor has expressed an interest in the paper and is thus a sensible person to suggest.

When I was an editor, I almost never read the cover letters accompanying the submission. I skipped straight to the paper and read it quickly as I was deciding who to ask to referee it. However, other current and former editors have told me that they do read the cover letters carefully and use the summaries that authors provide in them to guide their choice of referees. The cover letter provides the author with an opportunity to grab the editor's attention, to put the paper into context, and to explain to the editor why the paper is a good fit for the journal.

What the Journal Does with a New Submission

When a new paper is submitted to a journal, usually the first person who sees it is a staff member who makes sure that the paper meets the requirements of the journal. For example, some journals have maximum lengths or other restrictions, such as a minimum font size.[5] If the paper meets the specifications and the submission fee is paid, the paper is then looked over briefly by the editor in charge of assigning submissions, usually called the "managing editor." This person can reject the paper at

5. At the *Review of Financial Studies*, we adopted a minimum font size because one author submitted four or five papers every year that always seemed to be close to one hundred pages long in a very small font. Needless to say, none of the editors looked forward to handling this person's papers.

this point if it is obviously not suitable for the journal (a "desk rejection"). More often, the managing editor will assign the paper to one of the journal's other editors to handle, or she could decide to handle it herself.

At this point, the process differs somewhat from journal to journal. At *Review of Financial Studies*, we had a post-doc who read every submitted paper and suggested several names of possible reviewers for each paper to the editor who was handling it. Other journals assign each paper to an associate editor, who gives the editor an opinion on the paper and suggests potential referees. Eventually, the paper hits the editor's desk. The editor makes the call about whether the paper should be refereed or desk-rejected, and if it is to be refereed, who to ask to review it. Personally, I hated to desk-reject papers and rarely did so. Probably I could have saved referees' and authors' time if I had desk-rejected more often, but I hated the expressions I would see on the faces of desk-rejected authors when they saw me later at conferences. Other editors, however, regularly desk-reject papers that are extremely unlikely to be published, which is probably a good policy. Some journals, such as the *Quarterly Journal of Economics*, desk-reject over half of the papers that are submitted.[6]

If the paper is not desk-rejected, the editor must decide how many and which referees to use. Most journals are moving to a policy of having multiple referees on each paper, although some still use only one referee most of the time. Editors normally choose referees who do research related to the paper, since they are better able to assess the paper's incremental contribution over the existing literature. When they use multiple referees, editors try to pick people with diverse backgrounds and skills. For example, if a paper describes both theoretical and empirical work, an editor might ask a scholar who is better at theory to be one referee and someone who specializes in empirical work to be the other. Or she might ask a more senior scholar to write one report and a younger scholar to write a second. (Younger referees frequently are the

---

6. But not my papers. Every time I have submitted a paper to *QJE*, the editor has sent it to referees and then rejected it.

ones who are more likely to go through the entire paper more and to give the author detailed suggestions.)

Editors view referees as valuable resources, especially the ones they trust the most. For this reason, they tend to use their favorite referees only on papers they think have a real shot at getting accepted. What this means, unfortunately, is that the papers of more senior and better-known researchers are much more likely to get the referees more trusted by editors. These trusted referees tend to be senior scholars who have better perspectives on research. They are less likely than younger scholars to reject papers for minor methodological issues and more likely to focus on what is learned from a paper than on what is wrong with it.

Referee Reports

After an editor decides on which referees to use for a submission, she sends them an email request to referee the paper. The email will contain a copy of the paper, a deadline by which the editor would like to receive the paper, and details about any (small) payment that will go to the referee if he completes the report on time. Traditionally, papers were "double-blind" refereed, meaning that neither the referee nor the author knew the identity of the other. Today, however, blind refereeing has become something of a joke because referees can almost always find out the author's name by Googling the paper's title. Some journals have nonetheless kept up the facade of double-blind refereeing, while others have gone to a single-blind system in which referees are told the author's name, but the author does not know who the referees are.

Research-active scholars generally are asked to referee far more often than they would like. They agree to write referee reports as a professional obligation and as a favor to the editor, not because they want to do the work. If a scholar wishes to publish her own work in a particular journal, she is generally expected to referee for that journal when asked, unless there are mitigating circumstances. But writing referee reports is painful, takes a lot of time, and is trivially compensated. For most academics, refereeing papers ranks with grading exams and attending faculty meetings as an aspect of their job they try hardest to avoid.

That being said, when reviewers reluctantly agree to referee a paper, most try to do a good job.[7] Reviewers want to help the editor make better editorial decisions and to help the author improve her paper. So they read the paper carefully and try to provide useful suggestions to the author. But reviewers get grumpy when they are writing their third or fourth report in a busy month. They really don't like reviewing a paper that is hard to read and to understand, that has obvious mistakes or omissions of arguments, or that includes too much extraneous material. Authors' efforts to make their papers more readable do affect referees' reactions to them and can substantially increase the likelihood that their paper will be accepted for publication.

A referee provides the editor with advice about how she should handle the paper. Could the paper make a sufficiently large contribution to the literature to warrant publication in the journal? What do the authors need to do to the paper to make it publishable? Are there any ways to improve their analysis that the editor should encourage the authors to pursue? The answers to these questions, especially the first one, can vary from journal to journal. Very often, a paper whose contribution is not large enough for the *American Economic Review* would make a nice addition to a more specialized journal.

Referees convey their advice fairly bluntly in a private note to the editor, and they usually repeat this advice in the report itself for the authors to see. Sometimes referees sugarcoat the report a little if it is negative. For example, if a referee tells the editor, "This paper is really awful," he might say in the report that the authors see: "In my opinion, the incremental contribution is too small to warrant publication in this journal." Not all referees are so nice, however, and too often write negative reports that are unnecessarily hurtful.

In addition to the note to the editor, the referee writes a formal report that is forwarded to the authors. A referee report usually starts by providing a summary of the paper. It then gives an overall evaluation and

7. A very good paper about the refereeing process and how a scholar should go about writing a report is: J. B. Berk, C. R. Harvey, and D. Hirshleifer, "How to Write an Effective Referee Report and Improve the Scientific Review Process," *Journal of Economic Perspectives* 31 (1, 2017): 231–44.

recommendation regarding the paper's publication. Referee reports also contain suggestions to help the authors improve their paper. The quality and quantity of referees' suggestions vary tremendously. Sometimes referees provide five or six single-spaced pages of detailed comments that can be extremely valuable to authors when they revise their paper. Other referees write only a paragraph or two and focus their comments on the big picture, ignoring the details.

When they feel that they are going to recommend acceptance of a paper eventually, most referees want to work with the author to make the paper as strong as possible prior to publication. When they are going to reject a paper, they still want to help the authors improve it, but are unlikely to devote as much time to doing so. Therefore, when recommending that authors be invited to resubmit a revised version, referees usually try to be extremely thorough and make whatever suggestions they think will improve the paper. When recommending rejection, they tend to write shorter reports that explain why the paper is not suitable for the particular journal and spend little time making helpful suggestions.

When the Editor Gets the Paper Back from the Referees

Although it sometimes takes longer than the editor (and the authors) would like, the referees eventually send their reports to the editor.[8] At this point, the editor must decide how to handle the paper: she can reject the paper, ask for a revision, or, in rare circumstances, accept the paper as is. Most of the time the decision is fairly easy. At good journals, the majority of submitted papers are clear rejections. Editors can usually tell that a submission is a clear rejection after a quick read of the paper or after receiving the referee reports. The analysis in these rejected

---

8. When things go well, it should take referees only a month or two to return their reports. However, sometimes referees can be very slow, and papers will sit on their desk for six months or even a year. Occasionally, an editor has to give up on a particularly delinquent referee and will either make a decision on the basis of the reports received or solicit another report.

papers is not usually wrong, in that the authors made errors in their proofs or used inappropriate statistical techniques. The reason why most submitted papers are rejected is that they do not make a sufficient incremental contribution to warrant publication in the journal considering them. Journals compete with one another to publish the papers that will have the greatest impact, so editors try to publish papers that will burnish their journal's reputation. Most papers are rejected because editors and referees judge them to be ordinary and not likely to have an impact that would enhance the journal's reputation.

When an editor rejects a paper, she normally writes a short note to the authors and attaches copies of the referee reports. Some editors use a form letter for all the papers they reject. When I was an editor, I preferred to personalize my rejection letters. Having been rejected many times myself, I felt that I should explain in a few sentences exactly why the paper's contribution was insufficient to justify publication. Authors were still upset when they received my rejection letter, but I hope most of them felt that they had been treated fairly and received useful feedback from the submission process.

With papers that are close calls as well as papers that the journal is likely to publish, the editor's job becomes harder. She normally will carefully read the paper she is thinking seriously about publishing, as well as the referee reports. The referee reports provide guidance, but the authority to make the final decision on a paper belongs to the editor. A good editor will sometimes overrule referees, in both directions. Sometimes she will reject a paper that the referees like, and sometimes she will invite a resubmission on a paper the referees recommend rejecting.

Editors take a variety of approaches to the resubmission process. Some are not willing to invite resubmission unless they are fairly certain the paper will eventually be accepted for publication. Others are lenient on the first round and reject a lot of papers after they are resubmitted the second or third time.[9] Editors who like to give authors a second

9. This experience can be extremely upsetting for authors, especially those just starting out in the profession. A former student had one of the top economics journals reject his job market paper on the *fourth* resubmission. He was so upset that he left academia and went on to have a successful career in the money management industry.

chance tell a fair number of them that their paper is a "reject and resubmit": the paper is rejected, but unlike with most rejections, the authors have the right to revise the paper substantially and resubmit it as a new paper.

When requesting a revision, the editor explains to the authors exactly why the current version is not acceptable and the direction in which the editor would like the authors to take the paper. Often these instructions are very detailed. For example, the editor could tell an author that she should forget about the first set of tests presented in tables 3 through 5 and expand the second set of tests discussed later in the paper. Or she could tell the authors to increase their sample size dramatically, change the econometrics completely, come up with a valid instrument, or make any number of different changes. Revision requests vary dramatically in the amount of additional work they suggest—some suggested revisions are simple and can be completed in a few days, while others essentially call for writing a new paper and can take over a year to complete.

When I was an editor, I wanted to avoid rejections at later rounds, so I was very selective when deciding on the papers that I would ask authors to revise for potential publication. I very rarely rejected a paper after the first round, so virtually all of the papers for which I requested revisions were ultimately published. That being said, each time I wrote a letter requesting a revision, I did not know if the paper would ultimately be accepted. Hence, I was always firm and stated clearly what the authors had to do before the paper could be accepted. I further emphasized that I had the right to reject the paper in the future. However, the authors I dealt with almost always turned out to be extremely diligent, and they usually succeeded in doing what I asked them to do.

After the Author Receives the Editor's Letter and Referee Reports

Today authors hear news from journals through emails with subject lines like "Decision on Your Submission." When an author sees that subject line, her heart starts beating faster and she braces herself, knowing that most of the time the news conveyed in the email will be upsetting. The vast majority of submissions to good journals are rejected. No matter how long a scholar has been in the profession, getting rejected is still not easy. Indeed, as a former classmate of mine once told me: "The day you cease caring about a rejection is the day you should hang it up."[10] Even when the news is good and the response is a request to "revise and resubmit" the paper, reading the reports can be painful. The reports tend to focus on what the referees do not like about the paper and therefore can be unpleasant to read. Few scholars enjoy reading criticism of their work, even when the criticism is intended to be constructive.

The thing to remember when reading an email from a journal editor is that it (almost) always seems worse than it actually is. If the paper is rejected, there will probably be something useful in the reports, and the author can eventually submit an improved paper to another journal. If the editor gives the author the option to resubmit her paper, it is good news even if the letter includes a lot of negative comments about the paper's analysis. The author gets advice on what she can do to her paper to move it toward publication, and taking the paper in that direction will probably improve the paper irrespective of the publication process. The trick to learn is how to take negative feedback in a positive manner and use it to improve the work. Criticism is an integral part of academic life, and the ability to engage with unpleasant feedback and use it in a positive manner is a skill that is necessary for academic success.

Rejection

Top journals in most fields now reject over 90 percent of submissions. When authors receive a rejection, it can be very painful. They put their heart and soul into the paper, and most of the time they truly believe that the paper deserves to be published. When their paper is rejected by editors and referees, often in what can appear to the authors to be a cavalier manner, it can be hard to take. Yet the ability to take bad news in a productive manner is a necessary skill for a successful academic.

Why do so many papers get rejected? The simple answer is that a journal receives many more submissions than it can publish. But that

10. Perhaps this classmate took his own advice to heart—he became a dean last year!

answer begs the question of why so many papers are submitted to journals at which they will be rejected. Some rejected papers had a real shot at getting accepted, but the majority are fairly obvious calls to the editors; the *Quarterly Journal of Economics* desk-rejects over half their submissions within a few hours of receipt because it is obvious to the editors that these papers are not appropriate for their journal. Other journals are not as aggressive about desk rejections, but their editors still know before they send papers to referees which ones have a realistic shot at getting accepted and which do not.

One reason why so many clearly unacceptable papers are submitted has to do with the incentive structures that authors face. There is a very large payoff to having a paper appear in a top journal, while the cost of trying is low. Submission fees are usually trivial and often paid by grants or research budgets, and if an author is lucky, only a few months are lost. So why not try? Perhaps the paper will get a sympathetic referee or editor. This logic compels research-active faculty to submit a paper to at least one or two top-tier journals before trying a more specialized journal. The puzzle to me is why, when an author submits to a top-tier journal knowing her paper is not likely to be accepted, she is so often upset when the paper is rejected.

A number of papers are rejected because the author had an inflated view of her own work, so submitted it to a journal for which others thought it was clearly inappropriate. The same scholar who is a trusted resource for colleagues and editors can think her own work is far more important than it actually is. Persistence and a high level of confidence are two qualities that help people become successful scholars, but the tendency to overvalue their own work can lead scholars to submit to higher-ranked journals than is warranted by their papers' contributions.

What to Do upon Receiving a Rejection

It can be extremely disturbing to hear that others do not like the paper you have been working on for years. When authors receive a rejection, they often first react by being upset with the review process and complaining about it to anyone who will listen. Many will contact the editor and ask for a better explanation for the rejection than is in his letter.

From the author's perspective, the editor has made a mistake. It is natural for the author to think that the editor might realize his mistake and change his mind. However, no matter how much she wants to, an author should not contact the editor (except through the formal appeal process I discuss later). Complaining will not change the editorial decision, but the editor might lower her opinion of the author.

After a rejection, usually the best thing for an author to do is to spend a few weeks dissecting the rejection by herself and with her coauthors, close friends, and advisers. A rejection is one of those times when close friends can be extremely valuable. Sometimes it is useful for an author to take out her frustrations by screaming at her close friends (in private), then letting the friends scream at her in turn when their papers get rejected. But in public, and especially when communicating with senior colleagues and editors, she should do her best to remain calm, cool, and collected. She should try to come across as a professional. Her colleagues will know from their own experiences how difficult it is to be rejected, so if she reacts professionally, they will think more highly of her.

Although referees do make mistakes, typically there is some validity to their points. Perhaps one section of the paper isn't as clearly written as the author thought, or a result is less surprising than the paper makes it out to be in light of other work, or some omitted variables could also explain the paper's findings. Give the referees a fair hearing—even if you think they didn't do the same for you when they read your paper. Keep in mind too that in matters of opinion (the paper is too long, the introduction is hard to follow, and so on), it is possible that other readers will share the referees' opinions. In short, if a referee has done a diligent job, there is likely to be something in the report that can be usefully incorporated into the paper.

Of course, unlike when a paper has received an invitation to "revise and resubmit," the author is not required to address each point. If she thinks the referees' points are stupid, she can ignore them. But she will be ignoring them at her own risk. There is some chance that the next journal to which she submits the paper will ask the same referee to review it.[11] The referee will not be happy if, having spent a lot of time

11. Some referees have a personal "no double jeopardy rule"—they won't review a paper a second time from another journal. However, if a referee tells the editor that is the reason why

writing a report to help the author, he discovers that she appears to have ignored his suggestions.

More likely, however, the negative report has accurately identified something that is wrong with the paper, either with the formal analysis or with the author's explanation and interpretation of the results. Even if the referee misinterpreted something, the author should revise the paper with the goal of making sure that the next referee does not react in a similar fashion. Otherwise, the new referee is likely to reject the paper for the same reason the first one did.

One way to view negative referee reports is to see them as the referee's reaction to the choices an author made in constructing her paper. Which specifications did she report and which did she leave out? Which order did she put them in? How did she interpret the results? The list of decisions an author must make is endless. Referee reports can help authors make better decisions about how to write their papers. Authors sometimes have opinions about their own work that differ from others' on the issues that are most important, the parts of the paper that are most interesting, or the appropriate interpretation of the results. A negative referee report is a chance to rethink these opinions and to use others' opinions to guide the structure of the paper. Hopefully the result of this reassessment is to make the paper more interesting to future readers.

Revise and Resubmit

When an editor likes a paper, she rarely accepts it outright. The referees almost always have some suggestions, and in their own readings editors have often thought of ways to improve the paper. Hence, the editor normally doesn't wish to publish the paper exactly as it was submitted but

---

he won't do a review, the editor often asks to see the report submitted to the other journal. In this situation, I once made the mistake of sending the earlier report to the editor, who forwarded it to the authors and rejected the paper on the basis of my report. It turned out that one of the authors was the chair of a department in which I had a job seminar shortly after he received this report on his paper. When I was visiting his department, he improperly confronted me and told me that he thought I was the referee who rejected him twice. I lied and said I wasn't, but I don't think he believed me. I didn't get offered the job.

believes that, with significant work, a revised version will be acceptable for publication. In this case, the editor returns the paper to the authors and invites them to resubmit the paper after they revise it.

These outcomes are typically referred to as "revise and resubmits" or "R&Rs." With an R&R, editors are often very explicit about how they want the paper to be modified. The editor says exactly how she thinks the authors should restructure the paper, what referees' points she thinks are most important, and what she thinks are the appropriate inferences for the authors to draw from their analysis. With this type of editorial letter, the editor is effectively saying that if the author does what she asks, then the paper is very likely to be accepted for publication.

Alternatively, the editor may be more vague in the R&R, saying something like: "Your paper would be quite nice if you can solve this problem (these problems) with the paper. I have no idea if what I am asking is possible, but I would be willing to consider a resubmission if you can." Implicit in this open-ended response is that the authors shouldn't bother resubmitting unless they can solve the problems the editor raised in her letter. With this type of letter, the issue identified by the editor is often a fundamental one that the authors may not be able to address. For example, the editor could ask the author to solve a model via a closed-form solution rather than through a simulation, or to come up with a better instrument for their dependent variable.

The goal in the editor's letter is to give the authors a direction to push the paper so that the revision will be publishable. I personally think of an editor's R&R letter as essentially a contract: if the author does what has been asked, the editor will eventually accept the paper for publication. That being said, not every editor views revision requests as contracts. Editors can ask for substantial revisions and still reject the paper after the author faithfully does what they asked. In fairness to those editors, they often state explicitly that they do not view the R&R as a contract and make clear that what they are asking for is necessary but not sufficient for the paper to be publishable. Also in fairness to those editors, as with any contract, authors and editors can disagree over whether the terms were met and the authors actually performed what was asked of them.

R&Rs vary a lot in terms of the amount of work they ask the authors to do. Sometimes their suggestions are quite easy to implement and can be completed in a few days. For example, the editor might ask the author to expand her discussion of the editor's favorite alternative interpretation of her results, to add a few extra tests, or to cut out a section that seems superfluous to the editor. At the other extreme, the editor could ask for essentially a new paper, with a totally different focus and methods. As mentioned earlier, these decisions are sometimes referred to as "reject and resubmits." In a reject and resubmit, the editor is telling the authors that she likes something about the paper—maybe the data, the question they asked, or the overall methodological approach. However, the current version is so far from being acceptable that the editor does not wish to make any implicit promises and stresses that the revised paper would have to be sufficiently different from the original to be considered a new paper. Between these two extremes is a typical R&R, which asks the authors to rethink some parts of their existing analysis and perform some new work.

When an author receives an R&R, she should be happy—it means she has a shot at getting a revision of her paper published in the journal considering it. But it is only a shot. Papers often do get rejected in the second, third, or even fourth round. It is important to respond to every point that the referees and editors make in their reports and letters. Even more important is that the author understand what is bothering the referees and address the underlying cause of their concerns.

Appeals

Sometimes referees do make serious mistakes. Referees are human like the rest of us: they sometimes miss key assumptions or explanations, they can get the impression that the authors were doing X when they actually were doing Y, and occasionally they do not devote enough time to understanding the paper. Editors realize that the review process is imperfect and want to be fair to authors.

For this reason, most journals have set up an appeals process. This process differs from journal to journal, but typically the author writes a letter explaining why the decision was incorrect and the editor sends the paper to an associate editor or other senior person in the profession to review the decision. Decisions do, on occasion, get overturned on appeal. At *Review of Financial Studies*, we found that the acceptance rate for appeals was surprisingly similar to the acceptance rate for initial submissions, probably because authors appealed only rejections that were close calls.

That being said, I recommend appealing decisions only when there is a clear and substantive mistake in the referee's analysis. Some authors regularly appeal rejections. Editors know who these people are and find their constant appeals to be annoying. But editors do want authors to appeal decisions when they reject a paper because of an error by the referees. Editors put a lot of time and effort into their work for the journals and want very much to make the correct calls in their publication decisions.

As an author, I have appealed only one rejection in my career. My coauthors and I had what we thought was an airtight identification strategy, but the referee misunderstood what we did, argued in the report that the identification we used was problematic, and rejected the paper. I first ranted to my old friends for a few days. (I get really upset after rejections—I don't know anyone who takes them with total equanimity.) I then wrote a letter that explained, as clearly as I could, exactly what we did and why the identification strategy in the paper was valid. I let my coauthors tone down the letter because it was too strongly worded (I was pretty angry). We then sent the letter to the journal, and the editor immediately forwarded it to the referee. To his or her credit, the referee immediately realized the mistake and understood why the identification strategy in the paper was correct. Not too long after we made the initial appeal, we converged to a version that the referee thought was acceptable, and the paper was eventually published in that journal.

Starting a Revision—The "Response Document"

Where should authors begin when they receive a revise and resubmit? How should they go about revising their paper? Where to begin? A few years ago, when an editor asked us to revise and resubmit one of our coauthored papers, Isil Erel convinced me to organize the revision around the cover letter to be included with the revised document, which I always refer to as the "response document." I liked the approach so much that I now use it for all my papers.

The response document for a resubmission contains a detailed summary of the changes the authors have made since the original submission. It can also convey other information, such as a polite explanation of why a certain approach was used and why the referee's comments are or are not relevant. It can even contain results that the authors do not want to include in the paper itself. A good response document makes editors' and referees' jobs much easier and can sometimes persuade them that they don't need to spend a lot of time on the revised paper because the author has done what they asked. The response document enables the editors and referees to skip over the parts of the paper that presented no issues for them in the previous round. They can focus their attention on the author's response to what they asked—which is easily available to them in the response document.

Like some authors, I used to wait until the revision was complete before writing the response document, but Isil persuaded me that it makes more sense to start this document right after receiving the editor's letter. The response document provides a way to structure the revision process in a very productive way.

Here is what I do: I first copy the editor's letter and the referee reports into a file (omitting trivial bits, like "Dear Mike") and italicize the text of these documents. I then go through the report in detail with my coauthors. When we agree on how we will address each point, we make a note on the response document of what we will do (often in a bright color). When we make the changes to the paper, we delete the colored note and replace it with a short description of what we changed, written in language appropriate to use with editors and referees. When all the colored text is gone from the response document, we have basically completed the revision. After I add a short introduction to the response document explaining exactly how it is structured, the response is finished.

There are several advantages of this approach to revising a paper. First and perhaps most important, it gets all coauthors on the same page, as everyone sees clearly what the team has agreed to do. Second, it ensures that every point the referee made is addressed; it is easy to forget some of the points while juggling several long reports and an editor's letter, all of which contain issues the authors must address in the revision. And finally, by composing the response document during the revision process and not afterward, the document is complete as soon as the paper is done, so we can resubmit immediately.

The Substance of the Revision

In a typical R&R, a paper will receive one or two referee reports, each of which can be five or six single-spaced pages full of suggestions. Sometimes the ideas overlap, but referees do disagree with one another from time to time; if they disagree, satisfying both of them can get a bit challenging. A good editor will try to give the author guidance by highlighting the referees' points that he thinks must be followed, which suggestions he views as optional, and which he thinks the author should disregard. In addition, the editor could have some of her own suggestions on how to revise the paper, and her letter may include some suggestions from an associate editor as well. The author typically will find most of the suggestions useful, but some will probably be pointless and others completely wrong.

How does an author think about responding to an R&R? Before submitting the paper, she probably struggled to cut out as much extraneous material from the paper as possible. Does she really want to add a bunch of new material that will satisfy the referees but make her paper longer and cause most readers' eyes to glaze over? At the same time, appearing nonresponsive to referees and editors, who spent a lot of time making suggestions and have the right to reject the paper, is nearly always a fatal strategy. Responding carefully to every point the referees made while keeping the paper relatively short and readable can seem like an impossible task.

There are a few principles to adhere to in revising a paper for a journal. First, the author must address *every* point made in the referee report. Not addressing a point that referees think is important can upset them enough to recommend rejection on a paper they otherwise like.

Second, an author should strive to use the revision as a chance to improve the paper, and not only to jump through hoops to satisfy the referees. But if the author adds a lot of material to the paper in response to every point the referee made, there is a decent chance that the referee will decide that the new version of the paper is too long and boring, and will not recommend publication for that reason. Third, and perhaps most important, the author should always remember that her name is on the paper for all eternity. After the paper is published, the referees will always remain anonymous and soon will probably forget the details of their reviews (or the fact that they even reviewed her paper). The author, not the referees, will be the one who gets credit or blame for anything in the published version, regardless of whether or not it's something that appears there because of the referees' suggestion.

How do you go about this seemingly impossible task of adding material without making the paper longer, addressing pointless comments without implying to a reader that you think specious arguments are correct, and satisfying multiple referees who want you to push the paper in different directions? One thing to remember as you revise is that although you must address every comment in the referee reports and editor's letter, you have a lot of freedom about where and how to do so.

When I revise papers to address referees' concerns, my rule is to only put things in the paper that my coauthors and I truly believe will improve it. If a referee makes suggestions that improve our paper, we will, of course, incorporate them. Especially important to include in the paper are replies to concerns that have been raised by a number of readers and brought up in seminars. If we do include additional robustness checks at this point, we try to follow the strategy outlined in chapter 7: putting them in a separate subsection that can be easily skipped by readers who don't share the referee's concern. If a referee suggests that we do something that addresses a concern that seems minor, we might put our reply in an appendix (possibly an online one). We would usually mention in the text or a footnote that the test is available in the appendix, perhaps together with a short description of the results.

To respond to suggestions that seem to us to be specific to one referee and are unlikely to matter to most readers, my coauthors and I often address it directly in the response document and make no changes in the paper. My response documents frequently contain a number of tables intended to alleviate referees' concerns. Because space in the actual paper is precious, I often include tests requested by the referee that might not be of interest to a general reader in the response document. Hopefully, when the referee sees that the additional control he sought is not significantly different from zero, he will be persuaded that these new tests don't warrant space in the paper.

If my coauthors and I put an additional test in the appendix or response document, we always tell the editor and referees that we would be happy to move it to the document itself if they would like. Editors and referees appreciate when authors make sensible choices over where to put additional analyses and offer to move them at the editor's discretion. In practice, though, editors rarely take authors up on this type of offer. Over my career, I have offered to move additional tests requested by the referee to the main text many times when I submitted a revised paper. Not once has an editor or referee taken me up on the offer and asked that I move something from the response document or an appendix to the body of the paper.

In a typical R&R, the referees and editor basically like what the authors are doing—the question, data, methods, and so on—but have a problem with one aspect of the authors' approach. It could relate to the author's statistics, modeling, interpretation, or pretty much anything. The referees or editor will usually suggest a specific response to this issue—perhaps a statistical test or a different way of modeling the problem. Sometimes an author, who has usually thought about the issues for much longer than the referees and editors, has a reason not to adopt the suggested remedy. If so, it is perfectly fine for her to explain in the response document why she doesn't want to do what the referee suggested. But if she doesn't do what is suggested by the editor and referees, she should clearly explain why. In addition, she should discuss, politely and deferentially, why the concern of the referees or editor isn't really an issue, or how it was addressed by an alternative test she performed. The key is to understand exactly what is bothering the referees and address it head on, so that the referees know the author is taking their concern seriously.

Most of the time, if authors are thoughtful in their use of appendices and response documents, it is possible to address the concerns of referees and editor in ways that do improve the paper. However, sometimes referees are insistent. One time a referee decided that my coauthors and I had to include a particular calculation that I thought made absolutely no sense. My coauthors and I went back and forth with the journal a few times and tried to explain why we didn't want to include a nonsensical calculation in our paper. Eventually, it became clear to me that the referee was not going to change his mind, the editor was not going to overrule him, and the paper was not going to get published unless we included it. So I held my nose a bit and put the calculation in the paper. (My coauthors didn't care by this point and just wanted the paper published.) But I made sure to add a footnote "thanking" the referee for suggesting the calculation; I wanted readers to understand that it wasn't our decision to include the nonsensical calculation in the paper.

After Resubmitting to the Journal

Once the paper is resubmitted to the journal, the process repeats itself. Unless the revisions are trivial, the editor will send the paper back to the referees, who write new reports. Usually the same referees are used, but occasionally there is a new referee; perhaps one of the original ones could not do a second report, or the editor wants an additional opinion. As in the first round, the editor considers these reports upon receiving them, then sends the authors a second decision letter. Just as they did the first time, the authors edit the paper in response to the second set of comments, write a new response document, and eventually submit the revision to the journal.

This process is repeated until the paper is either accepted or rejected. At each round, the authors do not have to resubmit the paper to the same journal, but it is usually advisable to do so. Occasionally authors will decide that the revised paper is so much better than the original that they can try to submit it to a higher-ranked journal rather than resubmit to the original one. The idea is that they can always resubmit to the original journal if they get rejected by the higher-ranking one. Although there is nothing unethical in this strategy, I am reluctant to recommend it. The author could draw the same referees recruited by the editor of the original journal, who will not be happy at the authors' disregard for the work they did in their earlier reports. Additionally, taking the revised paper to a higher-ranking journal risks burning bridges with the original journal's editor, who will undoubtedly realize that another journal realized the benefits of his efforts and those of his referees to improve the paper. For these reasons, I have always resubmitted my papers to the same journal so long as it is an option; I have never tried submitting to a second journal in the middle of this process.

Ideally, the authors and referees converge to a version that is acceptable to both and eventually the editor can accept the paper. Sometimes, however, things do not go so well and papers are rejected at later rounds. Revising a paper and then getting rejected can be quite upsetting to authors. One of my closest friends had his job market paper rejected from a top economics journal in the second round. He had spent several years waiting for the journal to respond to both submissions and then revising the paper in response to the original reports. The reason the journal ultimately gave him for the rejection was that the paper was not interesting enough for the journal. How could it possibly have been interesting enough for them to ask him to spend so much time revising it if it wasn't interesting enough to publish after he did all the work? My friend has had an extremely successful career, so that setback wasn't the end of him, but the experience was needlessly painful for him and should have been handled better by the editor.

Once the Paper Is Accepted

Once a journal accepts a paper, the uncertainty is resolved and the stress reduced. But there is still work to be done. Most journals send their papers to copy editors, who send the authors a marked-up copy of the paper. These copy editors are usually excellent writers but not specialists in the subject of the paper. In their zeal to improve the paper's prose, copy editors sometimes accidentally change the meaning of something they edit. Consequently, it is important to go through the copy editor's comments carefully and not just accept all of the suggested changes without thinking about each one.

The rule for copy editors is that the formatting changes they make are required but all other changes are optional. Each journal has its own style: references must be done in a specific way, sections enumerated in a particular way, and so forth. Authors must comply with copy editors' edits that impose these styles, and they usually have no reason not to do so. Changes to the writing that are designed to improve the paper's prose are optional. However, unless you are an experienced writer, it is usually a good idea to accept whatever changes are suggested unless they change the meaning of a sentence.

After copyediting, in the last stage before publication, authors are sent page proofs. Journals usually will wait six months to a year to send page proofs to the author, and then they want a response in forty-eight hours. This deadline can be ignored; journals will always publish the paper if it has been accepted by the editor. The worst thing that can happen to an author at this stage is the paper being rescheduled to appear in a later issue of the journal.

In the olden days before word processors, journals had to manually typeset papers in order to publish them. So authors had to go through every word and number in the proofs for their paper to ensure that there were no typos or other errors. But any errors in words or numbers found today are usually the authors' fault and were there prior to the final submission. They can still be corrected at this stage, but publishers get upset if authors try to make too many changes at the page-proof stage.

One important thing to be careful about when going through page proofs is to check the formatting of the tables. For some reason, journals seem to want to publish papers in which the numbers in a column are not underneath the column headings. Or the entries in the table may be right-justified so that all of the numbers are in the rightmost part of the cell and look very strange to a reader. Or the headers are hard to read for one reason or another—either they are in too small a font or the line that is supposed to be beneath them actually goes through them. I have had these problems and been obliged to send proofs back to the journals multiple times before they were formatted in an acceptable fashion.

The rule here is to be tough and not approve a paper until it is perfect. An author should never approve a page proof until it is 100 percent correct. There is no need to compromise. The paper will have the author's name on it forever, and the person laying out the tables for the journal might be working for a different company a year after the paper is published. There is clearly a misalignment of incentives; it is in the author's interest—and the journal's too for that matter—to be persistent and to make sure everything about the published paper is right.

PART IV

Being a Successful
Academic

12

How to Be a Productive Doctoral Student

WHEN I ENTERED graduate school, my father, who had a PhD in organic chemistry, explained to me the most important difference between doctoral programs and other graduate programs. He told me that my friends who went to medical school, law school, or business school (for a nondoctoral degree) would work at least as hard as I would. They would stress out over their exams and have sleepless nights worrying about them, just as I would. However, virtually all of my friends who entered these programs would graduate. And they would know with sufficient certainty exactly when they would graduate that their parents could reserve hotel rooms for the graduation ceremony on the day they first entered the program.

In doctoral programs, students' progress is much more uncertain. Many students end up leaving doctoral programs, both voluntarily, if they change their mind about their chosen career, and involuntarily, if they do not pass their exams or cannot write acceptable dissertations.[1] And for the students who do graduate, the time it takes to complete the degree can vary tremendously. Both the average time to completion and its variation across students have increased in recent years. When my

---

1. One study of economics departments' doctoral programs finds an attrition rate of 26.5 percent in the first two years of the program. See W. A. Stock, T. A. Finegan, and J. J. Siegfried, "Attrition in Economics PhD Programs," *American Economic Review* 96(2, 2006): 458–66.

father received his PhD in the 1950s and I received mine in the 1980s, most students finished their degree in four years. Now, in economics and related fields, five years is the norm, and many students stay six or seven years. In short, when a student enters a PhD program, there is much uncertainty about whether she will eventually receive her PhD, and if she does receive it, how long the process will take.

Why are PhD programs so different from other programs? What makes students' progress in these programs so uncertain? Is there anything that faculty and students could do to improve the process?

I think the answers to these questions lie in the expectations of doctoral students, which are different from those of students in other graduate programs. Most graduate programs, such as law school or business school, are essentially extensions of undergraduate education. Students take a series of classes, some of which can be difficult, but all they need to do to graduate from these programs is to pass their classes. Students who are accepted to good programs are usually excellent students, so the vast majority of them do pass their classes. In some programs, such as medical schools or dental schools, there are clinical aspects to the education that can be extremely time-consuming and difficult. But it is rare for a student to flunk out of medical school, for instance, because of her performance in rotations. In the end, most students graduate from these programs on time.

In contrast, in a PhD program the goal is to teach students how to do research. The main graduation requirement is a dissertation, which is an original piece of research that meaningfully moves the frontier of our knowledge. The ability to write a good dissertation requires skills that are not easy to identify. Sometimes the student who could always solve any problem handed to her on an exam and has never received anything but A's is unable to come up with a research idea. Another student, a marginal admit to the doctoral program who barely passed the qualifying exams, may turn out to be the best researcher. The most important attribute of successful doctoral students is a knack for selecting interesting problems and solving them in creative ways. Since success at academic scholarship requires a different set of skills than success at taking classes, it is difficult for faculty or even a student herself to know whether she will be a natural fit for academic research.

It is a good idea for prospective students to spend some time learning exactly what they are getting themselves into when they begin a PhD program. Academic research in the economics-based disciplines tends to be much more abstract than many outside academia suspect. Entering students often think that in a PhD program they will do research about how to predict GDP, or how to become better at picking stocks. Sometimes PhD students are surprised to discover that empirical academic research tends to analyze systematic data sets rather than carry out case studies, and that theoretical research uses mathematical models to convey ideas rather than verbal arguments, emphasizing generality and abstraction more than specific institutional details.

One way that a prospective PhD student can learn whether academic research is right for her is to get involved in it before she starts graduate school. I would encourage anyone thinking about getting a PhD to work with their undergraduate or master's faculty on their research. If they write a thesis as an undergraduate or master's student, they should try to publish it. Another option is to do what is becoming known as a "predoc"—a job doing research prior to entering graduate school. An increasing number of such positions have become available. Some schools hire recent college graduates as research assistants for their faculty, and many of them go on to get a PhD. In addition, there are jobs available at government agencies and other organizations that do economic research. Such positions help prospective students learn what is involved with academic research and also make them more attractive to doctoral programs.

Approaching Life as a PhD Student

One problem for many students in a doctoral program is not approaching their time as a PhD student correctly. PhD students almost always have been excellent students throughout their entire lives; otherwise, they would have had neither the inclination to enter a PhD program nor the grades to get in. Entering students often think the PhD program is a continuation of their earlier studies, albeit at a higher level. In a certain sense, this view is correct—PhD programs do require a number of classes that can be quite difficult.

However, in an important way, PhD programs are fundamentally different from other academic programs. The underlying goal of any PhD program is to help the student become a serious scholar in her area of inquiry. The way a student establishes herself is by writing a dissertation that makes a substantive contribution to the academic literature. A good dissertation will extend the literature sufficiently that other scholars working in her area will want to find out what she did in the paper. Ideally, the dissertation will provide a launching pad for a career of meaningful scholarship.

Given that the objective in pursuing a PhD—to establish oneself as a researcher—is different from the objectives of other programs, a student should approach it differently. When a student enters a doctoral program, she should keep the ultimate goal of producing research in mind from day one. She should work to develop skills, to acquire a knowledge of the literature, and to come up with ideas that can lead to a successful research program.

With these goals in mind, I have a set of rules for doctoral students to follow throughout their years in the program. These rules cover both what students should try to do and what they should avoid. I will first go through the "don'ts" for doctoral students—what they should avoid during their time in the program.

The "Don'ts" of Being a PhD Student

1) Don't be too concerned with your grades. When you apply for a job, nobody will ever ask for them.
2) Don't be competitive with your fellow students. Your ultimate placement depends on the quality of your work on a national scale, not on your ranking relative to other students in your program. If you work well with your fellow students, they will be your future colleagues, coauthors, and lifelong friends.

3) Don't be too intimidated to ask questions of faculty. We are being paid to answer your questions, so ask them!

4) Don't go into hiding. Always keep a high profile in your department, even if things aren't going particularly well.

5) Don't restrict yourself to one area, or to the specialties of your adviser. Most faculty have knowledge and expertise broad enough to supervise the work you want to write, not just what they want to write.

6) Don't ever think that the first draft of a paper will be good enough. It won't. Most faculty papers go through multiple revisions before they are ready to be submitted to a journal; yours will probably go through five to ten major revisions before you are ready to send it out on the job market.

7) Don't think of research as a game. You are trying to teach the profession something meaningful, not just complete the PhD program. The same goes for the publication process: the best papers are written to pass along to others something important, not just to get published.

8) Don't write papers that are interesting only to academics. If you're in an economics program, try to explain the actual economy. It's more fun and interesting that way.

9) Don't write papers for the purpose of illustrating a technique. Find an interesting question and use the techniques appropriate for the question.

10) Don't write papers that are relevant today but are unlikely to be of interest in the future.

"DON'TS" 1–2: DON'T WORRY ABOUT GRADES AND DON'T COMPETE WITH FELLOW STUDENTS

Before a student enters a PhD program, her grades are almost a sufficient measure of her academic success. They determine her GPA, strongly influence the academic honors she earns, and are a major factor in her job placements and admissions to subsequent programs. The emphasis on grades can lead to a zero-sum-game mentality, however, as well as competitiveness between students. After all, the same number of students are chosen for Phi Beta Kappa, law review, and other prestigious positions each year. If a student helps her friend succeed, fewer honors will be available for her.

When the student enters a PhD program, she naturally assumes that the same rules apply, but they don't. Of course, it is always better to get an A than a B, and PhD program directors normally do an annual review of the students to ensure that each of them has done reasonably well in their courses. However, beyond these reviews, grades in PhD programs really don't matter very much. Unlike graduates of most other programs, academic job applicants do not provide their grades to potential employers. When a school is thinking of hiring a newly minted PhD from another school for its faculty, it is not just that the hiring committee doesn't care what grade she got in econometrics—they don't even know what that grade is, as it is not requested in the application materials. Grades are considered irrelevant by hiring committees at universities, and also by private-sector firms and government agencies considering hiring newly minted PhDs.

Since grades don't really matter, PhD students should not obsess about them. Instead, PhD students should approach every course as a researcher rather than as a student. Students should always be thinking about what they will learn in the course that can be applied to a research project, such as a research area or problem to be addressed, or a technical skill that will help them with a problem they have been working on, or an idea or way of thinking to explore further and possibly apply to other settings. Classes should be thought of as a means to helping students do better research rather than as an end in themselves.

Equally important as the way a PhD student approaches her classes is the way she approaches her classmates. Growing up in a zero-sum environment in which a classmate's achievement could take away from their own success can lead students to think of each other as competitors. This kind of thinking in doctoral programs can be extremely harmful. Most successful students learn at least as much from their classmates as they do from their professors.

A helpful, cooperative environment in which students have long discussions about research, read each other's papers, and encourage each other through the inevitable setbacks that PhD students experience can be as important to a student's success as the faculty's research prowess. I've always felt that one of the secrets of the success of the PhD program of the MIT Economics Department is that students always seem to help one another and write papers together. One of my closest friends, Ben Hermalin, who was a year behind me, specialized in contract theory. I lost track of the number of times he read the main essay of my dissertation, an empirical study about boards of directors. By the time I presented it on the job market, he was practically a coauthor. This experience led us to coauthor a paper on boards, which led to another one, and eventually to a research program that has continued for both of us throughout our careers. Over the past thirty years, Ben and I have published seven coauthored papers and coedited a book about boards of directors and other aspects of corporate governance. I think of this research as an outgrowth of the working relationship we formed as doctoral students.

The dynamic between students is especially important in smaller doctoral programs, such as the ones we have in business schools. I've been on the faculty of four business schools, all of which had small but successful doctoral programs. To my surprise, I found at each of these schools that the most important determinant of student success was not the qualifications of the students when they entered the programs, but whether the students in a cohort liked and cooperated with one another. At each of the schools in which I have taught, there were years when the students socialized with one another outside of school and helped one another. In those years, the students were usually happy during the program, wrote high-quality dissertations, and eventually got jobs at good universities. In other years, students didn't like one another, stayed away from each other as much as possible, and struggled to complete the program. I always tell first-year doctoral students that I can't tell them whom to like and to socialize with. But if they do happen to get along with one another and help each other through the program, they will all be happier and do better in the program.

"DON'TS" 3–6: HOW *NOT* TO INTERACT WITH FACULTY

Many PhD students think that they should write their dissertation by retreating to their apartment or some corner of the library and spending most of their time there polishing their paper. To impress a faculty member, a student might make her paper an extension of one of the professor's papers and conclude it by providing evidence that supports the professor's favorite theory. While writing this paper, the student doesn't ask any questions of the faculty member or make any effort to get to know him, but she does work hard on making the paper perfect. Then, after not seeing the professor for a long time, she hands him her paper, expecting him to tell her that it's brilliant.

Unfortunately, what usually happens when students adopt this approach is that the faculty member doesn't like the paper and gives tough feedback, after which the student ends up being very upset. Sometimes these students recover and write good dissertations, but other students drop out of the program and find jobs outside academia. What is particularly sad about this situation is that it is entirely preventable. Had these students approached their interactions with faculty in a different way, the writing process would have had a much happier outcome.

Faculty are paid to teach students. They understand that most students don't have the experience or knowledge to put together a research paper that extends our knowledge without a lot of help. Faculty know that the vast majority of PhD students need to have many conversations with their advisers and classmates, as well as make many unsuccessful attempts, before they can write a high-quality dissertation. Most (but not all) faculty view these conversations as one of the best parts of their jobs, since they love to spend time chatting with PhD students about their research and helping them make it better.

But PhD students usually have to make an effort to initiate a dialogue with the faculty members with whom they wish to work. Some students find these conversations difficult, especially those from countries in which the culture is for faculty to be distant from students. Such students most likely have never had to seek faculty help in order to succeed.

Their natural tendency is to go into hiding until they have something that they think a faculty member will really like.

The problem with this approach is that most academic research, with a few exceptions such as Andrew Wiles's proving of Fermat's Last Theorem (see chapter 1), is not conducted in this manner. By cutting themselves off from contact with advisers and classmates, students who go into hiding are depriving themselves of the very resource they need to write a good dissertation. For the vast majority of PhD students, regular conversations with faculty and other students are a necessary ingredient of a successful research paper. Each student should try to find some faculty with whom they are comfortable talking and make sure these faculty think a research project is promising before spending too much time on it.

Another problem with the way that some doctoral students interact with faculty is that students can misinterpret a faculty member's feedback on their research. It is sometimes more difficult than one might think to understand the comments of a faculty member. At a university where I used to teach, I had a colleague with a very negative disposition. He hated most ideas, and if he said an idea was "okay," that was high praise. A different faculty member at the same university would describe almost any idea a student proposed as "great." It was sometimes hard for the doctoral students to realize that receiving an "okay" from the first faculty member was higher praise than receiving "great" from the second one!

A mistaken belief that many students have is that faculty are interested in helping only students working in the subfield where they work themselves. In my experience, both as a student and as a faculty member, this view couldn't be further from the truth. My adviser, Jim Poterba, has published papers in virtually every area of economics—except the one on which I wrote my dissertation, corporate governance. However, when I asked him for help with my research, he could not have been more helpful.

When I have been a thesis adviser, some of my most successful students have written dissertations in subfields in which I have never worked myself. I found supervising these dissertations to be particularly interesting and rewarding, and I later worked with the some of these students in their chosen area following their graduation. Their dissertations in areas outside my own research interest led to successful research programs not only for my students but also for me.

One final misperception concerns students' expectations about the reactions to first drafts of their work from faculty. These students have gotten A's their entire lives and are very proud of the papers they give to faculty to read. But faculty often tell the students, sometimes not very politely, that their paper isn't good. This reaction can be devastating to the students.

PhD students should always keep their expectations low about the reception that their first draft of a paper will receive from the faculty. If a faculty member tells them that the paper is "not that terrible," the student needs to learn to take that admittedly depressing feedback as good news. Maybe the next draft will be "okay." The one after that might be "pretty decent," and the next one may be "getting there." A paper usually doesn't become "really good" until the sixth or seventh draft. That is just the way it is in PhD programs, and if a student has trouble dealing with that kind of feedback, she should probably go into another line of business!

"DON'TS" 7–10: THE KIND OF RESEARCH
I DON'T ENCOURAGE

The final set of "don'ts" concern the type of research that I think young scholars should avoid, and how they should pick topics. Obviously, the choice of research topics is a matter of opinion, and there are excellent dissertations written on many different subjects. My concern is that PhD students tend to gravitate to topics that do not serve them well in the long run. Students are anxious to impress their advisers and fellow students, and they find out what topics are currently the subject of papers being published in the top journals. Sometimes students choose a topic because it seems fashionable, not because they have a deep interest in it or because it is fundamentally important.

A research idea often can take on interesting dynamics. An idea that is novel when first proposed can get boring pretty quickly after a few papers have been written about it. Suppose a scholar develops a model with two firms that illustrates a new idea of hers. Then someone else will undoubtedly write about a similar model with three firms, even if the inclusion of a third firm doesn't add anything interesting to the analysis. Eventually, the model will include an arbitrary n firms, someone will add taxes, someone else will test it in continuous time, and on and on. A topic like this can take on a life of its own, especially if someone thinks there is a mistake somewhere in the analysis, and the original author gets upset and responds. All of the follow-up papers usually contain basically the same idea, just different details. Publishing articles on this topic becomes a game in which participants try to "win" and show off their skills, rather than explain anything about the world.

Rather than play these games, my preferred approach to research, which I encourage my students to follow, is to explain something interesting about the world that non-academics care about. I try not to fight with other academics about the details of their papers. My rule for research topics, especially for PhD dissertations, is that the author should be able to explain how any research project she undertakes answers an important question in a way that makes intelligent non-academics care about it. I find that this rule grounds academics in reality and encourages more relevant research. Academics who find this rule constraining should remember that research topics that non-academics are concerned about tend to be ones that are of fundamental importance. Because papers on topics that are interesting to non-academics tend to appeal to academics as well, they are more likely to lead to successful outcomes in the job market and publication process.

I should emphasize that this view of research is not universally accepted among academics. I have a former colleague and good friend who always told doctoral students to write "technique-oriented theses." He thought that students should pick topics that showed off their skills, so as to impress other academics and have successful careers. This friend was not alone in disagreeing with me on this point. Many prominent faculty push students toward attacking the work of other scholars in their dissertations or urge them to focus their research on technical issues of interest only to academics.

I don't write papers myself that are intended to show off my skills, attack other papers, or make methodological contributions, and I don't encourage my students to write such papers. I would never write a paper for the purpose of illustrating a technique; my first order of business is to study interesting problems. It is the problems themselves that determine whether a research project is worth tackling. Of course, I always try to use the appropriate methods for the problem I am studying, I do not hold back when I disagree with other scholars, and I draw attention to any methodological improvement I have made that someone else could use. But the main point of my papers (and my students' papers) is never to spark interactions with other scholars; the purpose is always to shed light on the problem I am studying.

A final "don't" concerns the time horizon of the topics on which students choose to work. Every student writes one and only one dissertation, unless they get a second PhD. Ideally, the dissertation should help her reputation for the remainder of her career. Consequently, when picking a dissertation topic, it is preferable to choose one that people are likely to care about in the future. While it is impossible to know for sure what topics people will care about in the future, it is clear that some topics will have much shorter half-lives than others. Even if many people care about a topic when a student is in school, it does not do her much good later in her career if people aren't interested in it at that point.

For example, when I was a PhD student in the 1980s, there was much interest in the Tax Reform Act of 1986. This act, which substantially lowered both corporate and individual rates while raising capital gains rates, was one of the largest changes ever made to the US tax code. It was very controversial at the time, and to some extent still is today. Many papers about it were published in the 1980s, and I presume there were dissertations written about its likely effects on the economy. But today's doctoral students view 1986 as ancient history; most of them were not even born at that time. My guess is that the vast majority of economics PhD students today have not even heard of the Tax Reform

Act of 1986, let alone have an interest in spending valuable time reading old papers that speculate on its future effects. It is likely that most scholars today who do not specialize in tax policy have forgotten about any dissertations in the 1980s about the Tax Reform Act of 1986.

The "Do's" of Being a PhD Student

1) Do develop a comparative advantage. This can be a unique data set, institutional knowledge, or an econometric or modeling technique. Try to use this comparative advantage to develop a reputation for being the best scholar addressing certain kinds of questions.

2) Do try to apply ideas you learn in one course to another. Often approaches that are standard in one field can also be used productively in other fields.

3) Do incorporate your own experiences and knowledge into your research. Sometimes a student's background allows her to start with a comparative advantage in a particular area.

4) Do get all of the data you can. Don't limit yourself to the particular sample that happens to be at hand. Be imaginative about different types of data sources. Sometimes unusual kinds of data can lead to the most interesting projects.

5) Do make sure you are proactive but polite in your dealings with faculty. Remember that they want to help you out but are very busy themselves.

6) Do pick an adviser whose scholarship you admire and whom you like personally. No matter how good a scholar he is, if you don't get along with him, your life will be miserable.

7) Do bring something on paper to every meeting with a current or potential adviser. It doesn't need to be perfect, and it can be only a paragraph long; the idea is to give your adviser something to react to. If you have done some analysis or modeling, email it in advance to get a more informed reaction when you meet.

8) Do be strategic in sharing drafts with your adviser. If you overwhelm your adviser with requests, the quality of the feedback will decline.

9) Do take advantage of the resources you have access to, especially chances to get to know people who visit town for seminar series (and not just those offered by your department).

10) Do get involved in research as early as possible. The sooner you discover what research is all about, the more likely you are to ultimately succeed.

11) Do present early and often, at every brown bag workshop and mini-workshop you can get invited to.

12) Do act professionally in all of your dealings with students, faculty, and administration.

13) Do work hard. Work really hard. But remember to enjoy yourself. Your time in a PhD program can be one of the happiest times in your life!

"DO'S" 1–4: DEVELOPING A RESEARCH PROGRAM

By the time a doctoral student is about to write a dissertation, she has done well in many different classes. She has acquired a substantial knowledge of the literature and can solve (almost) any problem that is handed to her on an exam. However, in the economics-oriented fields, a dissertation topic is not handed to her. Getting started on a dissertation is likely to be the hardest part of her PhD program. Ideally, the dissertation will turn into a research program that continues long after she leaves graduate school and will change the way others think about an important issue. Coming up with a dissertation topic that can turn into a successful research program is often a daunting task, which not every young scholar is able to complete. Choosing a dissertation topic amounts to creating a personal brand for which a scholar will be known throughout her career.

There is no magic formula for developing such a personal brand. If there were, academic research would be much easier than it actually is. I discussed the issues involved in developing research programs at great length in chapters 2 and 3, so I will not repeat myself here. But I do have some suggestions that seem particularly relevant to doctoral students in economics, if not all the social sciences, that I will outline in this section.

My first suggestion has to do with developing a comparative advantage. Graduate school is a time when, although it doesn't seem so, students actually have a lot of time on their hands. Most students spend an amazing amount of time worrying about exams, gossiping about faculty, and wasting time in other ways. When I was a doctoral student, many of my classmates and I found the time to become addicted to computer games, to play a lot of tennis and softball, to attend Boston Symphony Orchestra concerts, to go skiing as often as possible, to learn to folk dance, and to be involved in many other activities. Most of us still managed to take four or five classes per semester in our first few years, attend many seminars, graduate in four years, and go on to have successful careers. The key is to spend a lot of time working and to work intensively. But it is a perfectly fine—and in fact can increase productivity—to take some time off and enjoy other activities as well.

Students should try to use their time in a doctoral program investing in as many kinds of human capital as possible. For a young scholar, valuable human capital includes not just a knowledge of the literature but also technical skills that go beyond what is taught in classes and are common to most scholars in the student's subfield. In economics, knowledge of the relevant economic institutions and available databases about a subfield is also important human capital that a scholar must acquire. A surprisingly large number of students go about writing a dissertation without the relevant institutional knowledge of their area. These students often fail to ask the most interesting questions, approach issues incorrectly from a methodological perspective, and ultimately end up doing less important research than they could have.

Both technical skills and institutional knowledge are much easier to acquire as a doctoral student with free time than after becoming a faculty member. Faculty have to teach classes, attend faculty meetings, help with recruiting, and do many other academic tasks in addition to their research. If a research project requires that a substantial amount of time be invested up-front, doctoral students actually have an advantage over faculty. Projects that more senior scholars are reluctant to undertake because they require time-consuming activities such as data work or programming can be excellent choices for dissertation topics.

Of the corporate finance scholars in my rough age cohort who have matured with me in the profession, a number of the most successful ones acquired valuable specialized human capital in a particular subfield when they were doctoral students or young faculty. Each of them used this capital to write a series of papers that are still among the most important papers in the area in which they work. For example, my former colleague Kevin Murphy wrote his dissertation on executive compensation before it was a commonly studied field, and his early work set the tone of that literature for many years. Jay Ritter had a similar influence on the literature on initial public offerings. Both Kevin Murphy and Jay Ritter were able to write these important papers as doctoral students because they became experts on the institutional features in their area of specialty and gathered the best available databases. This model—acquiring a competitive advantage through a deep knowledge of the institutions, data, and economics of a particular market while in graduate school—is not particular to corporate finance, but a recipe for success in most other fields as well.

Another advantage that doctoral students have over faculty is that they are taking up-to-date courses in a number of different subjects. In contrast, faculty struggle to keep up with what is going on in their own field and cannot hope to understand the developments in other fields at a deep level. Applying the approaches commonly used in one field to another one is a productive way in which doctoral students can contribute to a literature.

Before he was a public figure, Paul Krugman followed this model of applying advances in one field to another as the bases for his early work. He developed the "new trade theory" by taking ideas about increasing returns to scale that were becoming popular in industrial organization and applying them to international trade.[2] The outcome of this effort

2. See P. R. Krugman, "Increasing Returns, Monopolistic Competition, and International Trade," *Journal of International Economics* 9(4, 1979): 469–79.

was a revolution in the field of international trade that eventually led to Krugman's Nobel Prize.

In my field, corporate finance, much of the progress of recent years has stemmed from taking identification much more seriously, using both reduced form and structural approaches. Many of the reduced form approaches were popularized by Joshua Angrist and other labor economists, while industrial organization economists such as Ariel Pakes kindled interest in structural approaches.[3] Identification is a serious problem in corporate finance research, just as it is in labor and industrial organization. Therefore, it is not surprising that progress was made in corporate finance by applying approaches that were popular in those fields.

I always encourage students to take advantage of their background and knowledge and try to apply them to their research. All students enter graduate school with their own experiences, knowledge, and skills that can provide a competitive edge in their research. Some gain their competitive edge from a unique set of technical skills, while others benefit from their institutional knowledge. For an example of institutional knowledge being particularly useful, before entering graduate school a former student of mine worked at Goldman Sachs, where he became an expert in the "structured products" that helped lead to the 2008 Financial Crisis. He wrote an excellent dissertation on the topic that proved to be the start of a very successful career.[4]

Another thing that students should always consider is the possibility of using nonstandard sources of data. Sometimes the best insights into important problems come from different kinds of data than what has been standard in a particular subfield. Some influential papers in labor economics have taken advantage of unique data sources that led them to intriguing findings that appeared to be clear evidence of discrimination in the workplace. Claudia Goldin and Cecelia Rouse studied the

3. See J. D. Angrist and J.-S. Pischke, *Mostly Harmless Econometrics: An Empiricist's Companion* (Princeton University Press, 2009); S. T. Berry, J. Levinsohn, and A. Pakes, "Automobile Prices in Market Equilibrium," *Econometrica* 63(4, 1995): 841–90.

4. See T. D. Nadauld and S. M. Sherlund, "The Impact of Securitization on the Expansion of Subprime Credit," *Journal of Financial Economics* 107(2, 2013): 454–76.

impact of adopting "blind" auditions in the hiring practices of symphony orchestras. They find that when auditions are blind, more women are chosen than when judges can see who is playing, a finding that strongly suggests that sex discrimination was a factor in hiring decisions prior to the introduction of this practice.[5] Marianne Bertrand and Sendhil Mullanaithan created their own database by sending fake résumés with names that were either commonly associated with African Americans (Lakisha, Jamal) or whites (Emily, Greg). They find that the résumés with the white-sounding names were more likely to receive calls than the résumés with African American names. Since the résumés were constructed to be essentially identical in other respects, the obvious implication is that the hiring firms treated applications differently depending on the perceived race of the applicant.[6]

I sometimes try to utilize unique data sources in my own papers. I have had fun studying the letters written from a large institutional investor to companies as part of its activism program. I also was able to analyze the minutes of board meetings to study how boards actually function. In both cases, my coauthors and I were led to some interesting research projects by our access to private data.[7]

Some of my favorite finance papers are based on data from the market for used aircraft, data on the width of train tracks in the nineteenth century, and data on weather-related delays in maritime shipping in the eighteenth century. My guess is that most readers who do not know these excellent papers would not have guessed that these particular data sources would inform influential *finance* papers. Perhaps not surprisingly, all three of these papers were written by doctoral students as part

5. See C. Goldin and C. Rouse, "Orchestrating Impartiality: The Impact of 'Blind' Auditions on Female Musicians," *American Economic Review* 90(4, 2000): 715–41.

6. See M. Bertrand and S. Mullanaithan, "Are Emily and Greg More Employable than Lakisha and Jamal? A Field Experiment on Labor Market Discrimination," *American Economic Review* 94(4, 2004): 991–1013.

7. See W. T. Carleton, J. M. Nelson, and M. S. Weisbach, "The Influence of Institutions on Corporate Governance through Private Negotiations: Evidence from TIAA-CREF," *Journal of Finance* 53(1998): 1335–62; and M. Schwartz-Ziv and M. S. Weisbach, "What Do Boards Really Do? Evidence from Minutes of Board Meetings," *Journal of Financial Economics* 108(2013): 349–66.

of their dissertation. Creativity is an attribute that doctoral students have in abundance, and they often have success when they use it in their research![8]

"DO'S" 5–8: INTERACTING WITH FACULTY

The quality of a doctoral student's relationship with the faculty in her area is one of the most important factors determining her success. How should a doctoral student foster a productive relationship with faculty? Are there any particular things that a student should think about doing? How is the relationship with faculty different as a doctoral student than it is as an undergraduate or a master's student?

One might think that it is obvious that a doctoral student should work hard building relationships with faculty. But sometimes students don't make the effort. Many students have spent their entire lives doing well in their classes, more or less on their own, by paying attention in class, learning the material by themselves, and doing a good job with the assignments. These students naturally assume that the same approach will work well in a doctoral program. The problem is that it usually doesn't.

The goal of a doctoral student is to become a serious scholar, which normally happens only through an apprentice-type relationship with the faculty. It can be a problem if students do not establish good relationships with faculty and do not talk with them regularly. These students can drift aimlessly from topic to topic and never hit upon one that makes an impact on the literature. Most often, the students who have trouble contributing to the literature are the same students who don't spend much time talking with faculty.

To establish a good relationship with the faculty, a student should be somewhat proactive (but polite) in the way she deals with them.

8. See T. Pulvino, "Do Asset Fire Sales Exist? An Empirical Investigation of Commercial Aircraft Transactions," *Journal of Finance* 53(3, 1998): 939–78; E. Benmelech, "Asset Salability and Debt Maturity: Evidence from Nineteenth-Century American Railroads," *Review of Financial Studies* 22(4): 1545–84; and P. Koudijs, "The Boats That Did Not Sail: Asset Price Volatility in a Natural Experiment," *Journal of Finance* 71(3, 2016): 1185–1226.

Students should remind faculty from time to time that they do exist, and that they are interested in studying a particular area. They should read the papers before relevant seminars and ask good questions during them. In addition, they should make sure to keep the faculty who do work related to their own aware of their work and talk with them regularly about it. Faculty always like it when doctoral students are full of ideas and have a genuine interest in the subject they are studying.

It is also a good idea for students to quickly familiarize themselves with senior scholars' related research before approaching them. For example, their questions about the data may already be answered in detail in the published papers. It can be a waste of the faculty's time if students don't bother to read their related papers before approaching them.

Students should also do high-quality research assistant work to build a good reputation among faculty. In programs where students are not required to do RA work, students can volunteer to help faculty. A former student tells me that, as a faculty member, she has spent a lot of time helping two students who volunteered to assist her with teaching (paid work) and research (almost no pay).

Most faculty really do enjoy helping doctoral students and treasure their close relationships with their students. However, faculty are usually very busy, and there are other students who would like to interact with them. Unless a student makes the effort, she might not get to know the faculty member she is interested in working with.

THE THESIS ADVISER

Almost as important to a doctoral student as the subject of her dissertation thesis is her choice of a thesis adviser. Every doctoral student has one, or sometimes two, faculty members who serve as adviser and are formally responsible for the student's progress. Ideally, the adviser will guide her through the process of writing a dissertation, help her navigate the job market, and be her friend and a valuable resource for the rest of her career. In the hard sciences, a student often is linked to a particular adviser from the beginning of the program because the adviser is the one who provides the student's funding. In economics and its related fields, however, students can choose whomever they want, usually after the second year in the program. How should a doctoral student approach this decision?

Students often enter doctoral programs with a strong sense of which professor they would like to have as an adviser. Students interested in a particular subfield who enroll in a particular doctoral program often hope to work with the person there who is an expert in that subject. Sometimes this approach can work out well. But not always. The student could fail to impress this professor. Or the professor could become a dean, move to a different university, or leave academia for the private or government sector. The student could also become fascinated with a different area and realize that she is not really interested in the area she thought she would work in.[9]

Consequently, I always recommend that students try to enter programs with a number of potential thesis advisers who are experts in different areas of research. Regardless of what area a student thinks she is interested in studying, or whether she thinks that she would be interested in working with a particular professor, she should try to get to know all the subfields in which her department teaches classes, as well as all of the faculty, if possible. Many times students discover that the work that attracted them to the subject and led them to go to graduate school is no longer state-of-the-art, or that it is not in an area where significant work is currently going on.

An important factor that students usually don't know much about when they start their doctoral program is the personality of a potential adviser and that professor's approach to supervising students' dissertations. Some faculty are warm and like to socialize with students, while others are cold and tend to keep their distance. Some spend a lot of time talking to students at every stage of a research project, while others don't want to talk much with the students until after the students have

---

9. This last scenario describes my experience as a graduate student. When I entered graduate school, I thought I would do research on derivatives pricing, since I had been a research assistant on the topic and my undergraduate professor had told me that it was a good field to study. I ended up doing a dissertation on corporate governance. Since then, I have worked on many different topics, none of which have anything to do with derivatives pricing.

completed a draft. Some like to work with students with great technical skills, while others care more about creativity than technical ability. These and other differences in how faculty approach advising can have a big impact on a doctoral student's experience with a particular adviser.

Students should work hard to find a faculty member with whom they have a good fit, in both the type of research he does and his style of advising. The adviser-advisee relationship is a long-term one, and it is extremely important for the doctoral student's career (and her mental health) that the relationship be a productive one as well.

One thing that students often worry about too much when picking an adviser is what might be called academic politics. Some students think that it is extremely important that they choose the most famous professor in the department, or the one who they think is best connected to help them get good jobs after they graduate. It is true that the most famous faculty tend to be among the better scholars in a department and so are likely to be a good choice as an adviser. But not always. Sometimes the famous person is so busy that he is unwilling to spend much time helping students. Or he has a style that makes the student uncomfortable. Or he advises so many students that he is unable to give each one sufficient attention.

In any of these situations, an alternative choice might lead the student to write a better dissertation and to be happier while writing it. Ultimately, the only thing that really affects a student's career is the quality of her dissertation. Therefore, *a student should choose an adviser who she believes can help her write the best dissertation*. Period. Everything else should be secondary. Students who keep this choice as simple as possible and pick the person who can help them the most are usually the ones who are most satisfied with their choice several years later.

After a student selects an adviser, the real fun begins. And yes, it is fun! Research amounts to discovering something new about the world and then proving it, first to oneself and then to the world. If you have the DNA of a scholar, the process can be exhilarating.

The adviser's role is to guide a student through the process of writing her dissertation. A student should approach the relationship somewhat strategically to maximize the value that the adviser can add to it. It is a good idea for her to have regular meetings with her adviser and to keep in regular contact with him. When I am a student's main adviser, I like to meet with that student pretty often, usually every week or two, and to have informal discussions more often than that. However, other faculty have different styles than mine and prefer meeting less frequently.

Prior to a meeting with her adviser, it is a good idea for the student to prepare something in writing to focus the discussion. If what she writes is short, the student can just bring it to the meeting. But if it is longer and will require some time for the adviser to digest, the student should send it to the adviser in advance so that he can read it and think about it.

A doctoral student should try not to waste an adviser's time. Some students give faculty drafts of new papers every few days. These papers usually aren't well thought out and have problems that the students should have been aware of. Students should realize that professors' time and energy are limited and think about how to utilize their attention efficiently. Besides sharing drafts, if a student overwhelms her adviser with questions to the point of becoming annoying, the quality of the adviser's answers will decline. Running ideas by graduate student friends before approaching professors about them can be a good policy, especially for students who have many ideas and want to weed out the less promising ones.

"DO'S" 9–13: BEING A SUCCESSFUL PHD STUDENT

Much of a student's success in a doctoral program comes from her attitude and the way she goes about life as a doctoral student. No program is perfect, and in every PhD program there is always a lot of complaining. No matter how much quality control departments impose, some courses always end up being badly taught. Some departments emphasize certain fields over others, and that can be a problem for students interested in the neglected fields. Placements are often disappointing. Faculty tend to get out of date in their research, they sometimes do not care enough about the doctoral students, and they often fight with one another. The list of things that doctoral students complain about is endless.

However, the most successful students tend to be the ones who look past a program's deficiencies and take advantage of the resources that *are* available to them. Most universities have some areas in which they are strong; a student should learn those areas well regardless of what she wants to specialize in. For example, if a school has strong econometricians, students should take a few extra econometrics courses; if the school is good at theory, then she should take a lot of theory courses; and if her university has a lab for doing economic experiments, she should learn some experimental economics. In addition, if the university has a strong law school, accounting department, or statistics department, it might make sense for a student to think about research issues that take advantage of complementarities between those fields and economics.

Looking beyond the resources offered by the university, students should try to take advantage of other resources they have access to. In most fields, there are practitioners and government officials doing work in the area who can sometimes help a student understand institutional details of markets and provide useful data. These non-academics are often delighted to help bright graduate students, but many students don't make efforts to get to know them. When practitioners working in areas related to students' interests come to campus to give talks to MBA students and undergraduates, doctoral students should attend and introduce themselves to the speakers if there is an opportunity. Doctoral students should read newspapers, websites, and magazines for material related to their research and should not be bashful about cold-calling people who might help them with their work.

Every student has her own experiences, skills, and connections that can be helpful in writing a dissertation. In fact, sometimes something in one student's background can help another student with her research. For example, my job market paper was an empirical study of corporate governance that was not based on a publicly available database. Instead, the data on boards of directors that I used in that paper were hand-collected by one of my classmates, Jim Dana, when he was an undergraduate. Jim and his coauthors were kind enough to share them with me. If I had not known Jim, or if he and his coauthors had been less generous, my career would probably have gone in a completely different direction.

When I was writing my dissertation, it also helped that I had been doing research for a while before I began. I worked as both an RA and a coauthor with a number of faculty in economics, finance, and mathematics while I was an undergraduate. During my first few years as a doctoral student, I wrote several pretty decent papers on taxation that I should have published, but unfortunately did not. By the time I started working on my dissertation, I knew at least a little about the academic research process.

I encourage all students to get involved in research as early as possible. Research is a skill with a steep learning curve; the more involved a student is in research early on, the higher on the curve she will be when it comes time to write a dissertation. In addition, if a student is able to publish her early work, these publications will be a large boon for her when she looks for a job. Even if her research does not lead to publication, she will learn details about the literature, data, and modeling necessary to work in a particular area. More importantly, she will begin to understand how frustrating, but ultimately rewarding, academic research can be. This experience will be extremely valuable to her when she starts writing her dissertation.

Once a student starts doing research on her own, she should strive to present it as often as possible. There are always a number of places where a doctoral student can present her work. Most departments have regular seminars and brown bag workshops. In addition, students can sometimes present in classes, and they can organize their own mini–brown bags where they present their work to each other.

Students' presentations improve over time for a number of reasons. First, during presentations students hear tough questions about their analysis and can address those concerns as they revise their papers. Second, with practice students discover the best way to present a particular piece of work. And third, when students present more, they become more comfortable talking to a group about their work. They respond better to questions they have not heard before, and they're not as intimidated when a faculty member they wish to impress doesn't like their work. Presenting research can be hard work and stressful, but practicing as often as possible helps students develop skills that are necessary to succeed in academia (and elsewhere).

Graduate school is a transition period between being a student and being a faculty member. As she proceeds through the program, a student should try to act more like a faculty member. As she gets involved with undergraduate teaching, she should realize that she will be held to the same professional standards of conduct as faculty. For example, doctoral students should behave professionally around undergraduates and should be especially careful that any personal relationships with the students they teach are appropriate. Graduate students should even think a bit more about how they dress. If they would like faculty to think of them as peers who they can recommend to their friends at other universities, it can't hurt to dress like a professor, especially at public events like conferences.

An important part of the transition is to learn to think of faculty as peers. An easy first step in this transition process is to address faculty by their first names. More important is the way students approach their interactions with faculty. Some students think that the best strategy when talking to a professor is to nod yes and agree with anything that the professor says, even if they disagree. But academia is about the back-and-forth exchange of ideas. Faculty are most impressed with students who disagree with them from time to time, since it is these disagreements that help both faculty and students sharpen their ideas.

Successful doctoral students work extremely hard, usually harder than they ever have before in their lives. Any student entering a doctoral program should do so with the expectation that it will not be easy, and that they will struggle to keep up with the workload. When I was a doctoral student, my rule was that unless I had something better to do, I would work at the National Bureau of Economic Research every evening and every weekend. When I went there, I could always find the same group of friends working on their dissertations. All of my friends who were at the NBER every evening have gone on to very successful careers, and some of them became the top economists of my generation.

But graduate school can be fun too. Looking back, I remember it as one of the best times of my life. I was taught by famous scholars, learned many fascinating ideas, and met other students from all over the world. I loved listening to the high-level debates, over both academic ideas and their implementation in the real world. And despite the workload, there was time to enjoy life away from the university as well. If you decide to go to graduate school for a PhD, you should expect to have an intense but ultimately rewarding experience.

Racial and Gender-Related Issues

Throughout this book, I have discussed a number of potential pitfalls that a scholar can face when pursuing an academic career. Some of them are inevitable given the inherent difficulties in producing new knowledge, combined with the competition for tenure-track positions at research-oriented universities. But there are a number of solvable, in-principle issues that would both make academia a more attractive place to work and enable us to do a better job for our students and society. Particularly problematic are issues connected to gender and race. Many of us, perhaps naively, believed that by the twenty-first century we would be past these issues. However, academia, like so many other sectors of the economy, still has gender and racial problems, and they show no signs of going away. Doctoral students, regardless of their gender or race, should be aware of these issues and encouraged to make efforts to minimize their impact.

THE UNDERREPRESENTATION OF WOMEN AND MINORITIES

It is evident from even a casual glance at the data that women, Blacks, and Hispanics are substantially underrepresented in academia, particularly in the economics-oriented fields. In 2016, women made up just 31 percent of the assistant professors and 15 percent of the full professors in US economics departments. In the same survey, only 8.1 percent of assistant professors and 4 percent of full professors were Black or Hispanic, despite the fact that these groups make up about 30 percent of the US population. The situation is even worse in finance: very few women and minorities are on the faculties of most finance departments. Understanding why women and minorities are so underrepresented is an important ongoing topic of research.[10]

The underrepresentation of women and minorities among faculty members in economics and finance has substantial negative consequences. Faculty become role models for students, especially impressionable undergraduates. Students tend to go into fields in which they can relate to the faculty. If a department has faculty who "look like them," students will be more likely to enter that field. So to encourage young women and minority students to go into economics, it is important to have women and minority faculty as role models.

As social scientists, we produce research that is used to influence public policy; some of us even end up working in the government helping to make policy decisions. Since these policy decisions affect all of society, it is particularly important that all groups are represented. In fact, there is evidence that economic policy advice varies systematically with the gender and race of the economist providing it.[11] Consequently, for the economics profession to help guide public policy in a way that maximizes the welfare of all citizens, it is important that the advice comes from a group of scholars who reflect the population as a whole.

HURDLES FACING SCHOLARS

I have supervised many female doctoral students' dissertations, I have had a large number of female coauthors, and I am in a department with much better than average female representation for a finance

---

10. The statistics in this paragraph are from A. Bayer and C. E. Rouse, "Diversity in the Economics Profession: A New Attack on an Old Problem," *Journal of Economic Perspectives* 30(2016): 221–42. Bayer and Rouse also provide an interesting discussion of the potential reasons why women and minorities are so underrepresented in the economics profession.

11. See A. M.May, M. G. McGarvey, and R. Whaples, "Are Disagreements among Male and Female Economists Marginal at Best? A Survey of AEA Members and Their Views on Economics and Economic Policy," *Contemporary Economic Policy* 32(1, 2014): 111–32.

department.[12] I have observed that, unfortunately, there are obstacles facing female students and faculty that simply do not exist for men. I think that it is appropriate to end this chapter with some discussion of these obstacles, so that female doctoral students have some sense of what awaits them as they advance in the profession.

A number of studies have documented unsettling patterns about women economists. Female economists appear to be given a harder time than male economists, both by their students and by editors: in studies that try to hold quality constant, women tend to receive lower teaching evaluations and are less likely to receive favorable responses from journals. Women are tenured at lower rates than men, *even holding research records constant.* The effect continues at higher levels, where women are less likely to be promoted to full professors or awarded endowed positions.[13]

One particular problem that female academics face is that, even in liberated academic couples with each partner trying to share in care responsibilities, women end up doing more than half of the work involved with raising children. This fact was illustrated vividly during the 2020 Covid-19 lockdown—male economists who were stuck at home increased their output, but female economists, who ended up with extra child care responsibilities, saw their productivity decline.[14] Universities have tried to adjust their standards for time spent in child care by

12. I have not had comparable experiences serving on the thesis committees of any Black or Hispanic doctoral students, nor have I had many Black or Hispanic colleagues whose experiences I can share. For this reason, I focus the discussion in this subsection on the hurdles facing female scholars, although I'm sure that much of what is said here applies to minority scholars as well.

13. See F. Mengel, J. Sauermann, and U. Zölitz, "Gender Bias in Teaching Evaluations," IZA Discussion Paper, Institute for the Study of Labor (September 2017), http://ulfzoelitz.com/wp-content/uploads/JEEA-gender-bias.pdf; D. Card, S. DellaVigna, P. Funk, and N. Iriberri, "Are Referees and Editors in Economics Gender Neutral?" Working paper (September 2019), https://economics.harvard.edu/files/economics/files/ms30505.pdf; and M. G. Sherman and H. Tookes, "Female Representation in the Academic Finance Profession," Working paper (August 2019), http://affectfinance.org/wp-content/uploads/2019/08/ShermanTookes_Aug16_2019-1.pdf.

14. See N. Amano-Patiño, E. Faraglia, C. Giannitsarou, and Z. Hasna, "Who Is Doing New Research in the Time of COVID-19? Not the Female Economists," Working paper, VoxEU,

granting extensions of tenure clocks for the birth of a child. But as so often happens, universities' good intentions appear to have made things worse. Male faculty, who also receive extensions for the birth of a child, turn out to be the primary beneficiaries of this policy, while female faculty are actually disadvantaged by it.[15]

While there are undoubtedly many reasons for the obstacles faced by female scholars, one important reason is the sexist culture that permeates much of the profession. This culture is vividly illustrated in the Berkeley undergraduate thesis of Alice Wu.[16] She performed an internet "scrape" of the postings on a popular website, Economics Job Market Rumors (EJMR), to create a database of the postings. Wu examines how female economists are treated relative to male economists in this anonymous forum—which is likely to reflect the unfiltered opinions of the posters (who hopefully are not too reflective of the broader population)—to determine the different ways in which women and men are viewed by members of the profession.

Wu finds that, holding the prominence of the person fixed, women scholars tend to be discussed much more than men. But the discussion of women tends to focus on their appearance and personal life, while the discussion of the men centers on their research. I have spoken to some young women scholars whose appearance or personal life was discussed on this website, and the experience was extremely upsetting for them. But the larger concern is that the focus on appearance and personal lives reflects a lack of seriousness given to women's work. At least in the mind of EJMR posters, the scholarship of female scholars takes a backseat to other aspects of their lives that ought to be irrelevant to their professional success.

Center for Economic and Policy Research (May 2, 2020), https://voxeu.org/article/who-doing -new-research-time-covid-19-not-female-economists.

15. See H. Antecol, K. Bedard, and J. Stearns, "Equal but Inequitable: Who Benefits from Gender-Neutral Tenure Clock Stopping Policies," *American Economic Review* 108(9, 2018): 2420–41.

16. See A. Wu, "Gendered Language on the Economics Job Rumors Forum," *American Economic Review* 108(2018): 175–79; and A. Wu, "Gender Bias in Rumors among Professionals: An Identity-Based Interpretation," *Review of Economics and Statistics* 102(5): 867–80.

Reading the previous few pages must be upsetting to female scholars, especially those who are just starting out. However, it is possible to succeed despite these barriers; more and more young women scholars have been making a mark on the economics profession in recent years. There is an active network of female academics who make an effort to provide role models and mentorship for younger female scholars. They have set up a number of conferences where presenting authors have to be untenured women. These conferences provide opportunities for women scholars and potentially offset some of the hurdles they face.

The one attribute I have noticed of successful women academics is that they are all *tough*. What I mean is that although these successful women are generally nice, polite people, they have their own points of view and do not back down from them when challenged, especially when they are challenged by men. I have always thought that an unfortunate aspect of many cultures is that women are sometimes taught that they should be deferential to men. If you grow up in such a culture, it is important to disabuse yourself of this idea if you wish to be a successful academic. Academia is a place where we earn our reputation by having our *own* ideas, and by standing up for them.

DISCRIMINATION AGAINST ASIANS

Unlike Blacks and Hispanics, Asians are not underrepresented in academia. There are many scholars from Asia in our doctoral programs, as well as a number of US-born Asian Americans. Perhaps because Asians seem to be well represented, some people incorrectly believe that there is no discrimination against Asians.

There are not as many studies documenting discrimination against Asians as there are that document gender discrimination. However, many of my Asian friends in academia believe that, holding quality constant, it is harder for Asians than whites to: get into doctoral programs, receive tenure-track offers, publish their papers, and get promoted to associate and full professor. With the caveat that I have not seen formal studies documenting these patterns, I suspect that my Asian friends are correct—that it is in fact harder for Asians to succeed in academia than it is for whites who do comparable work. For some reason, while academia is so outspoken against discrimination against other minority groups, today it is perfectly fine to hold Asians to higher standards.

I do not understand why such discrimination against Asians persists and is considered acceptable by much of the academic world. There does not appear to be any easy way of addressing the problem. Perhaps the first step is acknowledging and stigmatizing this discrimination. Nowadays, it is unacceptable for scholars to makes sexist or racist comments, but some are not called out when they make a joke about or promote stereotypes about Asians. Hopefully, discrimination against Asians will be condemned to the same extent as discrimination against other groups and become less prevalent in the future.

13

How to Be a Diligent
Thesis Adviser

THE MOST important professional relationships doctoral students have during graduate school are usually with the members of their dissertation committee, the chair of which is their thesis adviser. Advisers teach their students how to do research and also how to earn a living as academics. Ideally, advisers will be lifelong friends to their students and will help to guide their careers for a long time after graduate school.[1] However, many students are not as fortunate as I was and do not have a supportive relationship with their adviser. Often a bad relationship is the student's fault: she may not work hard enough, or listen to what her adviser says. Sometimes, however, the fault is with the adviser. He may have unrealistic expectations or simply not care or know enough about them to help students in a productive manner.

Since I discussed in chapter 12 how doctoral students should approach their relationships with their advisers, I thought it appropriate to consider the relationship from the adviser's perspective. How should faculty view their responsibilities as thesis advisers? Is the opportunity to supervise doctoral students' dissertations an optional perk of being a professor, something to be indulged in by faculty who enjoy it and

---

1. When I started to write this book, one of my first calls was to my thesis adviser from graduate school. Even after over thirty years as a faculty member, I would never have completed the book if he had told me that writing it was a bad idea.

avoided by faculty who don't? Or is advising students an important element of the job of every scholar in a research university? How should a faculty member set his expectations for his doctoral students? How often should he meet with them, and how should he structure the meetings? What else can he do to help his students succeed?

Why Advise Doctoral Students?

Before I discuss *how* one advises doctoral students, I will first address the issue of *why* one would bother to do it at all. After all, the only instructional responsibility normally specified in a faculty contract is the number of courses he must teach every year. In addition, universities are pretty clear when they do their reviews that a faculty member's research is extremely important to his standing. Supervision of doctoral students' dissertations, by contrast, is somewhat amorphous. It is sometimes mentioned in a faculty member's annual review, but most departments treat advising doctoral students as kind of an extra, like serving on a departmental committee, helping with a student club, or meeting with an alumni group.

Yet advising a doctoral student represents an enormous commitment by a faculty member of time and energy that goes well beyond the work involved in being on any faculty committee.[2] To do the job correctly, the adviser must have many discussions with the students about research, career planning, and many other topics. He must spend a lot of time providing the student with detailed suggestions on numerous drafts of her papers.

So why do faculty members agree to advise doctoral students? Some do not; they avoid being on thesis committees, and especially avoid being the main adviser. However, most faculty are eager to help doctoral students and are honored to be asked to serve on such committees, especially if they are the main adviser.

---

2. Possible exceptions are the committees that do the particularly onerous work of selecting a new dean or president or that investigate ethical violations.

There are some explicit benefits from advising doctoral students. Departments put substantial resources into their doctoral programs and do appreciate the effort that faculty members put into supervising their dissertations. And it is a prestigious accomplishment for an adviser to have advised a student who places on the faculty of a good university, especially a student who subsequently has a successful career publishing in the academic journals.

However, most of the benefits from advising students are not so explicit. For instance, advising doctoral students can be a particularly rewarding form of teaching. Most academics chose their profession at least in part because they enjoy teaching, but teaching the same class every year can get boring. In contrast to a faculty member's regular teaching, which usually consists of going through the same material over and over, each doctoral student's dissertation delves into a new topic. These dissertations are usually state-of-the-art studies about issues that the adviser is interested in. Consequently, advising doctoral students can be a form of instruction that is both more interesting and more rewarding than a faculty member's usual teaching.

Faculty can enjoy productive relationships with their doctoral students for many years after they graduate. If the student ends up working in academia, the adviser will run into her at conferences, and the two are likely to continue to do research on related topics. Many of my co-authors are former doctoral students of mine, and a number of them have become very close personal friends.

A faculty member also can learn a lot from supervising dissertations. As I discussed in earlier chapters, getting sufficiently "up to speed" on a topic to do state-of-the-art research is quite difficult and time-consuming. For this reason, many faculty, once they get established in a narrow subfield, never do any research outside that subfield for their entire career. Being an adviser on a dissertation is one way for a faculty member to expand his horizons and understand a subject on a much deeper level.

A number of times I have advised students on theses about subjects I was interested in but of which I had only a cursory knowledge. After helping the students with their work on these topics, I learned enough about the related issues that I eventually coauthored papers with them. As a result, I found myself doing research in areas in which I had not previously considered working. This is how I began working on stock repurchases, cash management, public equity offerings, securitization, and insurance.[3] I would probably not have pursued these projects had I not had the opportunity to advise these excellent students on their dissertations.

The Main Goals and Issues in Supervising Doctoral Students

Advising a doctoral student is a form of teaching that is very different from the usual classroom instruction. When teaching a class, the professor's goal normally is to convey specific material to the students. If the students demonstrate that they have learned the material, they do well in the class, and if they fail to demonstrate that they have learned it, they do poorly.

In contrast, the goal is much broader when advising a doctoral student. A successful adviser will teach his doctoral students to become scholars who are capable of doing world-class research on their own. The "deliverable" a student must have to graduate is a dissertation, and an adviser usually helps the student a lot with its contents. But the real objective of doctoral student instruction is to teach the student how to think like a scholar, how to go about coming up with a creative research program, and how to execute and present the research according to the standards of the profession. The dissertation-writing process is a

3. See C. P. Stephens and M. S. Weisbach, "Actual Share Reacquisitions in Open-Market Repurchase Programs," *Journal of Finance* 53(1, 1998): 313–34; H. Almeida, M. Campello, and M. S. Weisbach, "The Cash Flow Sensitivity of Cash," *Journal of Finance* 59(4, 2004): 1777–1804; W. Kim and M. S. Weisbach, "Motivations for Public Equity Offers: An International Perspective," *Journal of Financial Economics* 87(2, 2008): 281–307; T. D. Nadauld and M. S. Weisbach, "Did Securitization Affect the Cost of Corporate Debt?" *Journal of Financial Economics* 105(2, 2012): 332–52; and S. Ge and M. S. Weisbach, "The Role of Financial Conditions in Portfolio Choices: The Case of Insurers," *Journal of Financial Economics* (forthcoming).

hands-on introduction to research that students can replicate throughout their careers.

In addition to teaching doctoral students how to do research, faculty must also judge the quality of their work. These students are expected to uphold, and hopefully raise, the departmental standards defining an acceptable dissertation. Sometimes an adviser must make the difficult decision to tell a doctoral student that her work isn't good enough. But he should strive to make these occasions the exception and not the rule. An adviser's goal should be to work with his students and to help them exceed the departmental standards, so that as many as possible can graduate.

One of my pet peeves is that some faculty who like to think that they have higher standards than everyone else seem to enjoy making it difficult for doctoral students to get through the program. The irony is that these faculty, while telling the world about their own high standards for doctoral students, often themselves produce many papers that they cannot publish. If these faculty held their own work to the same standards that they expect of their students' work, their careers would probably have taken a different trajectory.

Professional Ethics

Another goal of doctoral programs is to teach students about professional ethics and appropriate behavior. Ethical behavior for an academic goes beyond the self-interested incentives to establish a good reputation for oneself. The American Economic Association recognizes this idea in its recent Code of Professional Conduct, which requires "integrity" of economists, including honesty, care, transparency, and a "disinterested" approach to assessing ideas.[4]

Academics should conduct all aspects of their professional lives ethically. In research, we are expected to search for the truth, not just do research that leads to publication in top journals, especially if doing so

---

4 See American Economic Association, "AEA Code of Professional Conduct," adopted April 20, 2018, https://www.aeaweb.org/about-aea/code-of-conduct.

comes at the expense of the truth. The publication process is imperfect, and there are always ways in which scholars could massage their search for truth so as to increase the likelihood of publication. Authors have been known to tilt their interpretations toward editors' favorite theories, work on topics that are fashionable rather than ones that are important, and selectively trim samples and pick specifications in ways that produce statistical significance. Consistent with this last set of behaviors being far too prevalent, there are studies showing that published papers are much more likely to report t-statistics slightly larger than 2 than slightly below 2; such results are the opposite of what ought to be true in the absence of reporting and publication biases.[5]

Appropriate ethical behavior is also an important element of the nonresearch aspects of our jobs. Perhaps most importantly, ethical behavior concerns the way we treat each other in our professional lives. As I discussed in chapter 12, sexism and racism are too prevalent in academia. But there is more to treating people well than simply not being sexist or racist. Many academics are rude to colleagues, students, and staff, don't respond to emails, don't read students' or colleagues' papers, and don't even show up for departmental seminars and gatherings. When faculty are easygoing and pleasant to be around, everyone is happier, students learn better, and it is easier to hire and retain faculty and staff.

Learning ethical behavior goes hand in hand with learning to be a good colleague. Ethics and colleagueship are notoriously difficult to teach, as there are no formulas or set rules to follow. I believe that the key to teaching ethics and colleagueship is to set a good example for the students and talk to them regularly about how to go about all aspects of the job of being a professor. One thing that I am very proud of is that, to my knowledge, none of my former doctoral students has ever been involved in an ethical scandal, and the vast majority of the ones still in academia are beloved by their colleagues.

5. See D. Fanelli, "Negative Results Are Disappearing from Most Disciplines and Countries," *Scientometrics* 90(2012): 891–904; Harvey, "The Scientific Outlook in Financial Economics"; I. Andrews and M. Kasy, "Identification of and Correction for Publication Bias," *American Economic Review* 109(8, 2019): 2766–94; and C. Blanco-Perez and A. Brodeur, "Publication Bias and Editoral Statement on Negative Findings," *Economic Journal* 130(2020): 1226–47.

As academics, we are granted incredible benefits by society. We can teach what we are interested in, we have high social status and good pay, and perhaps most importantly, we are given indefinite tenure. It is important to teach our doctoral students not to take these benefits for granted. They should be made to realize that academics are not entitled to these benefits and should work hard to pay back some of this good-will. We do so by teaching well, doing research that non-academics find interesting, and providing non-academics with positive externalities (other than football and basketball) when they visit our campuses.

Motivating Doctoral Students

Perhaps the most important factor determining a doctoral student's success is her motivation. One might think that motivating students to do first-rate research would never be difficult, since that is what they went to graduate school to learn to do. But sometimes students stop caring about their work. In some fields, students can become "professional PhD students" who stop working seriously on research and don't make progress toward graduation. They can stay on campus for seven or eight years, or sometimes even longer, as doctoral students, since they enjoy life on campus and the financial package they receive as a teaching assistant is sufficient to live on.

In economics and its related fields, there are usually good jobs available for students who write high-quality dissertations and present themselves well on the job market. Nonetheless, it can still be difficult to motivate some doctoral students. They can become depressed and unproductive if their adviser doesn't like their ideas, if they decide that academic research isn't all it is cracked up to be, or if they are procrastinators who always find reasons to postpone finishing their work. The job market does motivate students to some extent. Furthermore, departments can use both carrots (financial aid) and sticks (threats to be dropped from the program) to provide incentives for students to finish.

Relying on these incentives, however, is a second-best approach. The most successful students are always the ones who are self-motivated and don't need explicit incentives to motivate them to do research. They do research because they love it, not because of any carrots or sticks they receive from their research success. The best students are fascinated by new problems that they can tackle and will write a good dissertation irrespective of any explicit incentives they receive.

The Effect of Strong Explicit Incentives on Doctoral Students

The job of a thesis adviser is to uphold high standards and push students really hard, while still making sure they enjoy showing up for the work. Unfortunately, when faculty set the bar too high and threaten to kick students out if they don't meet it, there can be a number of negative consequences for the program. If students are afraid of flunking out of the program, they do put in more hours. They also become extremely nervous and try to tailor their research to whatever they think the faculty will be most willing to approve (which might be different from what faculty will actually approve).

One of the most important aspects of research that often is lost when a student faces explicit pressure is her creativity. For a research paper to be influential, it has to address a new question or use a novel approach to address an existing one. The ability to think of these new questions and approaches is where creativity plays a key role.[6] Students may respond to pressure, especially when combined with negative feedback on ideas that are a little "different," with research that is sterile and not particularly innovative.

Earlier in my career, when I was on the faculty of a university whose professors were known for being tough on their students, I became a good friend of a student who was struggling to find a thesis topic. Every few months, he would come to me with a new idea. I almost always liked his ideas and encouraged him to write his dissertation about one of

6. Identifying the students who have the "creative gene" and will end up loving research is actually quite difficult. Admissions committees for doctoral programs struggle to identify which of the potential applicants will do best, and observing applicants' creativity and curiosity—the most important ingredients of a successful scholar—is very hard.

them. Unfortunately, some of my colleagues were never enthusiastic about his ideas, and my friend always ignored my advice and did not pursue the ideas he told me about. He was worried about being able to complete his PhD if he worked on an idea that some faculty were not excited about. In the end, he asked a very senior professor to work with him on a fairly boring but unobjectionable topic.

Several of my friend's ideas eventually did get published in top journals. Unfortunately, the publications had other people's names on them! What happened was that scholars at other universities had ideas similar to my friend's, but unlike my friend, these scholars pursued the ideas and published the results. My friend did graduate, but he never published his dissertation. Despite such an inauspicious start, he nonetheless has had a very successful career. But it would have been even more successful if he'd had a bit more backbone when he was a graduate student and resisted the pressure to satisfy the idiosyncratic tastes of his professors. In the end, he wrote a far less interesting dissertation than he was capable of.

Another problem with programs in which students are constantly worried about being dropped is that they become much less likely to do joint work and tend not to help one another with their dissertations. Students can feel that helping their classmates do better makes them look worse in the eyes of the faculty and could hurt their own chances of graduating. Consequently, they don't coauthor papers with one another or support one another in their research. Strong explicit incentives, especially the wish to avoid not graduating, can create an overly competitive environment, leaving all of the students worse off.

Fostering Self-Motivation

The best dissertations are not written by students who are worried about getting kicked out of their program. They are written by students who come up with creative ways to address questions to which they would like to know the answer. These students spend a lot of time thinking about the state of the literature, what questions have yet to be addressed, and innovative ways of answering them. The motivation for this work is students' fascination with the questions and desire to challenge themselves to provide satisfactory answers. The best students work hard not because of any incentives provided by their department, but because they love research and want to be the best scholar they can be.

The extent to which doctoral students are self-motivated, however, can vary tremendously depending on their environment. Almost all doctoral students are smart and enthusiastic when they begin their programs. There are a few students who are so talented and motivated that they will succeed in producing good work regardless of their surroundings. But for most students, the drive to produce first-rate research comes from seeing others produce it and wanting to become part of an exciting scholarly community. The type of scholarly environment that students are exposed to will determine how motivated they are and, consequently, the quality of their dissertation.

Faculty should therefore think about the environment to which students are exposed and come up with ways to make it as stimulating as possible. Each faculty member remembers what motivated them when they were doctoral students and naturally tries to emulate the good parts of their student experience and avoid the bad parts. As I discussed in chapter 1, I was very fortunate to be a student at MIT in the 1980s and also to have a desk at the National Bureau of Economic Research, where I got to know a number of Harvard students and faculty as well. The incredible research environment surrounding me when I was a student was a huge factor in whatever success I have had since then. In my work with students throughout my career, I have tried to make the environment my students face as much like Cambridge, Massachusetts, as possible.

Expectations of Students

In my first week as a doctoral student, I attended my first seminar, where Dale Jorgenson presented an applied econometrics paper. After the seminar, Peter Diamond, who years later would be awarded the 2010 Nobel Prize in Economics, introduced himself to me and asked what I thought of the talk. The only honest answer I could have given would have been: "I didn't understand a word of it." However, being a nervous new student, I didn't want to admit not understanding the paper, so I told him that I thought the talk was very interesting.

Of course, Peter knew that I was a first-year student who had not yet taken econometrics, so he probably surmised that I didn't understand the paper. But he wanted me to know that as a doctoral student, I was expected to be an active participant in the intellectual life of the department. Whenever I attended seminars as a doctoral student, I was supposed to read the papers beforehand, think about them, and form thoughtful opinions about them. The minute I stepped onto campus, I was treated as something of a peer. That being said, I still had to pass my classes and exams. I worked extremely hard to pass the exams, even though hardly anyone actually failed them and was asked to leave the program. What motivated me was not that I was likely to fail, but that I was surrounded by many brilliant people and wanted to fit in and earn their respect.

I was highly influenced by the quality of the work of the other students in the program. Everyone in our program had been one of the best students at their university before coming to MIT. The very best students in this highly select group were just incredible. A number of the papers we read in our macroeconomics course were by Greg Mankiw, who at the time was still a doctoral student in our program. Andrei Shleifer was a year ahead of me, and before he left graduate school, he published multiple papers in *Journal of Political Economy*, and a number of papers in other top journals as well. Two of his *JPE* papers were even the lead article.[7] For most of us "normal" students, who had always been the top student in our previous programs, it was quite a revelation. We came to understand that to be one of the better students at MIT we

---

7. The majority of tenured faculty at the top twenty departments go their entire career without having a lead article in one of the top general-interest economics journals such as *JPE*. Andrei's lead articles from his graduate school days were: B. D. Bernheim, A. Shleifer, and L. H. Summers, "The Strategic Bequest Motive," *Journal of Political Economy* 93(1985): 1045–76; and A. Shleifer and R. W. Vishny, "Large Shareholders and Corporate Control," *Journal of Political Economy* 94(3, part 1, 1986): 461–88.

had to become one of the top scholars in our field. And we had role models who showed us how to become exactly that.

I let my own doctoral students know that my expectations for them are very high. I expect them to do more than just show up for seminars—I expect them to form opinions on the work, participate in the discussion during the seminars, and be part of the culture that makes life exciting for the other students. I strongly encourage my students to read each other's work and to help them make it better. Whenever possible, I have older students and former students explain their work to younger students, to show them that it is possible for people just like them to produce excellent scholarship. The goal is to convey to students that faculty expect their work to be world-class, and that it is possible for them to produce such world-class work. Bright students who observe that other students are meeting these high expectations will work harder and strive to meet them as well.

Ideas Matter—Rank Doesn't

Perhaps the most important thing a professor can teach a doctoral student is that research should stand on its own, and that the student should judge the quality of a paper independently of its authorship. Regardless of whether a paper is written by a Nobel Prize winner or another doctoral student, they should give the paper's analysis the same scrutiny.

Many students spend their entire lives thinking that their job as students is to repeat everything their professors say and to be deferential to their professors' ideas. The deferential approach to learning is perhaps a good way to understand cut-and-tried material like mathematics. However, it is not a productive way to understand state-of-the-art research in a subjective area like economics, where it is acceptable for different scholars to have different worldviews. An important part of the job of a thesis adviser is to disabuse students of the reverence for faculty and for published work that they have been previously taught.

I always thought one of the great things about the NBER was that people sat around the table and argued about economic ideas, whether at lunch, late at night, or in the conference room after a seminar. The opinions of the more famous senior people were given more weight in the discussion, but only because their opinions were more credible than those of the PhD students. At the end of the day, what mattered was not the identity of those who spoke, but whether what they said was correct.

In regular discussions of recent research at the NBER, doctoral students often came to the conclusion that the work was wrong or misguided. When the students reached this conclusion, it did not matter if the work was done by one of their professors or by a friend. The students were not taught to worship at the feet of their professors. Rather, they were encouraged to challenge professors' ideas.

Great research often consists of challenging the prevailing worldview. Doctoral students must learn that the research of their own professors, even if they are the most famous scholars of the day, is not always correct. If students wish to write influential dissertations, they have to get used to the idea of challenging the prevailing viewpoint early in the program, even if their professors are the ones who created it. Most such challenges will not be correct, but once in a while they open up cracks in the arguments of the leading scholars that lead to fruitful new research.

The Value of Informality—Professors Are Human Too

I always felt that the informal mixing of students and faculty at the NBER helped create the atmosphere in which students were willing to challenge faculty's work. Faculty and students would go to lunch together, play tennis with each other, and socialize in various ways. Students would always call faculty by their first names, and they would come to realize that professors, even the most famous ones who taught at Harvard and MIT, were just people like they were. Professors had good days and bad days; sometimes they wrote excellent papers, and other times they wrote awful ones.

When they accept professors as individuals who make mistakes, students can go the next step and recognize that their papers are not perfect either. If the papers of Harvard and MIT professors aren't perfect, then the ones from faculty of other universities aren't either. Doctoral students' natural inclination should be to look skeptically at published papers. They need to learn that looking hard enough at established research might reveal flaws in it. Students can then figure out how to fix these flaws and eventually make a meaningful contribution to the literature.

An advantage of an informal atmosphere is that students become much more comfortable talking with faculty, asking questions, and bouncing ideas off of them. Students' creativity does not blossom when they're scared, but when they recognize that there is much that the literature does not know and then think of new ways to advance knowledge.

When I work with doctoral students, I always strive to create an atmosphere as similar to the NBER as possible. I spend time talking with them about non-research-related topics, hoping to make them comfortable in the office and to think of me as a normal human being. I try to go to lunch with the students I work with regularly, usually every week or two. At these lunches, we typically don't talk much about research but instead enjoy ourselves as we share good food and conversation. When the students get back to the office, they hopefully will be a bit happier and realize that the faculty are there to help them rather than to scare them. Ultimately, I believe, it is an atmosphere where students can feel comfortable and respected that helps them become excellent scholars.

Students Should Work Together

Another objective of graduate school is to give students an opportunity to begin working with one another and forming relationships that could last throughout their careers. Advisers should realize the importance of these relationships to the students and do what they can to encourage students to develop them. Of course, whether students develop relationships with one another depends mostly on the students: if they like one another, they will become friends, and if they don't like one another, they won't. But there are things an adviser can do to create a positive atmosphere in which students' relationships with one another will thrive.

Perhaps the most important thing an adviser can do is to base recommendations on students' absolute performance and not their performance relative to one another. Any rankings cited in letters of recommendation should be measures of the quality of the students' work relative to historical standards and to the overall market for new economists, *not* students' standing relative to their classmates. If students think that they will be hurt if another student in their year does well, they will tend to think of each other as rivals rather than friends and won't help each other with their work. Academia *is* very competitive, but the real competition is from the outside market and the historical standards that universities apply when evaluating their faculty. If multiple students at a school stand out on the national market, then they should all be able to do well on the job market. If a student is the top student from a weak class, then being the top student is unlikely to help her very much.

I try to do whatever I can to encourage students to work together. I have started research projects with several students as coauthors to get them thinking of each other as teammates. Research, even on sole-authored dissertations, is very much a team effort, and if students view it that way, they will do better in the long run. When I am working with several doctoral students at the same time, I like to have research group meetings in which students take turns presenting their work to one another. When they work well, I try to say as little as possible and let the students make suggestions for each other's work. Ideally, these sessions tend to encourage the students to work together and can even lead to coauthored work between them.

Know and Understand the Students

Finally, advisers should make sure that they know their students reasonably well. It might seem obvious that advisers ought to know their students, but so many do not. Many are not aware of the basic facts of their students' lives. Where are they from (more specifically than just "China" or "Russia")? Do they have siblings? Do they get along with their parents? Are they in a relationship or did one just end? Do they have other interesting skills or hobbies?[8] Are they dealing with any health issues? Students really appreciate their advisers' efforts to get to know them better. And any additional information that advisers have about students can help them do a better job supervising students' dissertations and providing guidance on the job market.

Equally important as knowing students personally is understanding their abilities. Some students are great at formal modeling, some have excellent institutional knowledge, and others are exceptional at handling databases. I always try to steer students into topics that show off their best skills. What matters in the end is the contribution to our knowledge from the student's dissertation. It is a lot easier for a student to make a meaningful contribution to the literature if what she attempts to accomplish takes advantage of her skill set.

Understanding students' lives and their skills allows advisers to do a better job of both setting expectations and helping students achieve them. Some students need to be helped through the dissertation one step at a time. These students should meet with their adviser regularly, sharing one test after another and rewriting each section of their paper many times before going on to the next one. Other students are more independent and can be left alone for a few months to write a draft by themselves.

A good adviser will set expectations differently for each student based on each one's abilities. Faculty should realize that advice is not "one size fits all." What is reasonable for faculty to ask a top student to do might overwhelm an average student. The goal is to tailor each student's workload to her ability, so that all students who enter the program can eventually leave with a high-quality dissertation.

---

8. I have one former student who was a champion figure skater and another who was an All-American rugby player before entering graduate school. Many faculty never find out that their graduate students are often very interesting people.

14

Managing an Academic Career

WHEN I WAS DECIDING what to do after graduating from college, one of the things that led me toward pursuing a PhD in economics was the number of potential employment options that were available after I graduated. I thought that I might enjoy being an academic, but wasn't sure if I would be able to get a good academic job. After all, when my father received his PhD, there weren't many academic jobs available so he took a non-academic offer and went on to a very interesting career in the private sector. One of the appealing aspects of studying economics was that if academics didn't work out, I might be able to follow a similar path and have an equally rewarding career.

The truth is that, even though my goal was to be an academic, I had no idea when I entered graduate school which way my career would proceed. I did not know if I would flunk out of the doctoral program, if I'd decide I didn't like economics, or if I'd find a private-sector job that would be more interesting and lucrative than one in academia.

Like everyone else, I had to find my own way throughout my professional career amid considerable uncertainty. This uncertainty was multidimensional, involving my own interests and abilities, the demand for economists both inside and outside academia, how the field would develop, and many other considerations. It was the kind of uncertainty that John Kay and Mervyn King refer to as "radical uncertainty"—uncertainty whose sources are so unclear that it is impossible to model or hedge.[1]

How should you think about managing your career in the presence of radical uncertainty? What can you do to prepare for the inevitable setbacks you will encounter? How can you make smart career decisions in an uncertain world?

General Principles

I think that management of an academic career, or really any career, comes down to two principles. The first principle is that, at every stage of her career, a scholar should always spend some time thinking realistically about new directions that her career could take. When first starting out, these might include different possible fields to study and different types of employers she could work for. Later on, possible options could be other schools or firms that might hire her away from her current job. Finally, when she is established inside an organization, other opportunities are likely to be found in other roles she could take on and in outside opportunities that could be available.

The second principle is that once an opportunity is identified, a scholar should make an effort to acquire the human capital necessary to pursue it. By human capital I mean the résumé, skills, and connections that will enable her to move her career in that direction. In other words, when you see a potential opportunity, you should actively pursue it by acquiring whatever capital is necessary. This point probably seems obvious to many readers but is often ignored by the many people who expect opportunities to appear magically without any effort on their part.

In this chapter, I suggest career management strategies a scholar can deploy at each stage of her career. I proceed sequentially, starting with career planning issues for graduate students, then for junior faculty members, and finally for senior faculty members. I explain how a scholar

---

1. See J. Kay and M. King, *Radical Uncertainty: Decision-Making beyond the Numbers* (W. W. Norton & Co., 2020).

can apply these two general principles to make better decisions at each stage of her career.

The overriding theme of this chapter is embodied in a saying that we have on the wall of our family's summer home in northern Michigan: "You are the CEO of your own life!" *You* have to take responsibility for your own career and make sure it is interesting and fulfilling. If you do not enjoy your job, it is your responsibility to take charge, address the problem, and try very hard not to blame others for the difficulties you are having. Far too many people are unhappy because they spend their lives complaining about their jobs and not doing what they can to improve their situation.

Keeping Options Open as a Graduate Student

I have talked throughout this book about the comparative advantage of developing a specialization to make a meaningful contribution to a literature. But sometimes students get so engrossed in their own literature that they forget about everything else. In addition to developing a specialty, graduate students should take advantage of the opportunity afforded by graduate school to develop a knowledge of the major subfields of their area of study and, most importantly, acquire skills that can be applied to different kinds of problems.

A path that graduate students commonly follow is to "fall into" a topic that sometimes but not always is related to the research a faculty member of theirs is interested in. Perhaps the student is a research assistant for the professor or takes a class from her, and she ends up working on a related topic. But sometimes students develop an interest in a topic on their own without help from the faculty. Once a student has found a topic that fascinates her, she can end up immersing herself in it throughout her time in the program.

It is wonderful when a student can come up with a good thesis topic and spends most of her time thinking about it. However, it can be a problem if the thesis topic is all the student ends up knowing anything about after she finishes graduate school. If the research works out well, then the thesis could help her get an academic job and a start on a productive research program. But sometimes things do not go as planned. The student might fail to get an academic job, or the research might hit a dead end, either before or after publication of the dissertation. Eventually, regardless of their initial success, most research programs reach a point of diminishing returns and subsequent papers become less interesting and influential over time. To be productive throughout her career, a scholar must be able to address new issues in addition to the ones she started working on initially. These new issues can require a different set of skills than those required for her dissertation. Graduate school is the time to gain a broad set of skills she will be able to use in addressing new topics throughout her career.

In addition, having a broad set of skills can make a doctoral student much more attractive to employers outside of academia. Private-sector employers, and sometimes government agencies as well, often don't care at all about a student's dissertation and whether it will be published. Instead, they want to hire people who can understand problems and apply the appropriate tools to solve them. In addition, private- and government-sector employers highly value the ability to write well and to give clear presentations. If a doctoral student makes an effort to become a good writer and public speaker, these skills will benefit her regardless of who is her future employer.

The ability to handle large databases well and understand modern methods of statistical analysis has become incredibly important for most social scientists in the economics-based fields. One significant change over the thirty or so years I have been an academic has been the profession's increased focus on empirical work. The information economy has vastly increased both the availability of data and the computing power to analyze them. The standards for empirical work have increased dramatically over the past thirty years, and statistical approaches such as Bayesian MCMC analysis and machine-learning algorithms are now regularly used in empirical papers by not particularly sophisticated non-econometricians (like me). There is every reason to think that the trend will continue. In my opinion, anyone getting a PhD in the social sciences today would be crazy not to do their best to get up to date on these and other empirical methods. Otherwise, they will find themselves hopelessly out of date in a few years when even more sophisticated techniques become commonplace.

It might seem obvious that students should learn empirical skills regardless of their specialty, especially if their future as an academic is uncertain, but many students don't. I often meet recent graduates who tell me that, as theorists, they don't need to know how to deal with data. Some mention that they generate their own data running economic experiments, so don't have to understand the problems inherent in working with data generated in the real world.

I still am amused when I think of a certain sign on a bulletin board when I was a graduate student, posted by a now world-renowned economist after he passed his second-year exams. It said: "For Sale, a copy of Theil. Only opened twice. A must for every serious economist, I no longer need mine!" (Henri Theil's *Principles of Econometrics* was the most popular econometrics textbook at the time.) This scholar has had a tremendously successful research career since then that, not surprisingly, has not involved empirical work. But if he had had bad luck publishing his work and decided to leave academia for the private sector, he might have had more trouble landing a job than if he had taken empirical work more seriously.

When planning their careers, graduate students should spend most of their time focusing on the dissertation they have to write. At the same time, however, they should be acquiring the skills that will help them pursue future opportunities, from potential research programs on topics they haven't yet thought about to job opportunities both inside and outside of academia that would open up after they acquire these skills. Students should remember that most scholars' research tends to become more applied over their career. It is common for scholars to do more theoretical work soon after leaving graduate school and then more empirical and policy-oriented work later on. Consequently, it is particularly important for a graduate student to acquire empirical skills, regardless of the field on which her dissertation is focused.

The Rookie Job Market

Perhaps the most talked about and time-consuming event on the economics calendar is the "rookie market"—the job market for newly minted PhDs (who are often called "rookies"). Every year at the annual Allied Social Sciences Association meeting held soon after New Year's Day, doctoral students and recent graduates interview with universities, firms, and government agencies for jobs. After these interviews, the students who receive fly-out invitations travel in January and February. Offers are made throughout this period, usually in a very strategic manner, and the market clears by the middle of March.

Most departments do a reasonably good job of preparing their students for the job market (but not necessarily for life as a junior faculty member after the market is over). A number of faculty have written about the job market and how students should navigate it. Some have been kind enough to post these documents online so students outside their own department can benefit from them.[2] I will not describe the details of the market and the standard advice that is given to most students, since readers can find this information in these publicly available documents. However, I will discuss a few points that I think are particularly important and that I always emphasize to my students when they go on the market.

THE IMPORTANCE OF ADVISERS. During the job market, it is particularly important for a student to have a good relationship with her

2. See A. Butler and T. Crack, "A Rookie's Guide to the Academic Job Market in Finance: The Labor Market for Lemons," August 7, 2019, available at SSRN: https://ssrn.com/abstract =3433785; J. Cawley, "A Guide (and Advice) for Economists on the US Junior Academic Job Market: 2018–2019 Edition," September 21, 2018, http://www.aeaweb.org/content/file?id =869; R. Hall and M. Piazzesi, "Bob Hall's (MP: Wonderful) Job Market Advice for Stanford Economics Students," 2001, https://web.stanford.edu/~niederle/Advice_Bob_Hall.pdf; D. Laibson, "Tips for Job Market," https://economics.harvard.edu/files/economics/files /jobmarketadvicehandout.doc.pdf; P. Iliev, "Finance Job Market Advice," June 11, 2016, available at SSRN: https://ssrn.com/abstract=2779200; and E. Zwick, "How I Learned to Stop Worrying and Love the Job Market," http://www.ericzwick.com/public_goods/love_the _market.pdf.

adviser and to feel that she can be open with him about important issues in her life. A student's adviser should be both the one who guides her through the job market process and her primary cheerleader helping her sell her work to the profession. Surprisingly, some students are not open with their advisers, making it hard for advisers to help them. If the student has some issues that she might not want to tell the market, she should still be honest with her adviser about them. For example, a student might want to keep the identity and locational preferences of her partner secret from the schools that are considering hiring her. Or she may have a medical condition that could affect her work. Or she may not wish to have her sexual orientation become publicly known. If her adviser is aware of all the facts, he can help her come up with an appropriate strategy for managing the issue and addressing it (or not addressing it) with potential employers.

Advisers can sometimes convey useful information credibly to the market. For example, because many schools in the United States are located in small towns, it can be hard for them to hire faculty. The majority of doctoral students would prefer living in a city, so for them a school's location in a small town is a minus. Students are told by their advisers to express interest in all jobs until they have an offer, but many students are likely to decline a potential job offer in a small town if opportunities in larger cities become available. Some students, however, are genuinely interested in living in a small town, perhaps because they have small children, or because they value the low house prices and ease of life in a small town. For such a student, it can help her case if her adviser lets schools in small towns know that she finds their location appealing. An adviser can sometimes communicate such information much more credibly than the student could herself.

DEADLINES MATTER. In the job market, there are a number of deadlines that students face. A particularly important one is the date by which applications must be uploaded. In most US departments, faculty start reviewing files during the week after they return from the Thanksgiving holiday in early December. Therefore, students' applications must be complete by this point in time.

I have attended a number of faculty meetings over the years in which we evaluated candidates from other schools to decide whom we would interview. Usually we would defer considering applications that were not complete until a second meeting, which was most often planned for the following week. Unfortunately for those applicants, however, we often had filled our interview schedule with the applications that were complete at the time of the original meeting, so the second meeting never happened. It always seems that students whose applications are not complete when faculty first meet to consider them always have much lower chances of getting an interview even if they become complete shortly afterwards.

A complete application includes letters of recommendation from faculty, and students are put at a great disadvantage when those letters are late. For this reason, our department, like many others, has a staff member who is responsible for bugging the faculty to complete their letters of recommendation and for uploading them with the students' applications. Students have to realize that the staff are human and that it takes time to upload the letters. So that staff have sufficient time to upload the letters, students should have their portion of the applications finished well before the Thanksgiving holiday.

One time, when I was teaching at a different university, there was a student who was spending a year in his home country working at the central bank. He had an excellent job market paper, and a number of schools would certainly have been interested in interviewing him. But it was mid-December before he decided to go on the market and asked me (and the other faculty on his committee) to write him a letter of recommendation. As a result, he got only one or two interviews and no fly-out invitations. This student ended up staying in his job in his country's central bank. I always thought this was a sad outcome for him. The student had a good job, but he most likely would have had a number of other options if he had completed his applications and submitted them a few weeks earlier.

CAST A WIDE NET. Students often go into the job market with preconceived ideas about the job they will end up taking. Perhaps they

think only about living in one part of the country, or only want to consider academic opportunities. For example, I once had a student who
wanted to consider only jobs in Chicago. I pointed out that there weren't
too many universities in Chicago and that two of them, the University
of Chicago and Northwestern University, were top-ranked departments
that were unlikely to be interested in hiring her. I eventually convinced
her to apply to universities in other large cities, and fortunately she was
able to find a job at one of them.

I always strongly encourage students to submit as many applications
as possible, for both academic and non-academic opportunities in the
United States and also in other countries. Students have to understand
that the market often doesn't go as expected. Places that students
think will be interested in them often turn out not to be. But sometimes students are offered the dream job that had seemed like a remote possibility at the beginning of the job market process. In addition, people can find that they enjoy living in a part of the world they
never really thought about. Our Ohio State finance department has a
number of European faculty who never envisaged living in Columbus,
Ohio, but now love living here. I spent most of my life in the North-
east and Midwest of the United States and never thought much about
living in the western part of the country. But when the University of
Arizona offered me a job in 1994, I accepted it and spent five wonderful years in Tucson.

An increasing number of students are taking post-docs prior to starting on tenure-track positions. Some of them, such as the ones offered
by the NBER, are designated as post-docs, and others are "visiting faculty" positions that students take before going on the market a few years
later. Visiting faculty positions sometimes involve a fair amount of
teaching, but they can be at fairly highly ranked departments, and they
enable recent graduates to make new connections. Post-docs can be a
smart career move since they also allow new PhDs to make progress on
their research before starting their tenure-track career. If a new PhD is
able to publish some work during her time as a post-doc, she may be
offered a much better job than she would have gotten directly from
graduate school.

DON'T IGNORE NON-ACADEMIC OPPORTUNITIES. Most students who enter PhD programs plan on teaching at a university. But there are many excellent opportunities in government agencies, think tanks, consulting firms, financial firms, and industry. Since I personally have not worked in any non-academic organizations, I cannot give much advice to PhDs on how to manage a non-academic career. I have observed, however, that most PhDs who did not go into academia have seemed very happy with their decision. I always strongly encourage students going on the job market to apply for as many non-academic positions as they can and to consider them seriously if they become realistic options.

An important consideration in any decision about whether to accept a job offer is the extent to which you can move from the job in the future. It is often easier to move from academia to industry than from industry back to academia. Unless you have a non-academic job in which you can publish articles—a possibility, for example, in government jobs—it can be extremely difficult to move to a tenure-track position in academia. Universities tend to prefer freshly minted graduates to people who have been out for a few years.

In some fields, however, it is possible to move from the private sector to academia. My brother, David Weisbach, is a tax lawyer who started his career at a prestigious tax-oriented law firm. At nights, while doing the demanding job of a young associate, David was able to write an excellent paper and take it on the law school market. After a short stint at Georgetown, he has taught at the University of Chicago Law School for many years and has become one of the leading tax law professors in the country.

THE FINAL DECISION IS YOURS. An adviser's job is to help students get as many opportunities as possible. Students should be sure to have many frank discussions with their adviser about career opportunities and to seek their opinions about which are the best. When juggling offers and thinking about which to accept, a new PhD should consider, in addition to the academic ranking of the departments, the location of the jobs and the quality of her personal interactions with the people she met during the hiring process. The organization's culture and the extent to which it supports new hires are particularly important factors in her decision.

But when making the final decision, a student should always remember the saying: "You are the CEO of your own life." She must figure out what the right job for her is, regardless of what others advise her to do.

Life as an Assistant Professor

New assistant professors who worked extremely hard as doctoral students are often surprised to discover that their workload only increases when they become faculty members. Their research expectations remain the same or even increase. In addition, assistant professors have to teach classes, go to faculty meetings, referee papers, help doctoral students with their research, be involved with faculty recruiting, and take on all the other responsibilities of a faculty member. These increased responsibilities come at a time when they are moving into a new house or apartment and finding their way around a new city; some are also helping family members adjust to the new environment.

With so much to do, time passes quickly and assistant professors begin to feel pressure. This pressure is especially high if their job market paper is rejected by a journal or two or their teaching evaluations are below average. The new responsibilities, together with high research expectations, can be overwhelming. What should young faculty do to maintain progress on their research in the face of so many responsibilities? What priorities should they set when they go about doing their job? How and when should they think about pursuing outside opportunities?

Young faculty realize pretty quickly that the most precious resource they have is their time. All aspects of research always end up taking much more time than planned, leaving less time to complete drafts of new papers and publish old ones. Teaching is also time-consuming: faculty have to prepare for class, answer questions in their offices, administer makeup tests, and assign grades. Before they realize it, their first year as a faculty member has soon passed.

BE ORGANIZED AND PROCEED WITH A PLAN. A new assistant professor should remember the basic principles outlined at the beginning of this chapter. First, she should think about all of her options for the future; and second, she should acquire the capital necessary to pursue these options. Of course, when a newly minted PhD joins the faculty of a university, her number-one option is to receive tenure at that university. But she should realize that not everyone gets tenure at their first job, and the majority of successful academics move at least once or twice in their career. Therefore, a second option that a new assistant professor should keep in mind when she joins a university is to move to a different university. A third option—the feasibility of which varies across fields—is to move out of academia to the private or government sectors. In finance, there are usually firms looking to hire recent PhDs, especially people who specialize in capital markets research. In other areas of economics, however, such as pure theory, the private-sector market is more limited.

Keeping these options in mind, young faculty should have a plan to acquire the necessary capital to make them realistic possibilities. If the capital necessary were substantially different for each of these options, faculty would face a difficult choice over which kind to acquire. Fortunately, the factors that help get junior faculty promoted internally and also keep their outside options open are largely the same. The most important factor is the impact of a scholar's research. Teaching also matters a lot. In addition, a scholar has to demonstrate that she can be a good colleague who is likely to provide high-quality service in the future.

I have already discussed the research process in detail in earlier chapters. But one thing I haven't focused on is the time element and its effect on how a faculty member goes about her research. Some faculty are such perfectionists that they never actually finish anything. However, there does come a stopping point on each paper when a scholar must finally send it off to a journal. A good approach is to set deadlines for yourself during each part of the research process. I set deadlines for most things that I do, and I try really hard to finish tasks by the deadline, if not sooner. I don't always meet those deadlines, but simply having one can be a useful motivator.

I would recommend that a new faculty member keep in mind something like the following, admittedly optimistic, schedule. A typical dissertation contains three essays. The first is normally the job market paper, and it should be very polished by the time a student graduates. She should try to submit this paper to a journal even before she moves to the location of her new job, and certainly before the school year begins at that job. Hopefully the second essay is in decent shape and won't require that much work prior to submission. She should try to submit that one sometime in the fall of her first year out (assuming her fall teaching isn't too onerous).

The third essay is often a preliminary draft at the time of graduation, so it might take a bit more time before that paper is ready for submission. Nonetheless, in addition to submitting the first two essays, the scholar should try to have the third paper in shape by the end of her first year as a faculty member. In addition, she should push herself to write a new paper in her first year. It is great if a new faculty can establish coauthoring relationships during that first year.

This schedule is intentionally somewhat aggressive. Most junior faculty, even the ones who eventually receive tenure, do not get their papers to journals as fast as I suggest. This schedule should represent a goal that a new faculty member strives to achieve. However, when pushing herself to produce papers and submit them, she always has to be mindful not to submit the paper before it is ready, using the criteria for submission I laid out in chapter 11. And before reaching that point, she should revise the paper as outlined in chapter 10.

Getting the papers you wrote as a student into shape and off to journals so quickly is a lot of work. But it is essential to start your career well and to work hard to publish your dissertation as soon as possible. Early publication will enhance your ability to move in the seasoned market if you choose to go that route. In addition, submitting the papers you wrote in graduate school shortly after starting a first job frees up your time and energy to focus on new research by the time you reach your second or third year on the faculty. A good start on the publishing front can be an incredible boon to your career.

In addition to research, the other main factor taken into account in promotion decisions is teaching. Many people may think otherwise, but teaching really does matter in these decisions. When a university grants tenure to someone, they are giving her a lifetime contract. If her teaching is problematic, then the university will be extremely reluctant to offer such a lifetime contract. It is worth making an effort to improve your teaching prior to coming up for tenure and to take advantage of the university's "teaching and learning" center, a service now available on most campuses. Improved teaching does more than simply raise your standing with your colleagues; it also increases your own job satisfaction, because it is much more fun to teach well than to teach poorly.

The Seasoned Market for Junior Faculty

Young faculty often ask me how the "seasoned market" works.[3] While the rookie market is fairly organized and a wealth of fairly standard advice on it is publicly available, the seasoned market is more of a mystery. Young faculty often hear gossip about outside interest being shown in colleagues, and wonder how they can get this kind of attention themselves. How does this market work? What should people do to be considered for faculty positions by other universities? Should they contact schools themselves? If so, how and when should they do that? Is the human capital necessary for a scholar to move to another university different from what she needs to be promoted internally?

In contrast to the rookie market, the seasoned market is mostly driven by personal relationships. For example, if a new graduate from a top-ranked department has written an interesting paper in an area in which our department is focusing our efforts on the rookie market, the odds are pretty high that we will find out about her and consider

---

3. The term "seasoned market" is somewhat of a misnomer, since it is the candidates, not the market, who are seasoned. The market itself is not particularly seasoned, and as I discuss later, it is much less organized than the rookie market.

interviewing her. But usually we won't consider someone who is exploring the seasoned market unless one of our faculty brings up the name. Most of the time, that faculty member either knows the potential hire personally or was given the name by a trusted third party. Occasionally, when our department wants to hire in an area in which we are short, we will spend some time going through the websites of other departments trying to come up with names of people who might be a good fit. In addition, like most departments, we receive a number of unsolicited applications from faculty at other schools, and we do sometimes contact these candidates for an interview or seminar.

I think of the seasoned junior market as almost two separate markets. In the first, some people who move to a new school a year or two out of graduate school are given full tenure clocks. This type of hire is sometimes referred to as a "rookie substitute." For departments, hiring a person who is a year or two out of school is similar to hiring a rookie—they get paid the same and take the same slot that a rookie would take. Departments can consider candidates as rookie substitutes at different points in the year. A particularly active time for this segment of the market is right after the rookie market closes, when schools whose rookie offers were turned down are looking for alternatives. From the school's perspective, scholars a few years out of graduate school can be excellent hires since they usually have had a good start publishing (otherwise they wouldn't be looked at) and have a track record of teaching and colleagueship.

When a scholar has been out of graduate school for more than two or three years, universities are often prohibited from giving her a full tenure clock.[4] In that case, the school would make her what is often called a "senior junior" offer. To receive this type of offer, the applicant should already have established herself to some extent. I have always felt that by making such an offer, the university is telling the potential hire that her record is essentially on track to receiving tenure at that school.

---

4. The rules on who can and who cannot be offered a full clock vary across universities and even within universities, where they are not always applied consistently over time and across departments.

Presumably, a person hired with a senior junior offer who continues to produce research at the same pace and proves to be a good teacher and colleague in her new department should have a tenurable record when she does come up.

I believe that most of the profession shares my view about senior junior offers: that such an offer is a school's implicit promise about the new hire's future tenure decision. Consequently, the bar for getting hired with a shorter clock is higher than for rookies or rookie substitutes, since schools hope to hire only those with a strong enough record to make tenure a high probability. Empirically, it is true that scholars who are hired midway through their time as a junior faculty member do have higher tenure rates than rookies hired straight out of school, although there are some who get turned down.

Some junior faculty do get tenured offers from other schools before they are tenured at their own school. This practice is especially prevalent at the very top departments, which are always trying to lure away star junior faculty from one another. However, most departments prefer to make offers to a junior faculty from other schools in which they would start as junior faculty and come up for tenure in a year or two. Deans are generally more comfortable with this type of offer than with a senior offer. An untenured offer gives the school the right to deny tenure if the new junior faculty member turns out to be a horrible colleague or teacher. (This rarely happens.) The bar for getting an untenured offer is normally lower than for a tenured offer, so scholars who are willing to move without tenure are likely to have more options than scholars who insist on having tenure the moment they arrive on campus.

MANAGING THE SEASONED MARKET. Moving to another university is one of the three options for a young faculty member. The other two are getting promoted at her own school and moving to a job outside of academia. Since a young faculty member does not know what will happen in the future at her home institution, it is prudent for her to develop whatever capital she can to maximize the possibilities with the other two options. A young scholar's goal is to make herself attractive to other schools in the academic market and to generate interest so that she has the option of moving if she wants to.

Most junior faculty would love to be approached by other schools about a potential move. Even if they are happy at their current school, being approached by a competitor is a positive signal about their value. Such an offer can improve a faculty member's standing in her own institution, since an outside offer from a peer department establishes to the deans that her research is valued by the profession. Sometimes (but not always) universities will even match outside offers financially.

However, the optimal strategy for encouraging these approaches is not obvious. Unless she is "on the market," it usually makes sense for a scholar not to solicit offers but to wait until she is approached (although dropping hints from time to time to schools that might be attractive is sometimes a good idea).

Generating interest without soliciting it can be somewhat tricky. One thing that can help is to be well known in the profession. If a scholar has more friends and her papers are recognized as important, she will have a better chance of receiving interest from other schools. Going to conferences, presenting work as often as possible, and getting to know people from other schools can help to increase a scholar's visibility. Visibility can be thought of as a type of human capital that is especially important for generating outside interest. To a lesser degree, visibility can also help with internal promotions, as it can make a scholar's work better known and heighten its impact.

One thing that every scholar should do is to establish a relationship with any university with which they have a personal connection. For example, a scholar should make an effort to meet the faculty of the universities located in the city she is from. It is especially important for non-US faculty to do this; regardless of whether they want to move back to their home country eventually, they should make efforts to get to know the faculty of the universities there. When she visits her family, she can also visit the universities nearby. If she ever wants to leave the university where she teaches, a university in her hometown may become a natural fit.

However, visibility and connections help only to a degree. The most important factor in generating outside interest is a scholar's productivity. Usually it is faculty who are doing well at their home institution who draw interest from other schools. Faculty who receive outside offers tend to be those who publish, who are good teachers, and who are well liked by their colleagues. And yes, schools do make an effort to find out about the teaching and colleagueship of a faculty member at another school before approaching her. Being a good teacher and colleague not only benefits a faculty member at her home institution but also increases her external market value.

GOING ON THE SEASONED MARKET. Sometimes a faculty member is looking to leave a university but wants to stay in academia. Perhaps she had a personality conflict with someone in the department, received bad signals about her tenure prospects, was denied tenure, or just wants to live in another part of the world.

Unlike the rookie market, on the seasoned market it is often a good idea to target schools selectively rather than send out a mass mailing. The exception is if a faculty member has been denied tenure, in which case there is no reason not to write to many schools. But a faculty member who does not have to leave her university should be more selective than when she was on the rookie market and not target places she is unlikely to move to. In addition, the element of fit is much more important as she becomes a more senior scholar; she should place more emphasis on where she wants to live and on being around colleagues she knows and likes than she did when she was on the rookie market. She should assume that her school will find out that she has contacted other departments, so if she contacts too many and eventually does not leave, it can get awkward for her around her own department.

On the seasoned market, even more than the rookie market, it can be very helpful to have someone else, usually someone more senior, initiate the contact with the other university. This person can be your thesis adviser, a senior colleague, a coauthor, or another respected scholar who knows you reasonably well and can vouch for you. This third party can credibly convey what you're like, why you want to leave your current university, and why the school being contacted is a good fit. For example, a third party can say: "She is a great researcher and teacher, but she's single and hates living in a little town in the Midwest of the United States. She would love to live in a cosmopolitan international city like yours and would fit in very well with your group." If a department looking to hire faculty receives this information from someone they trust, their faculty might very well contact you. Such a comment in a cover letter from someone they don't know, on the other hand, sounds a lot less credible and is less likely to generate a positive response.

At some point in a scholar's career, it is prudent to go on the market to explore outside options. However, it is a really bad idea to solicit an offer from a department unless you would seriously consider moving to that university. Making an offer requires a lot of effort, and departments are not happy if they think that someone feigned interest in an offer just to get a raise at her home institution.

A sensible time to consider moving to another university is before you come up for tenure, or slightly before. Since tenure is never certain, the other school will understand if you turn down its offer because you subsequently got tenure. But if things go badly and you do not get tenure, it is nice to have the option to move right away, rather than be compelled to do a full search the following year. While the standard faculty contract contains a "terminal year" after the tenure decision so that you can find another job, it can be awkward to hang around a department that just denied your promotion. For this reason, many scholars prefer to leave right away rather than stay another year at the university that decided not to grant them tenure.

Promotion Decisions in Universities

Reviews are probably the most stressful and consequential times in an academic's career. A typical US university contract stipulates three main reviews during an academic's career, aside from the annual reviews that are mainly to provide feedback and the small annual raises faculty members can receive. The first review normally occurs during your third or fourth year as an assistant professor. There may or may not be outside letters at this review, but aside from that, it follows the same process as tenure reviews. Usually a departmental committee votes on your case, the department head makes a recommendation, a college committee makes yet another recommendation, and then the dean decides what the college should recommend to the university. Eventually someone high in the university administration, typically the provost, makes the final call, often with the assistance of a university-level promotion committee.

Most universities rarely terminate a faculty member at this early review. Instead, they use it as a way to give detailed feedback and to provide junior faculty with an opportunity to improve in areas of weakness. Importantly, universities use this review as an opportunity to advise some faculty that they are unlikely to be granted tenure in the future, and that it would be wise for them to start looking for another job. If a junior faculty member who has little chance of being promoted finds another job prior to the tenure review, it saves the senior faculty the ordeal of a painful review process and allows the junior faculty member a chance to move on in her career without having been denied tenure.

The tenure review can be the most important review of a scholar's career, since passing it gives her a lifetime contract. Tenure reviews usually occur during the sixth year and follow the process described above, except that evaluation letters from senior scholars in the profession are now required. Most universities allow the candidate to suggest some names and the department suggests others. If too many people who are asked refuse to write a letter, it is usually taken as a bad sign about the candidate, since it is likely that they think the case for tenure is weak.

Finally, most universities have a third review when an associate professor is being considered for promotion to full professor. There is no fixed timetable for this review, but it usually takes place about five years after a scholar receives tenure. In my experience, most departments will encourage an associate professor to have their case considered for full professor only if the faculty are likely to support the case. Since tenured associate professors have the right to remain at that rank for the rest of their career, there is no reason to consider cases that are likely to be difficult. An associate professor does have the right to have her case for full professor considered even when she is discouraged from doing so by the department. Occasionally these cases succeed, but more often they do not. There can be hard feelings if a longtime associate professor asks to be considered for full professor and is denied.

In the United States, this review structure is fairly common at most state universities. At private universities, timetables tend to be a bit longer. At some, an associate professor can be untenured, although there is still a serious review with outside letters to achieve this rank. In other countries, the review structure can differ substantially, and in some countries faculty have essentially lifetime contracts starting the day they are hired.

HOW TO MAXIMIZE YOUR CHANCES. While the rules of the promotion process are well understood by most faculty, what is not understood is what a faculty member can do to put her best foot forward and maximize her chances. By the time of the promotion decision, she has done her best in publishing and teaching. Now she has to put together her packet, provide names of letter-writers to the department, and, most importantly, remain calm around the department during this very stressful and sometimes awkward period.

One thing she can do that actually makes a difference is maintain a good attitude. It does help to be a good colleague—to be helpful, cheerful, and active in departmental events. Faculty doing tenure evaluations try their best to be fair and to ignore personal feelings, but there is no doubt that, holding all other things equal, well-liked faculty are more likely to be promoted than faculty who are not so well liked.

Promotions can be very difficult for everyone involved, including the people doing the evaluation. Junior faculty up for promotion often can figure out when the senior faculty are meeting to discuss their case. They should be aware that the first thing that is always said at these meetings is a reminder that everyone is obliged to keep quiet about everything said in the meeting, and especially not to say anything to the candidate. This is why, after the meeting, there are always moments when a senior faculty member really wants to tell the candidate that her case went well, but isn't allowed to. Sometimes the candidate incorrectly infers from the lack of information from a friend who normally tells her everything that there is a problem with her case, when in fact everyone in the promotion meeting was very positive about the case.

THE RESEARCH STATEMENT. One thing that many junior faculty do not spend enough time on is the research summary that must be included with the packet. When I read these documents, I often suspect that the candidate just copied the abstracts from her papers, put them one after another in a file, and called it done. This kind of research document doesn't necessarily do any harm to the candidate, but it doesn't really help her either. If I am writing an outside letter, or serving on a college committee to evaluate a candidate from another department, and I want to read a paper's abstract, I can just look at the paper.

What I want to know, especially when I am evaluating someone whose work I don't already know well, is what the candidate views as her overall research agenda and what she thinks are her most important insights. How does she think? What is the theme that links her papers with one another? What do we learn from her papers together as a group beyond what we would understand from reading them individually? Ultimately, the most important issue in promotion decisions is what we learn from a candidate's work that we would not have learned had the person gone into another line of business.

I always encourage junior faculty to put together a research document designed to answer these questions. A candidate for promotion should explain in her research document why she chose her research program, what her general approach is to addressing questions related to this program, what she views as her most important contribution, and where her research is likely to go in the future. She should focus the discussion in her research document on issues rather than journal publications. The research document shouldn't say: "This paper got into *Journal of Political Economy*, which is a top-ranked journal." Instead, it should say how the paper affects how the profession thinks about an important topic and how it influenced the opinions of other scholars. A good way to do so would be to document the paper's citations by other scholars and appearances on reading lists at other universities.

An outside reader can look at a candidate's résumé to see where her papers have been published. The research document should explain what is in the papers and why a reader should care about them. It should make a case that her research has taught us important lessons already, and that there is more to come in the future from the candidate.

OUTSIDE LETTER WRITERS. A candidate also has to include a list of potential letter-writers in her package. Most departments pick some of the names from the candidate's list and some additional names not on the list. Many junior faculty obsess over which names to include on their list and don't really know how to think about which names to include. Is it more important to select big names, people from top universities, or people who are likely to say good things about you? Is it okay if you know the people on your list? What if your list includes a coauthor or your thesis adviser?

When proposing the names of potential letter-writers, it is useful to consider the letter-writing process from the perspectives of both the potential letter-writers and the faculty on the promotion committee who will be reading them. Senior faculty at other universities who are good choices for writing outside letters are scarce, and they are often overwhelmed with requests, sometimes receiving ten or fifteen requests for outside letters in a single year. Many senior scholars are not viewed as good choices for outside letters because they have a reputation for lateness, they have strong opinions and idiosyncratic tastes, they're not active in research anymore, or they always come across as overly negative. Consequently, senior scholars who are prompt, even-tempered, active in research, and generally positive in outlook can be besieged with requests.

Beyond a formal letter thanking them, letter-writers receive no compensation for writing a letter and normally are not even told about the outcome of the case they spent time on. In addition, even though schools try their best to preserve secrecy, the candidates sometimes do find out the identities of the letter-writers and what they said in their letters. Some schools have to respond to Freedom Of Information Act (FOIA) requests; at others, staff or faculty on the committee have been known to share details from the letters with candidates, especially if the letter contains anything negative.

In other words, when someone is asked to write a letter evaluating a tenure case, she is being asked to spend a day or two of her time working hard for no compensation, with a chance that some nice person will hate her forever if she writes anything negative. And she can be asked ten or fifteen times to write such letters in a given academic year. The dilemma for scholars who are asked to write letters is that if they don't agree to write a letter, they can be sending a negative signal about the candidate's quality. Since faculty really don't want to send negative signals about someone who deserves to be promoted, most faculty will write letters for candidates who they think have very strong records, but they are likely to be reluctant to do so for weaker candidates. It is painful to write negative letters, and there can be ramifications of writing one if the university does not keep it secret. These reasons for a senior scholar's reluctance to write letters for tenure candidates are, of course, known to department heads and people on tenure committees. Nevertheless, an inability to find senior scholars with good reputations who will agree to write for a candidate is commonly taken as a bad signal about the candidate's quality.

Once the letters are written, they go to the committees evaluating the candidate, usually at the departmental, college, and university levels.[5] Within departments, the senior faculty normally know pretty well what the profession thinks of their junior colleagues, and the letters most often confirm what the senior faculty already know. Outside letters are more important at the college and university levels, where the candidates coming up for promotion are usually not well known to the people on the committee. The scholars on these committees are mostly from fields different from the candidate's, so normally they don't know much

5. This policy varies across universities. Some do not allow most faculty members to read the outside letters, some do not have a college committee but allow all faculty to vote on the tenure cases, and some (like Ohio State) do not have a university committee.

about the people writing the letters except their title and a few qualifications, such as whether the letter-writer edits a major journal. Since outside letters are mostly positive (remember, no one ever wants to write a negative letter), committees tend to focus more on the university the letter-writer is from and whether there is anything at all negative in the letter, rather than on any detailed comments about the candidate's papers.

In light of all these factors, I would recommend the following to candidates as the optimal strategy for picking names of letter-writers. First of all, pick people who can evaluate your work. Second, pick people who you know and who seem to like you and your work. Third, pick people whose personalities are more easygoing and positive. Remember that there are some academics who think that "She's okay" is high praise, but the people reading this person's letter, being unfamiliar with their personality, could view such a comment negatively.

Fourth, think about how distinguished the person looks from the perspective of a potential tenure committee member, especially one from another department. A senior scholar at a good university who hasn't published much lately is likely to look much better than an up-and-comer who has a less fancy title but is up to date about the literature you work in. In addition, even though a department may be very strong in the candidate's field, if the letter-writer's university is not well thought of in the field of the person reading the letter, even a positive letter will have less impact on his opinion of the case. Therefore, it is a good idea to select names of scholars from universities that are highly ranked in many fields, not just the candidate's field.

Fifth, avoid any appearance of conflicts, even if they are not severe enough to bother your department. Coauthors and advisers are out, and I would recommend avoiding even people who weren't on your thesis committee but taught you in graduate school. The impression you want to give to the tenure committee is that there are many excellent scholars who like your work. If you include people who committee members think might be biased about you and your work, then their inference might be that there are no unbiased scholars who would have been willing to write a strong letter on your behalf.

If the Review Does Not Go Well

THE THIRD- OR FOURTH-YEAR ASSISTANT PROFESSOR RE-
VIEW. The main purpose of this review is to provide junior faculty with
feedback on their performance in their first few years. Ideally, this review gives junior faculty a chance to correct any deficiencies so that they
can have a better shot at earning tenure a few years later. Under certain
circumstances, however, some junior faculty are not renewed at the assistant professor review, though nonrenewals at this stage are rare at
most schools. Usually it is only faculty members who have done very
little research or are exceptionally bad in the classroom who are not
renewed at the review prior to the tenure decision.

Even though most faculty are renewed at this stage, the feedback they
receive can be harsh and upsetting. Senior faculty try to give the scholar
up for review an honest assessment of what they have to do to earn
tenure and to suggest specific changes that could help her do a better
job. Sometimes these suggestions are no surprise to the person up for
review. For instance, a common message is: "You have to publish your
papers," or "You have to improve your teaching ratings." But some feedback is more substantive. In our department we try to be as specific as
possible; we tell the faculty member which of her new projects we consider to be most promising, and whether she is making any mistakes in
how she is going about her job. For example, a junior faculty member
may be starting too many or too few new papers, traveling too much or
too little, or making correctable mistakes in the classroom, such as
pitching the class at too high a level or trying to cover too much
material.

After receiving the feedback, it is important for the candidate to be
honest with herself. Does she think she has a reasonable chance of getting tenure given the feedback she received? If so, does she want to
spend her life at this particular university? Is she enjoying herself
enough and being sufficiently productive that it makes sense to stay
longer at the current job even if she doesn't expect to be promoted?
Does she agree with the review committee's specific criticisms of her
work?

These reviews are a natural time to reflect on your career and think about strategies for the future. Most of the time, even if the review is negative, the right thing to do is to stay at your school through the tenure review, assuming that you are relatively happy and productive there. But you should be honest about what was said in the review. I know of several junior faculty members who misinterpreted negative reviews and bought a big house immediately after receiving them, only to lose money when they had to sell the house a few years later following an unsuccessful tenure review.

Sometimes, however, following a slow start and a negative review, it can be stressful to stay at the place that provided such feedback. In this situation, a move to a new environment with a fresh clock can rejuvenate a career. At this stage, it would probably be a mistake for a junior faculty member to send out a mass mailing of her résumé to many schools. A mass mailing makes her job search public, so she would have to be in the difficult position of her colleagues knowing about an unsuccessful job search if she decides not to move. For this reason, if a young scholar wants to move midway through her time as a junior faculty member, a sensible approach is to contact departments that already know her and have shown an interest in the past. She should try to do so as quietly as possible to minimize gossip among her current colleagues.

THE TENURE REVIEW. Unlike the review in the third or fourth year, the tenure review is an up-or-out decision. If the university promotes a faculty member, then she has a lifetime contract. If it does not, then she has a year to find a new job. When someone is denied tenure, word spreads pretty quickly, and the profession knows that the person will be looking for a new job. Consequently, the right strategy when denied tenure is to do a global search and to consider all possibilities.

One thing that can be difficult for people who are denied tenure is maintaining a reasonably professional relationship with their senior colleagues. Being denied tenure is extremely stressful and upsetting, especially when the faculty member truly believes that she deserves to be promoted. It is only natural to speculate on the people who drove the decision to deny tenure and to take it out on them. However, a scholar must try to do what is best for her career at this difficult time in her life, even if it means hiding her feelings about the decision from everyone except her closest friends. Some faculty complain publicly and loudly about tenure denials. Such complaining rarely serves any productive purpose. To other schools that hear about it (and they surely will), that person will come across as a complainer who is likely to be a poor colleague.

There are two things that anyone who is denied tenure must realize. First, the vast majority of tenure denials are not personal but professional. Senior faculty are most likely to deny tenure because they did not like either the quality or quantity of the candidate's papers, or because of some other issue regarding her research or teaching. Sometimes tenure denials have to do with service: for example, some schools expect a minimum amount of time spent on their campus before they are ready to give a person a lifetime contract.

Second, regardless of the reason for the denial, it is extremely helpful to someone denied tenure to have their senior colleagues say good things about them. Whichever school is thinking of hiring her in the future will almost certainly call someone at the school that denied her tenure and ask why she was denied. If the answer is: "She is a great colleague and teacher but didn't quite have enough to meet our standards," she has a good chance of being considered seriously for a job at the other (usually lower-ranked) university. If the answer is: "She has published some papers but is an extremely difficult colleague, and some faculty thought there were problems with these papers even though they were published," her chances become much lower.

THE FULL PROFESSOR REVIEW. The final promotion in a scholar's career, unless she is nominated for an endowed professorship or chair, is to full professor. The important thing to remember about full professor promotions is that they don't have to occur at a particular point in an academic career. Some people remain an associate professor their entire career and live perfectly happy lives. But most faculty would like to become a full professor at some point, and most departments would like to eventually promote all of their research-active tenured faculty to full professor.

Therefore, it is best if you and your colleagues agree on what is required for promotion to full professor. Departments should not put people up for full professor unless they plan on promoting them, assuming that the letters are fine and that no negative surprises about teaching or ethical issues come up in the review process. And it is usually a mistake to push your department to promote you to full professor before the department is ready. Doing so can create unnecessary conflict and hard feelings. Most of the time, if you wait, you will be promoted in a few years anyway.

Keeping Life Interesting after Tenure

One thing that always surprises me about academia is the number of tenured faculty who become very bitter about their job. I have always thought that being a professor was one of the greatest jobs in the world. Being a tenured professor is the dream job of most people who enter graduate school. How can so many people who get their dream job end up so unhappy with it? Is there anything they could have done that would have made them happier at work?

Most faculty members who end up bitter have experienced something like the following: He published three or four papers related to his dissertation and received tenure in his late thirties. He continued to write similar papers, but they appeared in lower-ranked journals because his approach to research had become less novel and outsiders were beginning to think of him as a bit dated. After a few rejections from top journals, he started being critical of the profession for its taste in research, which was changing from the way research had been done when he was a graduate student. Meanwhile, in his own department or college, he had a disagreement with a department chair, who took it out on him by giving him a bad teaching assignment, assigning him a bad office, or taking resources away from him (summer money, access to an RA, and so on). He started complaining about his situation to everyone he knew, and eventually his complaining got back to the department chair.

If this faculty member was tenured when he was in his late thirties, he could have become bitter by his forties. By this time, he probably did not have many options to move to another research university nearly as good as the one where he currently taught. He remained on the faculty for twenty or thirty more years, over which time he found it increasingly difficult to contribute in a productive manner.

The sad fact is that this situation is entirely preventable. Anyone who is smart enough to get a PhD and earn tenure is capable of being a valuable member of the faculty for his entire career. Academics are almost always bright, hardworking scholars when they complete their degree and when they earn tenure. They will end up much happier over the long run if they find a niche, continue to do interesting work, and contribute to their university and society throughout their lives. This interesting work could be new research, but it doesn't have to be. Many other kinds of opportunities can become important parts of an academic's professional life as well.

Academics should always be thinking of ways to expand their horizons and branch out to do new things that will keep them busy. All people, and especially academics, do best when continually given new challenges. But many faculty fall into the trap of teaching the same courses over and over again and writing essentially the same paper over and over again. Those who fall into this rut have forgotten about the two principles laid out at the beginning of this chapter: faculty should always be thinking about research and nonresearch opportunities that they are likely to have access to in the future. To make these opportunities realistic, faculty must invest throughout their careers in the capital to pursue the ones they find appealing.

Some faculty continue to focus on research throughout their career. I fall into this category myself. I am somewhat of an outlier in that I have become more interested in research and in understanding financial markets as I have gotten older. The typical pattern, however, is the opposite: interest in research peaks in most academics' younger years and their research slows down as they focus on other things later in life. Some faculty move into administration as they get older. There is always a shortage of good administrators in academia, and providing leadership in an administrative position is an excellent way to contribute to a university. Other faculty get more excited about teaching as they get older. Some write textbooks and teach extra courses, sometimes for additional compensation. Some scholars become "public intellectuals" who contribute to the public discourse in their area of expertise. Consulting is yet another way that an academic can keep life interesting. When expertise in a particular area is in high demand by the private sector or the government, having established yourself as an expert can lead to a rewarding and profitable consulting business.

If you focus your professional life on any of these (or other) options, you can avoid falling into a rut and not enjoying your professional life. But pursuing any of these options requires investment in the right kind of capital. To remain capable of state-of-the-art research, you must work to keep up with the latest techniques and issues that others care about. You also have to ensure that your research does not get stale and stay open to letting your research evolve in new directions over time.

To become a successful administrator, you should demonstrate interest in whatever positions come up. Taking one of these less visible positions—such as serving as the assistant head of a small program in your department, or as adviser to a student group—is important as a way to gain experience. Being good at such positions can pave the way to becoming a department head or dean later in your career.

Keeping your career fresh and interesting in these ways takes time and effort. Earning income through extra teaching requires an up-front investment in developing a unique course and marketing that course. Many people plan to write a textbook "someday," but most never get around to such a major time commitment. The same goes for writing newspaper columns about current events and attempting to become a public intellectual.

Finally, consulting opportunities usually don't appear magically. An academic who wishes to establish a consulting business usually has to develop it over time by investing in specialized knowledge that practitioners are willing to pay for, and by cultivating relationships with industry professionals that will allow her to exploit this knowledge.

A scholar should learn early on in her career that "you are the CEO of your own life." She will be happiest if she goes about her career with a purpose, rather than just drifting toward whatever seems interesting at the time. She should always spend time thinking about what her options are likely to be in the future, and what capital will be necessary to pursue the options she finds attractive. Investments in human capital that will make life more interesting in the future are likely to be well worth their cost.

Epilogue

Academic Success beyond the PhD

AS ACADEMICS, we receive little training in how to prepare for our careers. We do learn much in graduate school about the *science* of scholarship; for an economist, that consists mostly of learning economic theory, mastering econometrics, and becoming familiar with the literatures in the applied fields. However, we typically learn much of what we need to know to be a successful academic in a haphazard, word-of-mouth fashion. For example, almost every economics graduate student knows how to maximize a likelihood function and understands the conditions necessary for an instrument to be valid. But perhaps surprisingly, an astonishingly high fraction of them do not know how to decide which results to report, how to present them so that a reader can easily tell what they have done, or how to explain their results to a reader who is not a specialist in the subfield.

Much of what academics do can best be described as a *craft*. Like other kinds of craftsmanship, scholarly work is a combination of time-tested techniques, strategic thinking, ethics, and imagination. These things can be learned, but they tend to be acquired in a haphazard manner. What I have attempted to do in this book is to distill my own views of the craftsmanship of an academic working in the economics-based social sciences. While others will undoubtedly disagree with some of what I suggest, I am confident that the vast majority of readers will concur with the book's main thesis—that most scholars would be better off spending much more time thinking about the nuts and bolts of writing their papers, how these papers fit into their research portfolio, and the development of their careers.

I have made a number of recommendations throughout the book. All are designed to help scholars produce more influential research and have more satisfying careers. I thought it might be helpful to summarize what I thought were the most important suggestions.

A (Baker's) Dozen Points to Remember

1) Be an academic "hunter." Take a question you want to know the answer to and look for approaches that will allow you to provide insights into it. Don't wait for topics to come to you; instead, seek out research questions on issues that fascinate you. Make a "market map" of all the work that has been done around the issue you want to study and use it to determine the way that is likely to provide the most novel insights into the topic.

2) Try to choose research projects that are related to one another and form a coherent research program. Your goal should be to develop a portfolio of papers that establish your reputation as one of the top scholars in an important subfield. Remember that there is a limit on how many papers any of us can work on at any point in time. The opportunity cost of starting a project can be substantial, especially if a scholar is near her capacity so that starting a project today limits her ability to start others in the future.

3) Everyone has unique knowledge and talents. Start research projects that take advantage of what you are good at. In addition, always be open to learning new areas and acquiring new skills. Awareness of what the best young faculty in your area are working on and the tools they are using will be a useful guide for deciding on a direction to take your research.

4) Do not think about "research" and "write-up" as separate activities. The write-up *is* your research. A huge fraction of the time you spend on your paper should be on the writing and presentation of your analysis. The success or failure of a particular

research project will depend not only on the modeling and empirical results but also on how you motivate the work, explain your results to a reader, and interpret them appropriately.

5) Assume that your target reader will spend a fixed amount of time on your paper regardless of its length. Write the paper so that this reader spends her time focusing on what you want her to think about: the analysis *you* do and the implications of *your* work. Don't spend too much time on lengthy literature reviews, technical details that do not affect the paper's main idea, or discussions that readers will find confusing rather than illuminating. Otherwise, readers will become distracted and spend less time thinking about your paper's insights.

6) The introduction is the most important part of an academic paper because it is the only part that many readers will look at. Therefore, space in the introduction is precious and the opportunity cost of wasting it is high. The introduction to your paper should accomplish the following (and only the following): (1) grab the reader's attention; (2) state the question you are asking; (3) identify the approach you use; (4) report the results; (5) provide your interpretation of the results; (6) discuss other implications of the results; and (7) provide an outline of the paper.

7) The description of data and methods has to be sufficiently detailed to allow a doctoral student on the other side of the globe to replicate your results. But this description should be written in prose interesting enough to keep a typical reader from getting bored. Put only what most readers will find interesting in the main body of the paper. Details required for replication but for not an understanding of the paper's analysis should be placed in appendices.

8) The keys to a good seminar presentation are communication and control. You must convey the ideas of your paper to a typical seminar participant, who is not likely to be a specialist in your subfield. You also have to control the audience and not let them bog down your presentation with requests for clarification

or discussions that are unrelated to your paper. Be sure to get to the main points you want to make early in the seminar and *finish on time*. The purpose of the slide deck is to keep the audience's attention where you want it and to provide them with details. Keep the slides clean, do not put too much information on each one, and use a large, readable font. At the end of the talk, you want people talking about what they have learned from your paper. If instead they are talking about how cool your slides are or are rehashing the argument you got into with one of the faculty attending the talk, you have probably missed an opportunity to increase your paper's impact.

9) It is inefficient to give your paper to everyone you know at the same time. Instead, send papers out sequentially. First ask one or two close friends you can trust to read your paper carefully. Make revisions based on their reactions and then ask for feedback from a few more people. Continue the process, addressing comments as you receive them. Eventually, the feedback will reach the point of diminishing returns and become less useful. Only at this point should you make a paper publicly available and post it online.

10) View journal submissions as a continuation of the revision process. Don't submit a paper to a journal until it is as strong as you are capable of making it. Be realistic about your choice of journal; not every good paper belongs in the *American Economic Review*. Take rejections as a productive way to improve your paper. If the editor gives you an opportunity to revise the paper, take advantage of it. Carefully address each point the referees and editors have raised, and explain your responses in your revision document. Hopefully your paper will eventually be published in a good journal.

11) An important factor in a doctoral student's success is her attitude toward research and her relationships within her department. A student should think about research ideas from the day she arrives on campus and start getting involved in research as soon as possible. A graduate student's relationships with the

faculty and also with her fellow students are a key element of her success. The best doctoral students usually provide valuable help to other students on their research, which is one reason why in many departments the highest-quality dissertations tend to cluster in particular years. Graduate school is *not* a zero-sum game in which success for one student comes at the expense of other students.

12) Always think about potential new professional opportunities, and acquire the human capital necessary to move your career in the direction that seems most exciting to you. These may be research-related opportunities that could allow you to extend your earlier work or move into a promising new area. But they can also come in the form of a chance to move into academic administration, to write textbooks or policy pieces for the general public, or to apply your expertise in the private or government sector. Academics should strive not to let their lives become boring by teaching the same classes over and over without taking on new challenges.

13) Academia can be a wonderful career. But much more so than other professions, the scholarly life is only what you make of it. Take advantage of the good parts and avoid the bad parts. Spend your life making a difference in your students' lives, studying interesting problems, becoming good friends with colleagues both at your university and elsewhere, and traveling the world to visit other universities and to present your research. Avoid fighting with your colleagues and deans, complaining about the inevitable inequities and inefficiencies in your university, and letting the annoying students bother you too much. Never forget that you are the CEO of your own life. Make sure it is an interesting and enjoyable one!

BIBLIOGRAPHY

Akerlof, G. A. 1970. "The Market for 'Lemons': Quality Uncertainty and the Market Mechanism." *Quarterly Journal of Economics* 84(3): 488–500.

Almeida, H., M. Campello, and M. S. Weisbach. 2004. "The Cash Flow Sensitivity of Cash." *Journal of Finance* 59(4): 1777–1804.

Amano-Patiño, N., E. Faraglia, C. Giannitsarou, and Z. Hasna. 2020. "Who Is Doing New Research in the Time of COVID-19? Not the Female Economists." Working paper. VoxEU, Center for Economic and Policy Research (May 2). https://voxeu.org/article/who-doing -new-research-time-covid-19-not-female-economists.

Andrews, I., and M. Kasy. 2019. "Identification of and Correction for Publication Bias." *American Economic Review* 109(8): 2766–94.

Angrist, J. D., and J.-S. Pischke. 2008. *Mostly Harmless Econometrics: An Empiricist's Companion.* Princeton University Press.

Antecol, H., K. Bedard, and J. Stearns. 2018. "Equal but Inequitable: Who Benefits from Gender-Neutral Tenure Clock Stopping Policies." *American Economic Review* 108(9): 2420–41.

Ashenfelter, O., and A. Krueger. 1992. "Estimates of the Economic Return to Schooling from a New Sample of Twins." *American Economic Review* 84(5): 1157–83.

Axelson, U., P. Strömberg, and M. S. Weisbach. 2009. "Why Are Buyouts Leveraged? The Financial Structure of Private Equity Firms." *Journal of Finance* 64: 1549–82.

Backhouse, R. E., and B. Cherrier. 2017. "The Age of the Applied Economist: The Transformation of Economics since the 1970s." *History of Political Economy* 49: 1–33.

Barberis, N., A. Shleifer, and J. Wurgler. 2005. "Comovement." *Journal of Financial Economics* 75(2): 283–317.

Bayer, A., and C. E. Rouse. 2016. "Diversity in the Economics Profession: A New Attack on an Old Problem." *Journal of Economic Perspectives* 30: 221–42.

Benmelech, E. 2009. "Asset Salability and Debt Maturity: Evidence from Nineteenth-Century American Railroads" *Review of Financial Studies* 22(4): 1545–84.

Berk, J. B., C. R. Harvey, and D. Hirshleifer. 2017. "How to Write an Effective Referee Report and Improve the Scientific Review Process." *Journal of Economic Perspectives* 31(1): 231–44.

Bernheim, B. D., A. Shleifer, and L. H. Summers. 1985. "The Strategic Bequest Motive." *Journal of Labor Economics* 93: 1046–76.

Berry, S., J. Levinsohn, and A. Pakes. 1995. "Automobile Prices in Market Equilibrium." *Econometrica* 63(4): 841–90.

Bertrand, M., and S. Mullanaithan. 2004. "Are Emily and Greg More Employable than Lakisha and Jamal? A Field Experiment on Labor Market Discrimination." *American Economic Review* 94(4): 991–1013.

Blanco-Perez, C., and A. Brodeur. 2020. "Publication Bias and Editorial Statement on Negative Findings." *Economic Journal* 130: 1226–47.

Bordalo, P., K. Coffman, N. Gennaioli, and A. Shleifer. 2016. "Stereotypes." *Quarterly Journal of Economics* 131(4): 1753–94.

Butler, A., and T. Crack. 2019. "A Rookie's Guide to the Academic Job Market in Finance: The Labor Market for Lemons." August 7. Available at SSRN: https://ssrn.com/abstract=3433785.

Card, D., and DellaVigna, S. 2013. "Nine Facts about Top Journals in Economics." *Journal of Economic Literature* 51(1): 144–61.

Card, D., S. DellaVigna, P. Funk, and N. Iriberri. 2019. "Are Referees and Editors in Economics Gender Neutral?" Working paper. September. https://economics.harvard.edu/files/economics/files/ms30505.pdf.

Card, D., and Krueger, A. B. 2000. "Minimum Wages and Employment: A Case Study of the Fast Food Industry in New Jersey and Pennsylvania." *American Economic Review* 84(4): 772–93.

Carleton, W. T., J. M. Nelson, and M. S. Weisbach. 1998. "The Influence of Institutions on Corporate Governance through Private Negotiations: Evidence from TIAA-CREF." *Journal of Finance* 53(4): 1335–62.

Catton, B. 1952. *Glory Road.* Anchor Books.

———. 1953. *A Stillness at Appomattox.* Anchor Books.

Cawley, J. 2018. "A Guide (and Advice) for Economists on the US Junior Academic Job Market: 2018–2019 Edition." September 21. https://www.aeaweb.org/content/file?id=869.

Churchill, W., and R. M. Langworth. 2008. *Churchill by Himself: The Life, Times, and Opinions of Winston Churchill in His Own Words.* Ebury.

Coase, R. H. 1937. "The Nature of the Firm." *Economica* 4(16): 386–405.

———. 1960. "The Problem of Social Cost." *Journal of Law and Economics* 3: 1–44.

Cochrane, J. H. 2005. "Writing Tips for PhD Students." June 8. https://static1.squarespace.com/static/5e6033a4ea02d801f37e15bb/t/5eda74919c44fa5f87452697/1591374993570/phd_paper_writing.pdf.

Conway, J. H., and A. Soifer. 2005. "Covering a Triangle with Triangles." *American Mathematical Monthly* 112(1): 78.

DeAngelo, H., and L. DeAngelo. 1985. "Managerial Ownership of Voting Rights: A Study of Corporations with Dual Classes of Common Stock." *Journal of Financial Economics* 14(1): 33–69.

———. 1991. "Union Negotiations and Corporate Policy: A Study of Labor Concessions in the Domestic Steel Industry in the 1980s." *Journal of Financial Economics* 30(1): 3–43.

Djankov, S., R. La Porta, F. Lopez-de-Silanes, and A. Shleifer. 2003. "Courts." *Quarterly Journal of Economics* 118(2): 453–517.

Durlauf, S. N., and J. J. Heckman. 2020. "Comment on Roland Fryer's 'An Empirical Analysis of Racial Differences in Police Use of Force,'" *Journal of Political Economy* 128: 3998–4002.

Erel, I., Y. Jang, and M. S. Weisbach. Forthcoming. "The Corporate Finance of Multinational Firms." In *Multinational Corporations in a Changing Global Economy*, edited by F. Foley, J. Hines, and D. Wessel. Brookings Institution.

Erel, I., B. Julio, W. Kim, and M. S. Weisbach. 2012. "Macroeconomic Conditions and Capital Raising." *Review of Financial Studies* 25(2): 341–76.

Erel, I., L. H. Stern, C. Tan, and M. S. Weisbach. Forthcoming. "Selecting Directors Using Machine Learning." *Review of Financial Studies*.

Fanelli, D. 2012. "Negative Results Are Disappearing from Most Disciplines and Countries." *Scientometrics* 90(2012): 891–904.

Friedman, M. 1970. "The Social Responsibility of Business Is to Increase Its Profits." *New York Times Magazine*, September 13.

Fryer, R. G., Jr. 2019. "An Empirical Analysis of Racial Differences in Police Use of Force." *Journal of Political Economy* 127: 1210–61.

Gans, J. S., and G. B. Shepherd. 1994. "How Are the Mighty Fallen: Rejected Classic Articles by Leading Economists." *Journal of Economic Perspectives* 8(1): 165–79.

Ge, S., and M. S. Weisbach. Forthcoming. "The Role of Financial Conditions in Portfolio Choices: The Case of Insurers." *Journal of Financial Economics*.

Goldin, C., and C. Rouse. 2000. "Orchestrating Impartiality: The Impact of 'Blind' Auditions on Female Musicians." *American Economic Review* 90(4): 715–41.

Grossman, S. J., and O. D. Hart. 1980. "Takeover Bids, the Free-Rider Problem, and the Theory of the Corporation." *Bell Journal of Economics* 11(1): 42–64.

Hall, R., and M. Piazzesi. 2001. "Bob Hall's (MP: Wonderful) Job Market Advice for Stanford Economics Students." https://web.stanford.edu/~niederle/Advice_Bob_Hall.pdf.

Harvey, C. R. 2018. "The Scientific Outlook in Financial Economics." *Journal of Finance* 72(4): 1399–1440.

Hausman, J. A. 1978. "Specification Tests in Econometrics." *Econometrica* 46(6): 1251–71.

Hermalin, B. E., and M. S. Weisbach. 1988. "The Determinants of Board Composition." *RAND Journal of Economics* 19(4): 589–605.

———. 1991. "The Effects of Board Composition and Direct Incentives on Firm Performance." *Financial Management* 20(4): 101–12.

Herndon, T., M. Ash, and R. Pollin. 2014. "Does High Public Debt Consistently Stifle Economic Growth? A Critique of Renhart and Rogoff." *Cambridge Journal of Economics* 38: 257–79.

Hou, K., C. Xue, and L. Zhang. 2020. "Replicating Anomalies." *Review of Financial Studies* 33(5): 2019–2133.

Iliev, P. 2016. "Finance Job Market Advice." June 11. Available at SSRN: https://ssrn.com/abstract=2779200.

Ju, N., R. Parrino, A. M. Poteshman, and M. S. Weisbach. 2005. "Horses and Rabbits? Trade-off Theory and Optimal Capital Structure." *Journal of Financial and Quantitative Analysis* 40(2): 259–81.

Julio, B., W. Kim, and M. Weisbach. 2007. "What Determines the Structure of Corporate Debt Issues?" Working Paper Number 13706. National Bureau of Economic Research (December).

Kahneman, D. 2011. *Thinking, Fast and Slow*. Farrar, Straus and Giroux.

Kaplan, S. 1989. "The Effect of Management Buyouts on Operating Performance and Value." *Journal of Financial Economics* 24(2): 217–54.

Kay, J., and M. King. 2020. *Radical Uncertainty: Decision-Making beyond the Numbers.* W. W. Norton & Co.

Keynes, J. M. 1936. *The General Theory of Employment, Interest, and Money.* Palgrave Macmillan.

Kim, W., and M. S. Weisbach. 2008. "Motivations for Public Equity Offers: An International Perspective." *Journal of Financial Economics* 87(2): 281–307.

Koudijs, P. 2016. "The Boats That Did Not Sail: Asset Price Volatility in a Natural Experiment." *Journal of Finance* 71(3): 1185–1226.

Krugman, P. R. 1979. "Increasing Returns, Monopolistic Competition, and International Trade." *Journal of International Economics* 9(4): 469–79.

Laibson, D. N.d. "Tips for Job Market." https://economics.harvard.edu/files/economics/files/jobmarketadvicehandout.doc.pdf.

Leamer, E. E. 1983. "Let's Take the Con Out of Econometrics." *American Economic Review* 73(1): 31–43.

LeRoy, S. F., and R. D. Porter. 1981. "The Present Value Relation: Tests Based on Implied Variance Bounds." *Econometrica* 49(3): 555–74.

Lewis, M. 2016. *The Undoing Project.* W. W. Norton.

May, A. M., M. G. McGarvey, and R. Whaples. 2014. "Are Disagreements among Male and Female Economists Marginal at Best? A Survey of AEA Members and Their Views on Economics and Economic Policy." *Contemporary Economic Policy* 32 (1): 111–32.

McCloskey, D. N. 1998. *The Rhetoric of Economics.* University of Wisconsin Press.

Mengel, F., J. Sauermann, and U. Zölitz. 2017. "Gender Bias in Teaching Evaluations." IZA Discussion Paper. Institute for the Study of Labor (September). http://ulfzoelitz.com/wp-content/uploads/JEEA-gender-bias.pdf.

Miller, M. H. 1977. "Debt and Taxes." *Journal of Finance* 32(2): 261–75.

Nadauld, T. D., and S. M. Sherlund. 2013. "The Impact of Securitization on the Expansion of Subprime Credit." *Journal of Financial Economics* 107(2): 454–76.

Nadauld, T. D., and M. S. Weisbach. 2012. "Did Securitization Affect the Cost of Corporate Debt?" *Journal of Financial Economics* 105(2): 332–52.

Nasar, S. 1998. *A Beautiful Mind.* Simon & Schuster.

———. 2011. *Grand Pursuit: The Story of Economic Genius.* Simon & Schuster.

Neumark, D., and W. Wascher. 2006. "Minimum Wages and Employment: A Review of Evidence from the New Minimum Wage Research." Working Paper 12663. National Bureau of Economic Research.

———. 2008. *Minimum Wages.* MIT Press.

Pulvino, T. C. 1998. "Do Asset Fire Sales Exist? An Empirical Investigation of Commercial Aircraft Transactions." *Journal of Finance* 53(3): 939–78.

Reinhart, C. M., and K. S. Rogoff. 2010. "Growth in a Time of Debt." *American Economic Review Papers and Proceedings* 100: 573–78.

Roberts, A. 2014. *Napoleon: A Life.* Penguin Books.

Schwartz-Ziv, M., and M. S. Weisbach. 2013. "What Do Boards Really Do? Evidence from Minutes of Board Meetings." *Journal of Financial Economics* 108(2): 349–66.

Shapiro, Jesse. N.d. "How to Give an Applied Micro Talk: Unauthoritative Notes." https://www.brown.edu/Research/Shapiro/pdfs/applied_micro_slides.pdf.

Sherman, M. G., and H. Tookes. 2019. "Female Representation in the Academic Finance Profession." Working paper. August. http://affectfinance.org/wp-content/uploads/2019/08/ShermanTookes_Aug16_2019-1.pdf.

Shiller, R. J. 1981. "Do Stock Prices Move Too Much to Be Justified by Subsequent Changes in Dividends?" *American Economic Review* 71(3): 421–36.

Shleifer, A., and R. W. Vishny. 1986. "Large Shareholders and Corporate Control." *Journal of Political Economy* 94(3, part 1): 461–88.

———. 1993. "Corruption." *Quarterly Journal of Economics* 108(3): 599–617.

Smith, A. 1776. *An Inquiry into the Nature and Causes of the Wealth of Nations*. London: printed for W. Strahan, and T. Cadell.

Soifer, A. 2010. "Building a Bridge III: From Problems of Mathematical Olympiads to Open Problems of Mathematics." *Mathematics Competitions* 23(1): 27–38.

Stephens, C. P., and M. S. Weisbach. 1998. "Actual Share Reacquisitions in Open-Market Repurchase Programs." *Journal of Finance* 53(1): 313–33.

Stock, W. A., T. A. Finegan, and J. J. Siegfried. 2006. "Attrition in Economics PhD Programs." *American Economic Review* 96(2): 458–66.

Strunk, W., and E. B. White. 1999. *The Elements of Style*. Allyn & Bacon.

Thomson, W. 2001. *Guide for the Young Economist*. MIT Press.

Tufte, E. R. 2001. *The Visual Display of Quantitative Information*. Graphics Press.

Upper, D. (1974). "The Unsuccessful Self-treatment of a Case of 'Writer's Block,'" *Journal of Applied Behavior Analysis* 7(3): 497.

Weisbach, M. S. 1988. "Outside Directors and CEO Turnover." *Journal of Financial Economics* 20 (1): 431–60.

Wiles, A. 1995. "Modular Elliptic Curves and Fermat's Last Theorem." *Annals of Mathematics* 141(3): 443–551.

Wu, A. 2018. "Gendered Language on the Economics Job Rumors Forum." *American Economic Review* 108: 175–79.

———. 2020. "Gender Bias in Rumors among Professionals: An Identity-Based Interpretation." *Review of Economics and Statistics* 102(5): 867–80.

Wu, D.-M. 1973. "Alternative Tests of Independence between Stochastic Regressors and Disturbances." *Econometrica* 41(4): 733–50.

Zinsser, W. 2016. *On Writing Well: The Classic Guide to Writing Nonfiction*. Harper Perennial.

Zwick, E. N.d. "How I Learned to Stop Worrying and Love the Job Market." http://www.ericzwick.com/public_goods/love_the_market.pdf.

INDEX

abstraction, 201

abstracts, 55, 59–60, 62, 71–73, 171

accessibility, 63, 126

accounting, 11

Accounting Review, 11

acronyms, 126

administration, as career, 276–77, 283

advisers: for dissertation, 218–21, 231–34; during job search, 252–53

agency theory, 125

Akerlof, George, 70–71

Allied Social Sciences Association, 252

Amazon reviews, as database, 94

American Economic Association, 235

American Economic Review, 10, 62, 165

American Mathematical Monthly, 117

Angrist, Joshua, 215

"animal spirits," 114

anomalies, in financial trading, 96n3

appendices, 79, 96, 104, 111–12, 281; online, 65, 92–93, 107, 172, 191

Ash, Michael, 66

Ashenfelter, Orley, 29

Asians, in academia, 229–30

asset pricing, 9

audience: grabbing attention of, 76; non-academic, 209; for presentations, 139–41; for research papers, 62, 65, 89

Backhouse, Roger, 8

Bayesian statistics, 250

A Beautiful Mind (Nasar), 122–23

behavioral economics, 9, 167

Bertrand, Marianne, 216

beta estimates, 105–6

bias, in academic research, 235–36

Black, Fischer, 8

Blacks, in academia, 225–26

boards of directors, 77, 95, 98, 205

brevity, 60, 75, 80, 117

"brown bag" workshops, 157–58, 223

business plans, 13

business schools, 6, 11, 13, 63

capacity for work, 12–13, 42, 44–45, 280

Card, David, 28, 41

Catton, Bruce, 122

causal inference, 28, 81

Cherrier, Béatrice, 8

child care, 227–28

China, 6

Churchill, Winston, 56

clarity, 15, 40, 58, 61–62, 124

Coase, Ronald, 2–3

coauthors, 45–49, 155–56; avoiding misunderstandings with, 79; faculty and students as, 245; in revise and resubmit (R&R) process, 189

Cochrane, John, 32, 123

code, posting of, 103

collegiality, 236, 244–45, 267, 282–83

comma splices, 129

comparative advantage, 31, 213

competition, with fellow students, 204–5, 239, 245

conclusions, in research papers, 66–67, 97–98

conferences: acceptance rates of, 54, 159; decorum at, 224; selection process of, 54–55, 62. *See also* presentations
consulting, 277
Conway, John, 117
copy editing, 194–95
corporate finance, 30, 72, 76, 80, 214–15
corporate governance, 30, 33, 77, 95, 98, 125, 205
cover letters, in journal submissions, 175
Covid-19 epidemic, 32, 227
craft, in academic careers, 279
creativity, 12, 35, 43–44, 200, 217, 220, 234, 238–39
crediting others, 5, 18, 55, 56, 64, 77; to excess, 84–85; in literature reviews, x, 84–85, 88–92, 147, 281
criticism, 15, 161, 182; anticipating, 81; in promotion process, 272–73. *See also* rejections

Dana, Jim, 222–23
databases, 7–8, 94, 250
data description, 94–97
data sources, 216–17, 222–23
deadlines: in job search, 253–54; self-imposed, 258
DeAngelo, Harry, 111–12
DeAngelo, Linda, 111–12
delays: in finishing dissertation, 237; in journal publishing, 10, 15, 43, 165, 179n8
Diamond, Peter, 240–41
discrimination, in academia, 225–30
discussants, 150–52, 163
dissertation, 200, 202, 206–10; advisers for, 218–21, 231–34; getting started on, 212; journal articles from, 259; as learning process, 234–35; in non-academic job market, 250; topics for, 30, 31, 35, 210, 214, 238–39
"dividend puzzle," 72
"Do Stock Prices Move Too Much to Be Justified by Subsequent Changes in Dividends" (Shiller), 69

dot-com boom, 32
Durlauf, Steven, 35

Econometrica, 10, 118, 119, 164, 165
Economics Job Market Rumors (EJMR), 228
editing: by coauthors, 12; by copy editors, 194–95; for non-native speakers, 131; overzealous, 99
Editorial Express, 174
efficient markets theory, 96n3, 114–15
empirical research, 99–115; data description in, 94; growing importance of, 7–8, 9, 250–51; introductions to, 81; models described in, 92; robustness testing in, 73, 103–4, "writing up" results of, 101–3, 120–21
English-language fluency, 5, 116, 120, 124, 130–31
Erel, Isil, 189
errors: typographical, 47, 57–58, 104, 118; resolving, 65–66
ethics: investigations into, 232n2; in research, 235–36
Euler, Leonhard, 1
evaluations, by students, 257
examples, to illustrate theories, 93
excess volatility, 69

Facebook, 162
faculty: advice for, 231–46; early career on, 257–65; interaction with, 206–8, 217–18, 224, 243–44; junior, 257–65; non-native, 263; "rookie market" for, 252–57, 261; "seasoned market" for, 260–65; visiting, 255; workload of, 177, 213, 232, 257. *See also* promotion; tenure
Fama, Gene, 8
family responsibilities, 227–28
Feldstein, Martin, 121
Fermat, Pierre de, 1
Fermat's Last Theorem, 1, 207
Financial Crisis of 2008, 7, 32, 215
follow-through, 14–15

footnotes, 85, 91, 125
Freedom of Information Act (FOIA), 270
Friedman, Milton, 86, 140
Fryer, Roland, 35
future research, suggestions for, 98

General Theory of Employment, Interest, and Money (Keynes), 77
Goldin, Claudia, 215–16
Goldman Sachs, 215
Gompers, Paul, 105
government jobs, 256
grades, 203–4
graduate study, 199–230; attrition rate in, 199n1; do's and don'ts of, 202–18; uncertainty in, 199–200
Grammarly, 128
Grand Pursuit (Nasar), 123
grantsmanship, 38
graphic information, 109–11
Grossman, Sanford, 85–86
"Growth in a Time of Debt" (Reinhart and Rogoff), 65

Hart, Oliver, 85–86
Harvey, Campbell, 96n3
Hausman, Jerry, 118
Heckman, James, 35
Hermalin, Ben, 205
Herndon, Thomas, 66
Hilbert, David, 1
Hispanics, in academia, 225–26
historical writing, 122
Hitchcock, Alfred, 70
Hong Kong, 6
human capital, ix–x, 5, 248, 260, 278, 283; expedited research linked to, 156; types of, 213–14; visibility as, 263

infrastructure funds, 151
INSEAD (Institut Européen d'Administration des Affaires), 6
interpreting results, 82, 112–15

introductions, x, 62; common mistakes in, 83–86; goals of, 75–83, 281; prominence of, 55, 59–60, 74, 171, 281; as research preparation, 41

jargon, 122, 124
Jensen, Mike, 8
job search: applications in, 253–54; flexibility in, 254–56; non-academic opportunities in, 250, 256–57, 258, 262; "rookie market" in, 252–57, 261; scope of, 255; "seasoned market" in, 260–65; third-party help in, 264–65
job talks, 141
John Bates Clark Award, 8
Jorgenson, Dale, 240
Journal of Accounting and Economics, 11
Journal of Accounting Research, 11
Journal of Applied Behavioral Analysis, 117
Journal of Finance, 10
Journal of Financial Economics, 10, 167n4
Journal of Labor Economics, 165
Journal of Political Economy, 10, 62, 165, 241
journals: acceptance rates of, 54; delays by, 10, 15, 43, 165, 179n8; general-interest vs. specialized, 62, 165–66, 178; hierarchy of, 6, 9–10, 16, 38–39, 55, 164, 166, 193–94; "impact factor" of, 165; quality vs. quantity of, 39; in research evaluation, 38; review process of, 54–55, 169–96; for senior vs. junior scholars, 46; specifications of, 175. *See also* research; revise and resubmits (R&Rs); submissions, to journals; writing
junior faculty, 257–65

Kahneman, Daniel, 27–28
Kaplan, Steve, 36, 105
Kay, John, 247–48
Keynes, John Maynard, 77, 114, 140
King, Mervyn, 247–48
Krueger, Alan, 28, 29, 41
Krugman, Paul, 214–15

labor economics, 215
"Large Shareholders and Corporate Control"
   (Shleifer and Vishny), 85
Latex, 145
law reviews, 164n2, 173n3
Leamer, E. E., 69
length, of research papers, 171–72
Lerner, Josh, 105
LeRoy, Stephen, 114
leveraged buyouts, 105
LinkedIn, as database, 94
liquidity, 77
literature reviews, x, 84–85, 88–92, 147, 281
London Business School, 6

machine learning, 7, 98, 250
macro-finance, 9
Mankiw, Greg, 241
"The Market for 'Lemons'" (Akerlof), 70
Massachusetts Institute of Technology
   (MIT), 4, 118, 205, 240–42
McCloskey, Deirdre, 123
MCMC (Markov chain Monte Carlo)
   methods, 250
Merton, Robert C., 8
Microsoft Word, 128
Miller, Merton, 8, 69–70
Minard, Charles Joseph, 109, 110, 111
motivation, in doctoral study, 237–39
minimum wage, 28, 41
Mullanaithan, Sendhil, 216
Murphy, Kevin, 214
"mystery novel" form of organization, 108

Napoleon Bonaparte, emperor of the
   French, 109–11
Nasar, Sylvia, 122–23
National Bureau of Economic Research
   (NBER), 4, 71, 141, 162, 224, 240, 242–43,
   244, 255
nervousness, 146–47
networking, 156–57, 158
New Classical Economics, 77

Nobel Prize in Economics, 2, 8n6, 35, 38, 115,
   215, 240
non-academic jobs, 250, 256–57, 258, 262
non-native faculty, 263
non-native speakers, 124, 130–31
novelty, 80

online appendices, 65, 92–93, 107, 172, 191
online posting, of research, 160–62
On Writing Well (Zinsser), 123
option pricing, 30
organizational economics, 2
outlines, in introductions, 83
"Outside Directors and CEO Turnover"
   (Weisbach), 69

Pakes, Ariel, 215
passive voice, 127
payout policy, 72
peer review, 10–11, 43, 54–56; author's
   suggestions for, 174–75; in journal
   submissions, 38, 39, 54, 55, 57–58, 91,
   99, 100, 115, 165–66, 169–70, 176; by
   junior vs. senior scholars, 176–77;
   overzealousness in, 99; reports in,
   177–82; shortcuts taken in, 171
persuasiveness, 61, 63
planning, 13–14
playing to one's strengths, 31, 246, 280
Pollin, Robert, 66
Porter, Richard, 114
post-docs, 255
Poterba, Jim, 121, 207
PowerPoint, 143–44, 145
pre-docs, 201
presentations, x, 159; discussants in, 150–52,
   163; engaging listeners in, 139–40; humor
   in, 146; improving through, 223–24;
   keeping control of, 142, 149, 281–82;
   knowing the audience for, 140–41;
   noise and distractions in, 146; papers
   contrasted with, 135–36; planning of,
   136–37; questions from audience in,

147–49; slides in, 142–45, 282; time management in, 137–39, 145, 282

present tense, 129

price stickiness, 77

Principles of Econometrics (Theil), 251

private capital, 76–77, 104–5

production function, in academia, 12

professionalism, 16, 118

professional schools, 199, 200

promotion, 24, 260, 262, 265–71; to full professor, 274–75; negative reviews for, 272–73. *See also* tenure

proof corrections, 195

prose style, x, 116–31

prospect theory, 27

public intellectuals, 277

public speaking coaches, 147

quantitative skills, in job market, 250

Quarterly Journal of Economics, 10, 176, 183

question framing, 78–79

rankings: of journals, 55, 193–94; of students, 202, 245

readability, 65, 80

recommendations, in job applications, 254

regressions, 108

Reinhart, Carmen, 66

rejections, 38, 55, 58, 118, 167, 172, 179–80, 182–85, 282; appealing, 187–88; "desk" rejections, 55, 58, 175–76, 183; resubmission following, 180–81, 187

remote collaboration, 48

repetition, 126

replication, x, 47, 60, 64, 65–66, 80, 95–97, 103

research, 5–6; agenda for, x, xi, xii, 22; costs of, 41–42, 44–45; ethics of, 235–36; evaluation of, 38–41; getting suggestions for, 153–57; growth in, 6–7; hunting vs. farming in, 24–26, 40, 280; impact of, 38, 40; learning curve for, 223; marketing the results of, 23; mass-mailing of, 160;

for non-academic audiences, 209; online posting of, 160–62; presenting, *see* presentations; principles of, 12–17; publication process in, 9–11; reasons for doing, 17–18; sequential distribution of, 154–56, 282; staggered projects in, 43; structuring portfolio of, 43–45, 280; topic selection in, 21–36, 208–11; ways to publicize, 160–64. *See also* empirical research; journals; specialization; writing

research assistants, 155, 201, 218

research results, 80–81; how to report, 108–12; interpreting, 82, 112–15; organization and ordering of, 107–8; which to report, 104–6

research statements, in promotion and tenure reviews, 268–69

revise and resubmits (R&Rs), xii, 43, 100–101, 179, 182, 185; explicit vs. vague, 186; flexibility in, 192; principles for, 190–93; "reject and resubmits" vs., 180–81, 187; response document in, 188–90, 191–92; second-round review in, 193–94; successful, 194–96; time spent on, 167–68, 169–70, 187

Review of Economic Studies, 10

Review of Financial Studies, 10–11, 171, 176, 188

The Rhetoric of Economics (McCloskey), 123

Ritter, Jay, 214

robustness checks, 73, 103–4, 107, 191

Rogoff, Kenneth, 66

"rookie market," 252–57; substitute submarket in, 261

Ross, Steve, 8

Rouse, Cecilia, 215–16

run-on sentences, 129

Scholes, Myron, 8

search committees, 232n2

"seasoned market," for junior faculty, 260–62; going on, 264–65; management of, 262–64

"senior juniors," 261–62

sentence fragments, 128
Seoul, 6
Shapiro, Jesse, 138
Shiller, Robert, 69, 114–15
Shleifer, Andrei, 8, 70, 85, 241
significance, statistical, 112–13
Singapore, 6
slides, in oral presentations, 142–45, 282
Smith, Adam, 77, 124–25, 140
social media, 162–63
Social Science Research Network (SSRN), 71, 162
Soifer, Alexander, 117
Soviet Union, 32
specialization, 6, 7–9; peer review hampered by, 10–11; perils of, 249–51; reasons for, 22–24; topic selection aided by, 34
specification testing, 118–19
staleness, in academic careers, 275–76
statistical significance, 112–13
Stein, Jeremy, 8
Strunk, William, 123
submissions, to journals, xii, 15, 174–75; cover letters in, 175; fees for, 167n4, 183; peer review in, 38, 39, 54, 55, 57–58, 91, 99, 100, 115, 165–66, 169–70, 176; referee reports in, 177–82, 190; sequential vs. simultaneous, 164, 173; strategies for, 165–68; timing of, 164–65, 167. See also rejections; revise and resubmits (R&Rs)
subtitles, 71
summaries, conclusions vs., 97
Summers, Lawrence, 121
sunk-cost fallacy, 45

tables, x, 102, 108; on slides, 144; typesetting of, 195–96
"Takeover Bids, the Free-Rider Problem, and the Theory of the Corporation" (Grossman and Hart), 85–86
Tax Reform Act of 1986, 210–11
teaching: evaluations of, 257; in promotion decisions, 260

tenses, of verbs, 129
tenure, 11, 156, 258; denial of, 264, 265, 273–74; discrimination and, 227; job searches coordinated with, 265; journal submissions and, 165, 174; letters in support of, 24, 266, 269–71; life after, 275–78; in other countries, 267; in private vs. state universities, 267; publishing and, 16, 38; for "senior juniors," 261–62; specialization and, 24. See also promotion
textbooks, 277, 283
Theil, Henri, 251
theory, in academic papers, 92–93
Thinking, Fast and Slow (Kahneman), 27
"this," 127–28
time management, 35, 42, 213; for junior faculty members, 257; in presentations, 137–39, 145, 282; in revise & resubmits (R&Rs), 167–68, 169–70, 187
titles, 68–71, 88
Tufte, Edward, 109
Tversky, Amos, 27
Twitter, 162
"typos," 47, 57–58, 104, 118

uncertainty: in academic career, 247–48; in graduate study, 199–200
unobservables, 29
Upper, Dennis, 117

"variance bounds" test, 114
venture capital, 24–25
Vishny, Robert, 8, 85
visiting faculty positions, 255
The Visual Display of Quantitative Information (Tufte), 109

War and Peace (Tolstoy), 109
The Wealth of Nations (Smith), 77, 124–45
websites, for personal information and research, 163–64
Weisbach, David, 256

White, E. B., 123
Wiles, Andrew, 1–2, 207
winsorizing, 96
Wolfskehl Prize, 1
women, in academia, 225–30
working papers, 15–16, 44
workplace discrimination: in academia,
    225–30; research on, 215–16, 226
writing: audience for, 62, 65, 89; clarity in,
    15, 40, 58, 61–62, 124; common mistakes
    in, 126–29; in competitive marketplace,
    54–56; conciseness in, 60, 75, 80, 117;

formulaic, 87; goals of, 61–67; how to
improve, 120–23; importance of, 53;
research equated with, 56, 280–81;
roadmaps used in, 63; structure and,
58–60; style of, x, 116–31. *See also*
editing; journals; research
Writing Tips for PhD Students (Cochrane),
123
Wu, Alice, 228
Wu, D. M., 119

Zinsser, William, 123

A NOTE ON THE TYPE

This book has been composed in Arno, an Old-style serif typeface in the
classic Venetian tradition, designed by Robert Slimbach at Adobe.